IN SEARCH OF
THE ETHICAL LAWYER

Law and Society Series
W. Wesley Pue, General Editor

The Law and Society Series explores law as a socially embedded phenomenon. It is premised on the understanding that the conventional division of law from society creates false dichotomies in thinking, scholarship, educational practice, and social life. Books in the series treat law and society as mutually constitutive and seek to bridge scholarship emerging from interdisciplinary engagement of law with disciplines such as politics, social theory, history, political economy, and gender studies.

For a complete list of titles in the series go to www.ubcpress.ca. Recent titles include:

IN SEARCH OF
THE ETHICAL LAWYER
STORIES FROM THE CANADIAN
LEGAL PROFESSION

Edited by Adam Dodek
and Alice Woolley

UBCPress · Vancouver · Toronto

25 24 23 22 21 20 19 18   5 4 3

Printed in Canada on FSC-certified ancient-forest-free paper
(100% post-consumer recycled) that is processed chlorine- and acid-free.

Library and Archives Canada Cataloguing in Publication

In search of the ethical lawyer: stories from the Canadian legal profession / edited by Adam Dodek and Alice Woolley.

(Law and society)
Includes bibliographical references and index.
Issued in print and electronic formats.
ISBN 978-0-7748-3098-0 (bound). – ISBN 978-0-7748-3099-7 (pbk). –
ISBN 978-0-7748-3100-0 (pdf). – ISBN 978-0-7748-3101-7 (epub). –
ISBN 978-0-7748-3102-4 (mobi)

1. Legal ethics – Canada – Cases. I. Dodek, Adam, editor II. Woolley, Alice, editor III. Series: Law and society series (Vancouver, B.C.)

| KE339.I58 2016 | 174'.30971 | C2015-907423-1 |
| KF306.I58 2016 | | C2015-907424-X |

Canadä

UBC Press gratefully acknowledges the financial support for our publishing program of the Government of Canada (through the Canada Book Fund), the Canada Council for the Arts, and the British Columbia Arts Council.

This book has been published with the help of a grant from the Canadian Federation for the Humanities and Social Sciences, through the Awards to Scholarly Publications Program, using funds provided by the Social Sciences and Humanities Research Council of Canada.

UBC Press
The University of British Columbia
2029 West Mall
Vancouver, BC V6T 1Z2
www.ubcpress.ca

Alice:

To Michelle for her inspiration and for her friendship.

Adam:

To Jerry Ziskrout, one of the truly great storytellers,
who showed me the possibilities in thinking about ethics
and the Canadian legal profession.

Contents

Foreword

PAUL WELLS

Here is a book of the sort of stories that used to be the very stuff of Canadian newspapers. News coverage of Canada's courtrooms used to be measurably richer and more complete than it is now. A big trial would attract as many reporters as the room could fit, not only for the arraignment and decision but also for every twist and turn in the proceedings. Even less monumental cases would attract sustained attention in the local paper, illuminating for a general audience the judgment calls of lawyers and their clients and thereby contributing to a general understanding that the law is something more complex, and at times more troubling, than a set of rules straightforwardly applied.

It's not wickedness, venality, or bias that has brought those old days to an end. It's Craigslist. News organizations' traditional revenue base has collapsed. Social media have replaced the paid classified ads that we used to run by the hundreds in thick sections. Almost every big news organization has a fraction of the reporters that it once fielded. Keeping a reporter or two at the courthouse, with reinforcements in the main newsroom ready to call in on an hour's notice, is a luxury that few can afford. When reporters do show up, they are not courtroom regulars. They are novices and generalists, fresh from the city council meeting or the garbage strike. There is no room in their harried noggins for insight into nuance or the incremental evolution of a complex story. Much more often than even in the recent past, we simply report the verdict. If that.

So this book fills a lately expanded vacuum in our popular understanding of the moral challenges at the heart of the practice of law. There's so much in the craft that resists code and theory. We fail the humanity in law when we skip lightly over its human conflicts and imperfections. Yet, while I've focused, as a reporter would, on the growing inability of the popular press to capture the human subtlety in so many cases, I'm not particularly surprised to learn from Adam Dodek and Alice Woolley's introduction to this volume that it's much the same situation in the formal study of law. A courtroom is a machine for translating chaos, willy-nilly, into a measure of clarity. Of course, teachers would prefer, in many cases, to pay less attention to the messy inputs and more attention to the satisfying conclusions. But in real life lawyers are parts of the machine, and it would be surprising indeed if they could forever toil in it without getting the messy inputs all over themselves.

By the evidence of the tales told here, what you get when that happens is often a lesson worth contemplating. Consider Kenneth Murray, an earnest small-town lawyer of no great experience who accepted, in 1993, a collect call from Paul Bernardo. The rest of that harrowing tale is related in "Putting Up a Defence: Sex, Murder, and Videotapes," by Allan C. Hutchinson. Murray comes to possess disturbing evidence in a notorious case of multiple rapes and murders. In deciding what to do with the evidence, he must choose between the public interest and the interest of his client. His instincts fail him. The cost is heavy. Hutchinson suggests a different course that Murray could have followed. I found at least some of the advice that he gives unsettling. But that's a feature, not a bug, of these essays: they raise questions that don't have easy answers, and nobody should expect every reader to come down on the same side of each question.

One of the hallmarks of this volume is the variety of stories and experiences canvassed. I was taken with the tale of Gerry Laarakker, a sole practitioner in small-town British Columbia who lost his temper when a client showed him a threatening letter from a law firm about the client's teenaged daughter, accused of shoplifting. This was nothing but "extortion by letterhead," Laarakker decided, and he fired off a scathing (and really quite funny) letter to the offending firm. The firm took umbrage, Laarakker was hauled before a disciplinary panel, and ...well, read on. The story, told with real flair by Micah Rankin, turns out to be about the limits on a lawyer's obligation to treat colleagues with civility – and the limits of a good man's ability to tolerate outrage.

Readers might find themselves asking why some of these chapters belong in a book on legal ethics. I think that's habit talking, not any inherent incongruity in these stories. We have grown so used to discussing law as evidence and precedent that, when skilled and sympathetic practitioners and academics remind us of another dimension (which Faulkner called "the problems of the human heart in conflict with itself"), we're unsure how to assay its value. But these ethical dilemmas can inform, inspire, or derail lawyers' work as surely as any other aspect of law. All the more reason to ponder the questions posed herein.

Acknowledgments

Our decision to collect and edit stories of Canadian lawyers whose lives and legal experiences illustrate and reflect central themes in legal ethics was brought to fruition by the willingness and enthusiasm of our contributing authors – David Asper, Constance Backhouse, Janine Benedet, Brent Cotter, Richard Devlin, Trevor Farrow, Allan Hutchinson, Micah Rankin, and Lorne Sossin. We are grateful to all of them for their scholarship, commitment to this project, and dedication to bringing to life the stories of the men and women portrayed here.

We and our contributing authors are all part of the Canadian Association for Legal Ethics (CALE) – a community of lawyers, regulators, and academics who discuss ethical and regulatory issues associated with the practice of law in Canada. That community has played an integral role in the significant growth of legal ethics scholarship in Canada over the past decade, including this book.

We would also like to acknowledge Deborah Rhode and David Luban, whose American collection *Legal Ethics: Law Stories* helped us to appreciate the role of stories in understanding ethical issues.

We were also very fortunate to have the enthusiastic and diligent support of UBC Press in our development and completion of the book. Randy Schmidt supported our project from its inception, and Harmony Johnson,

Holly Keller, Valerie Nair, and Nadine Pedersen ensured that we brought it to a successful conclusion.

And finally we would like to thank our families – Nicole, Ben, Gerry, Emily, and John – for their patience and support.

IN SEARCH OF
THE ETHICAL LAWYER

Introduction

ADAM DODEK AND ALICE WOOLLEY

Legal Stories and the Law

American judge Oliver Wendell Holmes famously quipped that "the life of the law has not been logic: it has been experience."[1] Nearly a hundred years later another American highlighted the division between the life of the law and the study of it: "The study of law can be disappointing at times, a matter of applying narrow rules and arcane procedure to an uncooperative reality; a sort of glorified accounting."[2] This statement, written by Barack Obama in 1995 several years after graduating from Harvard Law School, might resonate with many students of the law.

All too often the common law appears to be pedantic. It is a system based on cases. It is a hierarchical system in which greater weight is placed on the cases higher up in the hierarchy. Students focus on the rules and "the ratio." Yet, when they have to think about the application of those rules and ratios, whether to a real situation or to a hypothetical examination, they face the "uncooperative reality," which submits uneasily, if at all, to logical analysis.

The paradox of the common law arises from the contrast between its origins in real-life disputes between ordinary people or between citizens and their government and the translation of those disputes into causes of action. Cases arise from disputes between a rancher and his wife, who claims a right to share in the profits from the sale of the ranch that she contributed to through her labour;[3] between a mother and the state, which wishes to take a child away from her;[4] between a woman and her ex-boyfriend, who wants to stop her from getting an abortion;[5] between a fifteen-year-old African Canadian boy and a white policeman;[6] and myriad other circumstances ranging from the mundane to the almost unbelievable. But as the cases move up the common law's hierarchy, the stories of the people are all too often pushed aside. The higher a case goes, the less it becomes about the people and dispute that gave rise to it. Lawyers, judges, law students, and legal scholars read, remember, distill, and use the cases for the law that they contain, not for the people whose lives they affected. In one of the most famous cases in Canadian law, the *Persons* case, the five women who spearheaded the case – known as "the Famous Five" – are mentioned only once.[7] No reference is made to their struggles or how the case came to be decided by the Judicial Committee of the Privy Council in London.[8]

Casebooks are used to teach law, and the treatises written to explain it further excise the facts. In both, it is not uncommon for cases to be reproduced or presented with no reference to the facts. The people and their stories – the facts of the case – are unwelcome distractions.

But any lawyer will tell you that in a courtroom the facts do matter. Indeed, they may determine the outcome to a far greater extent than an articulation of the legal rules abstracted from those facts. Moreover, when one considers the very concept of law, its purpose and its structure, the centrality of facts is inescapable. Without application to people, disputes, corporations, organizations, social structures, governments, or the goals of public policy, the law would have no meaning or purpose; it would be no more comprehensible than the random strokes of monkeys on a keyboard.

It is our belief that the facts – people, circumstances, disputes, entities, culture, and social structures – also matter in the consideration of ethical issues for the Canadian legal profession. Without a rich and rigorous understanding of the personal, social, structural, and cultural circumstances in which they arise, one cannot have a meaningful conversation about the ethical challenges of legal practice; the interpretation and significance of the rules of professional conduct; what it means to be a "good" lawyer; the solutions to vexing problems such as access to justice; the meaning of "professionalism"; or, indeed, any other issue of legal ethics and professional regulations.

Our goal in editing this book was thus to tell the stories around some of the most important and interesting issues in Canadian legal ethics, to put the people and their circumstances and stories back into the discussion. As President Obama also said after his observations of law's tendency toward "narrow rules and arcane procedure," "[b]ut that's not all the law is. The law is also memory; the law records a long-running conversation, a nation arguing with its conscience."[9] This book is part of that conversation, part of the argument with our collective conscience and our individual consciences about the meaning of ethical and unethical behaviour, both specifically and generally.

This is not to suggest that the law governing lawyers – the rules of conduct, case law, and statutes that determine lawyers' obligations to their clients and to the legal system – is less rigorous or doctrinally important than other areas of law. As the recent flourishing of legal ethics scholarship in Canada demonstrates,[10] the law relating to questions such as solicitor-client privilege,[11] conflict of interest,[12] and lawyer civility[13] merits analysis and critique. However, as was observed about the law in general, divorcing it from its factual context undermines the effort to understand it.

Furthermore, one of the specific challenges of the law governing lawyers is that the codes of professional conduct, which contain many of the central obligations of lawyers to their clients and to the legal system, are enforced relatively infrequently,[14] or their enforcement does not lead to a reported judgment setting out how the provision applies to a given set of facts. It can thus be difficult to understand the true import of their provisions, since their terms are divorced from any factual context. Indeed, one of us often tells his students that, if an ethical issue can be resolved by reference to a provision in the *Rules of Professional Conduct*, it is not worth discussing. This is an oversimplification, but the point is that, given how those rules have (or have not) evolved, most of the vexing issues of legal ethics cannot be easily resolved solely by reference to their terms. The rules might be a starting point or a way station in the discussion, but they are not usually the beginning, middle, and end of the debate. The stories of people, social structures, policy, and history in this book contribute to filling out that debate.

The stories in this book are not stories of "great men"[15] (though some are stories of men and women of greatness), nor could such a book provide the necessary context for understanding the obligations and challenges of ethical legal practice. The important background for ethical legal practice is the stories of ordinary women and men and the social and cultural contexts in which they lived. Those are the stories that provide the necessary personal, social, and cultural contexts for Canadian legal ethics.

In telling those stories, our book is part of a larger tradition of legal storytelling. Other works of authors featured in this collection – Constance Backhouse and Allan Hutchinson – have used stories to inform law, jurisprudence, and legal history.[16] And our book was inspired in significant part by David Luban and Deborah Rhode's *Legal Ethics: Law Stories,*[17] which describes the backgrounds and contexts of ten of the most significant legal ethics cases in the United States.

The case thus made for *In Search of the Ethical Lawyer* asserts the importance and utility of knowing the contexts and circumstances surrounding the law governing lawyers. But a non-utilitarian case can also be made. Many great tales arise in the law, tales of sadness and joy, of triumph and failure. This book tells a few of them.

Defending the Guilty, Defending the Innocent

Law mediates between the state and the citizenry, both legitimizing and constraining government power. This is true generally but is most obviously the case in the context of criminal law, in which the state exacts consequences on individuals found to have violated the law's requirements. Criminal defence lawyers practise at this intersection between the state and the citizen, helping to ensure that the law's consequences apply only where warranted and to protect the dignity of the accused.

The high stakes of criminal defence work heighten the ethical challenges faced by those lawyers. On the one hand, protection of the accused's dignity in the face of state power mandates zeal and advocacy; on the other, the morally wrongful conduct of the clients whom those lawyers represent can make that zeal seem monstrous rather than meritorious. As Allan Hutchinson says in his chapter, "[p]eople tend to identify defence lawyers with their unsavoury clients and their unforgivable deeds. However, when individuals are in trouble, they want the best and most dogged lawyer on their side and their side alone; they need to be assured about the unquestioned loyalty of their lawyer to their cause."

Furthermore, and significantly, unquestioning loyalty can lead lawyers astray, past the point of protecting a client's dignity, and ensuring that state power is exercised only when legitimately merited, to violations of the law and morality. And it can create challenges for regulators and legislators, who have to articulate the rules and boundaries of advocacy.

The opening chapter of this book – Adam Dodek's "Keeping Secrets or Saving Lives: What Is a Lawyer to Do?" – illustrates both of these problems. Dodek describes the people and circumstances underlying the Supreme Court's decision in *Smith v. Jones,* in which the Court held that a lawyer can disclose privileged information when there is an imminent threat of serious bodily harm or death to an identifiable group or person. In that case, the

Court permitted a psychiatrist retained by an accused's lawyer to reveal the violent criminal intentions that the accused had disclosed to the psychiatrist. As Dodek shows, while the Court articulated a relatively clear rule to govern the conflict between duty to the client (of confidentiality) and duty to the administration of justice (to protect the public from harm), that rule does not reduce the tension experienced by a criminal defence lawyer faced with the choice of disclosing information. That lawyer might still feel, as does the lawyer who represented the accused in *Smith v. Jones*, that "it was not my place to unilaterally displace solicitor-client privilege," even as he knows that the non-disclosure of information can place people in harm's way; the discretionary nature of the Court's rule leaves him with that ethical choice to make and its consequences to bear.

The dual challenges of articulating the appropriate rules to govern lawyer advocacy, and for the individual lawyer to identify the appropriate limits on resolute advocacy, are also illustrated in Allan Hutchinson's "Putting Up a Defence: Sex, Murder, and Videotapes." His chapter tells the story of one of the most infamous and controversial episodes in the annals of the Canadian legal profession. Lawyers still talk about it fifteen years after its occurrence and likely will continue to debate its merits for decades. Ken Murray's decision to take videotapes from the home of murderer and rapist Paul Bernardo, and not to reveal the existence of those tapes to the authorities for fourteen months, led to his being charged with obstruction of justice. In describing the circumstances of Murray's representation of Bernardo, the decision that Murray made about the videotapes, and the consequences that he faced, Hutchinson shows the difficulty for Murray in balancing the need to represent his client's interests, including protection of his client's confidentiality, with the need not to interfere with the administration of justice. Murray's resolution of this dilemma was wrong, but as Hutchinson notes, the dilemma that Murray faced was real, and no response would have been entirely satisfactory; his case "highlights the fact that the challenges to the criminal bar in meeting its ethical and professional responsibilities are difficult and many." Indeed, as Hutchinson describes, so difficult is the problem of how criminal defence lawyers ought to handle physical evidence received from their clients that the law societies have arguably failed to articulate rules to govern it.

One might think that the ethical challenges of the defence lawyer who represents an innocent person are less acute; in that instance, advocacy and the administration of justice ought to orientate toward the same end – acquittal. But "'No One's Interested in Something You Didn't Do': Freeing

David Milgaard the Ugly Way," David Asper's account of his attempts to free Milgaard, after his wrongful conviction for sexual assault and murder, illustrates the false oversimplification of that thought. Asper discovered that the intense advocacy that results from knowledge of a client's innocence, the resistance of individuals in the government to establishing that case, and the structural impediments to demonstrating innocence after conviction create their own ethical challenges. Ordinary zeal did not suffice; only extraordinary zeal, employing judicial and extrajudicial mechanisms such as the media, was enough to obtain the exoneration of his client. Although Asper believes that his actions were justified given the result, he also recognizes in hindsight the absence of malice in many of his opponents, the difficult and sometimes troubling decisions that his advocacy required, and that extraordinary zeal will inevitably create disquiet in those subject to it. It might be worth it, but it is not easy.

Lawyers in Social Context

Criminal defence lawyers work for the cause of law and justice and for the protection of the accused persons whom they represent, whether innocent or guilty.[18] But the causes that inform the work and lives of lawyers range widely.

Of course, not all lawyers define their careers and practices through the pursuit of a particular vision of justice, but for those who do, legal practice brings a unique set of rewards and challenges – rewards, because legal practice reflects an alignment between those lawyers' moral beliefs and their discharge of their role in the legal system that other lawyers may not enjoy in the same way. At the end of her career, the justice-pursuing lawyer might think that through her work she has helped to make the legal system more fair and just. Challenges arise, however, because a system of laws is not always a system of justice, and lawyers who seek to move the law toward justice may personally bear the brunt of that system's resistance. Agents of social change are not always welcome by the society that they are changing. This is particularly so when they themselves belong to the legally and socially marginalized group whose circumstances they seek to make more just.

In "'Begun in Faith, Continued in Determination': Burnley Allan (Rocky) Jones and the Egalitarian Practice of Law," Richard Devlin describes the life and work of Rocky Jones, one of the first Black lawyers in Nova Scotia and a man who worked tirelessly against racism. His efforts accomplished social change, working with Dalhousie Law School to create a program for

Indigenous, Black, and Mi'kmaq students and being one of the first graduates of that program. He also achieved legal victory in "one of the most significant Supreme Court of Canada decisions on race in Canada," obtaining an acquittal for a young Black man who had been charged with assault and resisting arrest. That acquittal, based in part on the judge's observation that "police officers do overreact, particularly when they're dealing with non-white groups," was challenged to the Supreme Court, where it was ultimately upheld.

Jones's work also resulted, though, in his spending seven years defending himself from a defamation action. The action arose as a result of statements made in his representation of three Black girls who had been searched by a police officer investigating a minor robbery at their school. As Devlin notes, Jones had the support, admiration, and collaboration of some members of the Nova Scotia legal profession, while "others resented and reviled him." As an egalitarian lawyer, his efforts effected real social change but also sparked social resistance, much of which Jones himself had to bear.

Similar instances of success and difficulty affected the women portrayed in Janine Benedet's chapter, "Feminist Lawyering: Insiders and Outsiders." Benedet recounts the professional accomplishments of Carole Curtis, now a justice of the Ontario Court of Justice but formerly a bencher of the Law Society of Upper Canada. Curtis was notable for her leadership in the areas of family law and small firm practice. Yet her career was nearly derailed by a complaint brought to the Law Society and a hearing in which it was alleged that Curtis had advised a client to violate the law. That allegation was unanimously rejected in "a complete vindication" for Curtis; however, as Benedet describes, Curtis can justly claim that the Law Society prosecuted the case aggressively, pushing for ethical obligations to be imposed on her that have never been viewed as part of a lawyer's duties.

Benedet also tells the story of Beth Symes and her legal challenge of the tax treatment given to child care expenses incurred by businesswomen, in this case partners in law firms. Benedet notes the complexity of this sort of litigation, how it can be framed as an attempt to instantiate certain types of privilege, but also the failure of that framing to recognize changes to the unfair treatment of women by the law that the litigation sought to accomplish.

Benedet links these stories together, and with her own experiences as a feminist lawyer, by noting the complex place that feminist lawyers occupy: they both challenge the legal system and operate within it, occupying positions of privilege and power. She suggests that the challenge – and the opportunity – for feminist lawyers is allowing those two positions, insider and outsider, to exist together in pursuit of "bettering both the lives of women and the legal profession."

Benedet's and Devlin's chapters describe lawyers in a world of social change in which they could move the law toward greater justice. Their experiences were not unambiguously positive or wholly successful, but as Benedet notes there is a real sense in which those lawyers became part of the establishment as they challenged it. That aspect of their experience sets them apart from lawyers from an earlier time, whose struggles to enter the profession were met with fiercer resistance and overt discrimination. That history of the legal profession, and of those men and women, is described by Constance Backhouse in "Gender and Race in the Construction of 'Legal Professionalism': Historical Perspectives." She suggests that the very idea of professionalism cannot be properly invoked without "successfully grappling with the gendered, class-based, ethnoracist, heterosexist, or able-bodied presumptions welded onto the concept of professionalism at the outset." Backhouse supports her claim with a description of the challenges (and successes) of Delos Rogest Davis, Canada's first Black lawyer; Clara Brett Martin, its first female lawyer; and Andrew Paull, an Aboriginal man who never managed to obtain admission to the legal profession. She also notes the discrimination experienced by some of the first female judges, including Bertha Wilson and Claire L'Heureux-Dubé, the first two women appointed to the Supreme Court of Canada. Backhouse concludes her chapter with a challenge to lawyers to move past "professionalism" and "civility" to focus on "different ideals, such as anti-racism, gender equality, respect for Aboriginality, religious tolerance, reduction in wealth disparity, and social justice."

Backhouse provides important context for considering lawyers' ethics and duties. She demonstrates the limits that cultural and social contexts can place on creating a society that reflects the legal and moral norms that it purports to embody, reminding us that our own efforts to ensure the ethics of Canadian lawyers are surely more limited in their accomplishments than we appreciate. She also pushes lawyers to consider which ethical principles truly matter: the principles of social justice that, in the end, are the most critical for ensuring that lawyers help to accomplish a just society.

Lawyers and Access to Justice

The importance of Backhouse's exhortation to lawyers to focus on social justice becomes clear when viewed in the light of Canada's growing problem of access to justice – what Trevor Farrow refers to in his chapter as the "divide between what legal services people need and what they can afford and access." The problem of access to justice necessarily implicates the legal profession, whether because lawyers or regulation of the profession might be held responsible (in whole or in part) for the inaccessibility of legal services, whether because lawyers participate in trying to solve the problem of access, or whether because the focus on lawyers distracts us from the true nature of the problem or its solution.

The chapters by Lorne Sossin and Trevor Farrow consider access to justice and the role that lawyers can – and cannot – play in resolving it. Sossin's chapter – "The Helping Profession: Can *Pro Bono* Lawyers Make Sick Children Well?" – describes the initiative to provide *pro bono* legal services to families with children at the Toronto Hospital for Sick Children – "PBLO at SickKids." Sossin uses the *pro bono* initiative at SickKids to illustrate the important role that lawyers can play in helping families with complex social needs while also using that initiative to assess some of the ethical dimensions of legal practice. He explores some of the ethical challenges of *pro bono* work – such as the choice of clients to represent – as well as the question of whether *pro bono* work truly creates ethical opportunities for the profession. Sossin notes the different ethical standards that can apply to *pro bono* work and addresses the broader moral question of whether it ought to be viewed as truly altruistic or whether, like other legal work, it is tainted by a lawyer's pursuit of self-interest. Ultimately, Sossin concludes, *pro bono* work does present an ethical opportunity for lawyers and the profession in general: "If lawyers can help to heal sick children, and act in the interests of vulnerable groups without expectation of personal benefit, there might be hope yet for the legal profession."

In "A New Wave of Access to Justice Reform in Canada," Trevor Farrow puts access to justice in perspective, identifying the true nature of the problem, in which legal problems and social issues are inextricably connected, and neither can be understood if we do not see the relationship between them. Moreover, law and justice are not the same; to provide access to justice requires a much broader focus: "We need to start seeing our role as providers of justice in terms of the real stuff of life: help with addictions, food, housing, empowerment, and dignity." Farrow describes the initiatives of the Action Committee on Access to Justice, its collaborative approach, and its attempt to begin a fundamental shift in how we approach justice reform, and he articulates a "concrete plan for action" on the problem of access. He describes how that plan ultimately involves the legal profession, seeking "to encourage innovation and creativity at the bar (and in all legal sectors) so that clients and their problems are handled by the right people, at the right time, in the best way possible."

On Being a Lawyer

Lawyers' lives and work can be part of broader social movements, causes, and contexts but are also their own experiences, accomplishments, and challenges. The final section of the book describes the lives of three lawyers with widely varying practice experiences and public renown, but all of whom found purpose and meaning through the practice of law. Their stories provide a portrait of the possibilities and opportunities that a legal career presents, even if lawyers are viewed, as Hutchinson puts it in his chapter, as being "among the least trustworthy and least respected of all professionals."

In "Michelle's Story: Creativity and Meaning in Legal Practice," Alice Woolley considers this question directly: can being a lawyer be constitutive of a meaningful life? She does so through the life and legal practice of Michelle, an employment lawyer who lost her ability to practise law after being diagnosed with multiple sclerosis. The ways in which her legal practice fulfilled her, and the nature of the loss that she experienced when she was no longer able to practise law, illustrate how the practice of law can be something that a person can love, that is worthy of love, and that can be actively pursued – i.e., can be a source of meaning. As described by philosophers such as Bernard Williams and Susan Wolf, meaning is a part of the accomplishment of an ethical life, a part distinct from morality: that is, doing "the right thing." Michelle's life in law was an ethical life in that broader sense, and the loss created by her forced retirement was existentially difficult.

Ian Scott, the lawyer portrayed by Brent Cotter in "Ian Scott, Renaissance Man, Consummate Advocate, Attorney General Extraordinaire," also accomplished an ethical life in the fullest sense. His career both in private practice and in public service as an attorney general was noted for its accomplishment of justice; Scott worked as counsel for several public inquiries into matters of public importance, and as an attorney general he spearheaded a truly remarkable number of reforms to law and the legal process. Scott also pursued his legal career with passion, commitment, and an orientation to excellence. Cotter places Scott's work, including Scott's writings, in the context of the ethical obligations of the government lawyer, noting the tension between that lawyer's orientation to the political goals of the government of the day and maintenance of the rule of law, focusing on

Scott's attempt to articulate the appropriate relationship between matters of principle and matters of policy.

In the concluding chapter, "Gerry Laarakker: From Rustic Rambo to Rebel with a Cause," Micah Rankin similarly places his subject in the context of an important ethical issue: the regulation of lawyer civility. Laarakker, a lawyer in British Columbia, was disciplined by the law society for his incivility in response to a demand letter sent on behalf of a major retailer to the parents of a shoplifter, a letter, Laarakker noted with justification, that indicated no real intention to pursue the matter in court. Rankin describes Laarakker's background and his commitment to redress the injustice of unmeritorious demand letters (routinely issued by some members of the profession), his discipline case, and his subsequent response to the problem of demand letters; Rankin uses these aspects to illustrate what he describes as "the profound difficulties that arise from the regulation of civility."

A Concluding Thought

The system of laws cannot be understood through one lens. A legal story incorporates legal norms, cultural contexts, history, institutions, structures, and the people whose lives, whether willingly or not, come into contact with the law. In the stories collected here, we have tried to reflect these various aspects, particularly those that might not be evident when one studies the law governing lawyers on its own – the culture, institutions, structure, history, and human beings of legal ethics. Although we have spent most of the past decade of our professional lives focused on legal ethics, reading (and telling) these stories have given us a new and broader perspective.

Notes

1 Oliver Wendell Holmes, *The Common Law*, ed. Mark DeWolfe Howe (Boston: Little, Brown, and Company, 1963) at 5.
2 Barack Obama, *Dreams from My Father* (New York: Times Press, 1995) at 437.
3 See *Murdoch v. Murdoch*, [1975] 1 S.C.R. 423.
4 See *New Brunswick (Minister of Health and Community Services) v. G. (J.)*, [1999] 3 S.C.R. 46.
5 See *Tremblay v. Daigle*, [1989] 2 S.C.R. 530.
6 See *R. v. S. (R.D.)*, [1997] 3 S.C.R. 484.
7 See *Edwards v. Attorney General of Canada*, [1929] U.K.P.C. 86, [1930] A.C. 124, [1929] J.C.J. No. 2, [1930] 1 D.L.R. 98, [1929] 3 W.W.R. 479.
8 Fortunately, others have written about these women and this case. See, for example, Robert J. Sharpe and Patricia I. McMahon, *The Persons Case: The Origins and Legacy of the Fight for Legal Personhood* (Toronto: Osgoode Society for Canadian Legal History, 2007).

9 Obama, *supra* note 2 at 437.

10 Adam Dodek, "Canadian Legal Ethics: Ready for the Twenty-First Century at Last" (2008) 46(1) Osgoode Hall Law Journal 1.

11 Adam M. Dodek, *Solicitor-Client Privilege* (Toronto: LexisNexis, 2014).

12 Alice Woolley, *Understanding Lawyers' Ethics in Canada* (Toronto: LexisNexis, 2011).

13 Alice Woolley, "Does Civility Matter?" (2008) 46 Osgoode Hall Law Journal 175; Alice Woolley, "'Uncivil by Too Much Civility'? Critiquing Five More Years of Civility Regulation" (2013) 36 Dalhousie Law Journal 239.

14 See Harry W. Arthurs, "Why Canadian Law Schools Do Not Teach Legal Ethics" in Kim Economides, ed., *Ethical Challenges to Legal Education and Conduct* (Oxford: Hart Publishing, 1998) at 105, 112. See also Harry W. Arthurs, Richard Weisman, and Frederick H. Zemans, "Canadian Lawyers: A Peculiar Professionalism" in Richard L. Abel and Philip S.C. Lewis, eds., *Lawyers in Society: The Common Law World*, vol. 1 (Berkeley: University of California Press, 1988) at 123; Harry W. Arthurs, "Climbing Kilimanjaro: Ethics for Postmodern Professionals" (1993) 6(1) Westminster Affairs 3; Harry W. Arthurs, "The Dead Parrot: Does Professional Self-Regulation Exhibit Vital Signs?" (1995) 33 Alberta Law Review 800; and Alice Woolley, "Regulation in Practice: The 'Ethical Economy' of Lawyer Regulation in Canada and a Case Study in Lawyer Deviance" (2012) 15(2) Legal Ethics 243.

15 Thomas Carlyle, *On Heroes, Hero-Worship, and the Heroic in History* (New York: Fredrick A. Stokes and Brother, 1888).

16 Constance Backhouse, *Petticoats and Prejudice: Women and Law in 19th Century Canada* (Toronto: Women's Press, 1991); Allan Hutchinson, *Is Eating People Wrong? Great Legal Cases and How They Shaped the World* (Cambridge, UK: Cambridge University Press, 2010).

17 Deborah L. Rhode and David J. Luban, *Legal Ethics: Law Stories* (New York: Foundation Press, 2006).

18 See *How Can You Represent Those People?*, Abbe Smith and Monroe H. Freedman, eds. (New York: Palgrave Macmillan, 2013).

1

Keeping Secrets or Saving Lives

————————— What Is a Lawyer to Do?

ADAM DODEK

Prologue: Ottawa, June 1, 1998

Paul Schabas found himself in a strange position. Schabas, an experienced and gregarious Bay Street lawyer, frequently represented media clients. He was no stranger to the Supreme Court of Canada, but on this day he was being treated like a pariah. It was June 1, 1998, and Schabas had flown from Toronto to Ottawa to participate in a rare oral hearing in a leave to appeal application at the Supreme Court. The judges would decide whether the Supreme Court would take the case. Schabas saw this as a sign that something about the case was important. The judges almost always decided these matters based only on the written arguments of lawyers. Schabas was representing Southam News, whose legal affairs correspondent, Stephen Bindman, had got wind of a strange case in which the high court had imposed a total sealing order and a sweeping publication ban.[1]

As a media lawyer, Schabas was used to challenging publication bans on behalf of his clients.[2] Such bans are not unusual in Canada; they protect the identities of victims and minors and ensure a fair trial. However, in this case, the publication ban was unusual because the entire file was sealed. The lower courts had given the parties pseudonyms: "*James Jones v. John Smith.*" Could anything be more clichéd?

Schabas knew only three things about the case: (1) it involved solicitor-client privilege, the rule that protects the secrecy of communications between a lawyer and his or her client; (2) it was from British Columbia; and

(3) the courts did not want the media to obtain any information about the case, let alone report on it.

Bindman closely followed the Supreme Court and had discovered that it had inadvertently disclosed information about the case in its Bulletin of Proceedings, seemingly in violation of its own publication ban.[3] The Court discovered the error after an hour and immediately took the bulletin off its website and retrieved the hard copies that had been distributed to staff in the Press Gallery. According to Registrar Anne Roland, the Court's chief administrator, "[m]embers of the Press Gallery whom we contacted for assistance were very co-operative in this regard."[4] Bindman, apparently, was the only reporter who actually got hold of the bulletin. He was never asked to return it, but obviously he knew of the Court's snafu and wrote a story about the incident entitled "Supreme Court Violates Its Own Gag Order."[5] This was the first public revelation of the case that would become known as *Smith v. Jones.*

The limited information that Schabas had about the case had come from Bindman. The Court's inadvertent disclosure gave Schabas information about the case in British Columbia. He sent lawyers from his firm's Vancouver office to check the court files there, but they were stymied, finding the files totally sealed.[6] It was a dead end. Thus, when Schabas left his Toronto office, he knew less about the case that he was about to argue than any case in his legal career.

It was unusually chilly for early June when Schabas arrived at the Supreme Court. He faced a more frosty reception inside the building. After he proceeded through security and checked in, Schabas made his way to the "Barrister's Robing Room," slightly above the main floor of the courthouse. Despite its fancy name, the room is little more than a glorified high school changing room for lawyers. And much smaller. But it is here that lawyers don their court attire, exchanging their suit jackets and ties for the black robes and tuxedo-style shirts with white tabs protruding from the neck. The robes are supposed to make all lawyers look the same. They do, but they also add much formality and many would say stuffiness to the proceedings. Schabas was not alone in the small robing room. There were two other lawyers there. He did not recognize the two lawyers from British Columbia, and they did not speak to him beyond exchanging pleasantries. Schabas would not even learn their names until later.[7]

The strangeness of the case would continue. Bindman had been convinced that there was a story to tell. Before Schabas even entered the courtroom, he had reached the same conclusion. Both of them were right.

Introduction: Vancouver, September 1996

Michael Leopold – later known in court proceedings by the pseudonym "James Jones" – came to Vancouver lawyer Les Mackoff in the usual way: through a referral.[8] Mackoff had graduated from the Faculty of Law at the University of British Columbia in 1981. He had begun his career as a federal prosecutor before moving to Los Angeles, where he had practised law with a large firm from 1985 through 1990, primarily in the field of aviation product liability litigation or what might be considered airplane crash law. Mackoff had returned to his hometown of Vancouver in 1990, established his own firm, and started to concentrate on criminal defence work.[9]

On September 14, 1996, Leopold attacked a prostitute in an alley in the Downtown Eastside. She suffered significant injuries as a result of the attack. The police had descriptions of the car and attacker, which they broadcast on the radio. Leopold heard the description and surrendered to the police on September 17.[10] The next day he was charged with aggravated sexual assault, which carries a maximum penalty of life imprisonment.[11] Leopold remained in custody for three months until he was released on bail on December 19. The trial was scheduled for October 1997.[12]

In a criminal trial, the Crown is required to provide "disclosure" of all relevant information to the defence.[13] This duty is not reciprocal. Subject to a few limited exceptions, the defence does not have to disclose any information to the prosecution.[14] The delay between an arrest and the trial is usually required in order for the defence to prepare for trial, which includes reviewing Crown disclosure. During this time, there are often discussions between Crown counsel and defence counsel on a possible disposition of the case: that is, a plea agreement.

In order to prepare for Leopold's defence, Mackoff arranged to have his client evaluated by Dr. Roy O'Shaughnessy, the Head of Forensic Psychiatry at UBC Hospital. He was clearly one of the top forensic psychiatrists in the province. Mackoff had used Dr. O'Shaughnessy before and respected him. When a doctor participates as an expert in a court case, he or she does not bill medicare but is paid by the party who retains him or her – and paid well, usually several hundred dollars per hour. Mackoff retained Dr. O'Shaughnessy to interview his client in order to produce an evaluation that might assist in preparing either the defence or submissions for sentencing if Leopold entered a guilty plea.[15]

The interview took place on July 30, 1997, and lasted approximately ninety minutes. Before Leopold went to see Dr. O'Shaughnessy, Mackoff told him that talking to the doctor would be like talking to a lawyer: whatever

Leopold told Dr. O'Shaughnessy would be protected by solicitor-client privilege.[16] Indeed, Mackoff likely already knew much of what his client would tell the doctor.

Leopold clearly felt at ease with Dr. O'Shaughnessy, who later described him as cooperative, candid, and open.[17] Leopold detailed what transpired when he picked up the prostitute and assaulted her.[18] He explained that, after engaging in sexual activity with the woman, he proceeded with what he described as "Phase II" of his plan to kidnap a woman and make her his "sex slave." Leopold had deliberately sought out a small woman whom he thought he could control physically. He had brought rope, duct tape, and a ball to put into her mouth to restrain her. Leopold told Dr. O'Shaughnessy that he did not attempt to hide his identity from his victim because he planned to kill her eventually by strangling her and then place her body in a trailer and bury it in a bushy area. He further indicated that he planned to shoot his victim in the face with a shotgun in order to prevent her identification by dental records or facial features.[19]

Leopold told Dr. O'Shaughnessy that he intended this first kidnapping and murder to be a "'trial run' to enable him to determine if he could 'live with' what he had done."[20] If he could, he intended to seek out other victims and commit similar crimes. He mentioned that he was unsure if he was capable of actually killing someone. However, Leopold believed that, by the time he had kidnapped his victim, he would have little choice but to kill her in order to protect himself. Leopold shared with Dr. O'Shaughnessy his detailed plans for the kidnapping and murder, including preparing a holding area in his basement with deadbolt locks on all doors and arranging the pretense that he was on vacation to ensure that no one would visit his home.[21]

Leopold described his sexual fantasies in detail to Dr. O'Shaughnessy. He said that around puberty he began to experience deviant sexual arousal fantasies triggered by reading hard-core pornography containing images of bondage, domination, and rape. During his teenage years, Leopold had rape fantasies and was sexually aroused by imagining forced sexual behaviour. He would have thoughts of raping specific women whom he had seen in school or on the street. During his late teens, Leopold began to fantasize about kidnapping a woman, taking her to a secluded location, and raping her. Later his fantasies expanded to torturing and then killing his victims.[22] In his twenties, Leopold began to hire prostitutes on Vancouver's skid row to engage in sadistic acts; he needed to cause them pain in order to achieve sexual gratification. Aged thirty-five at the time of the interview, Leopold told Dr. O'Shaughnessy that during the past ten years his sexual fantasies had been primarily sadistic and that he had had some fantasies about pre- and postpubescent children; he also confirmed that he was interested in other deviant sexual behaviours.

Leopold revealed to Dr. O'Shaughnessy that the incident with the prostitute that led to his arrest had been his first attempt to act out his sex slave fantasy and that he had been considerably relieved upon his arrest. He further advised Dr. O'Shaughnessy that his sadistic fantasies had returned. He admitted having violated the terms of his bail by continuing to frequent the skid row area of Vancouver and changing his licence plates to avoid police detection. Leopold expressed concern about his fantasies and his behaviour and appeared to recognize that he needed treatment.[23]

Dr. O'Shaughnessy discussed treatment options with Leopold and informed him that he needed psychiatric intervention, including medication. O'Shaughnessy considered Leopold "to be a dangerous individual in that he would more likely than not act on these fantasies unless he had sufficient treatment."[24]

The day after the interview, Dr. O'Shaughnessy called Mackoff and told him that in his opinion Leopold was dangerous.[25] It is likely that Dr. O'Shaughnessy provided Mackoff with the basis for his opinion. In an affidavit that he filed in a later court proceeding, Dr. O'Shaughnessy opined that Leopold showed "evidence of a 'paraphilic' [*i.e.,* deviant sexual] disorder[26] with multiple paraphilias, in particular sexual sadism,"[27] and evidenced "Personality Disorder with Mixed Features and some antisocial features and drug abuse difficulties."[28]

Such revelations might be shocking, but in the normal course they would never have seen the light of day because of solicitor-client privilege. Ordinarily, when an expert is retained by a party in litigation and offers an opinion or produces a report not helpful to the party, the lawyer decides not to use the expert. The lawyer thanks the expert for the work, pays the bill, and buries the opinion or report under the protection of solicitor-client privilege (recall that, in a criminal case, only the Crown has a duty of disclosure, not the defence).[29]

This is what appears to have happened in this case. After O'Shaughnessy called Mackoff the day after the interview, he sent along his bill, which Mackoff promptly paid, and he did not expect to hear further from the doctor.[30] In his mind, O'Shaughnessy's role was over, but this was not to be the case.

A Defence Lawyer's Duty of Loyalty

Despite being warned by Dr. O'Shaughnessy about his client's dangerousness, Mackoff did not consider revealing this information to the authorities – to the Crown or perhaps to the police. Reflecting on this decision fifteen years later, Mackoff was straightforward and somewhat poetic in his rationale. He explained that the practice of criminal defence law often involves representing people whom the lawyer might believe have ongoing intentions to pursue a violent criminal lifestyle. In criminal defence parlance, repeat clients are known as "rounders," probably because they keep coming "'round the law office."[31] By occupational choice, criminal defence lawyers such as Mackoff deal with clients who have done horrible things. Many such lawyers deal with dangerousness on a daily basis.

Mackoff said that, if a criminal defence lawyer thought about turning in such clients based on expressions of future criminal behaviour, he would be constantly second-guessing himself.[32] It is simply not the role of criminal defence lawyers to worry about what their clients might do in the future. Their job is to do everything in their power to help their clients deal with what they might have done in the past that has led to their arrest. Thus, in our criminal justice system, the prosecution (or "the Crown") and the defence have very different roles.

Roles of the Prosecution and the Defence

In *R. v. Boucher* (1955),[33] the Supreme Court of Canada explained that the purpose of a criminal prosecution is not to obtain a conviction but to provide the court with what the prosecution considers to be credible evidence relevant to what is alleged to be a crime. In an oft-quoted line, Justice Ivan Rand of the Supreme Court stated that "[t]he role of prosecutor excludes any notion of winning or losing; his function is a matter of public duty than which in civil life there can be none charged with greater personal responsibility. It is to be efficiently performed with an ingrained sense of the dignity, the seriousness and the justness of judicial proceedings."[34] The Crown prosecutor has a duty to see that all available legal proof of the facts is presented: "[I]t should be done firmly and pressed to its legitimate strength but it must also be done fairly."[35]

Codes of conduct for lawyers incorporate the same ideas.[36] Thus, the *Model Code of Professional Conduct* provides that the prosecutor's "primary duty is not to seek to convict but to see that justice is done through a fair trial on the merits."[37] The *Model Code* explains that the prosecutor "exercises a public function involving much discretion and power and must act fairly and dispassionately."[38]

The role of the defence counsel is decidedly different. In *R. v. Boucher*, the Supreme Court recognized that the counsel for a person accused of a crime has no obligation to assist in the prosecution and is entitled to assume a purely adversarial role.[39] This role has long been entrenched in the common law and is part of the unshakable duty of loyalty that the criminal defence lawyer owes to his or her client.

In *R. v. Neil* (2002),[40] the Supreme Court of Canada quoted the following statement made by Henry Brougham, later Lord Chancellor, in his defence of Queen Caroline in 1820 against the charge of adultery brought against her by her husband, King George IV. Lord Brougham proclaimed before the House of Lords during the trial that

> an advocate, in the discharge of his duty, knows but one person in all the world, and that person is his client. To save that client by all means and expedients, and at all hazards and costs to other persons, and, among them, to himself, is his first and only duty; and in performing this duty he must not regard the alarm, the torments, the destruction which he may bring upon others. Separating the duty of a patriot from that of an advocate, he must go on reckless of consequences, though it should be his unhappy fate to involve his country in confusion.[41]

In defending Queen Caroline, what was at stake was not only her life but also King George's Crown.[42] Lord Brougham's statement has become part of the dominant model of the role of the lawyer – especially the defence lawyer – in the adversarial system.[43] This duty of loyalty is essential to the independence of the legal profession in a free and democratic society.

If Mackoff had revealed information about Leopold's case against his client's wishes, he would have placed his client in jeopardy and possibly helped to convict him. One of Canada's leading criminal defence lawyers, Eddie Greenspan, said that "[h]elping to convict someone is the very opposite of a defence lawyer's function."[44] If Mackoff had revealed any information against his client's wishes, at the least he would have been in a conflict of interest and could not have continued as Leopold's lawyer because he would have become a potential witness against his own client.[45]

It was Mackoff's job and his duty to take Leopold's side. Greenspan has explained that "[a]n accused or convicted person has no friends in society ...

No official of his country will be on his side." When a person is accused of a crime, the entire justice system moves against the individual, and the "encounter between one individual and the entire judicial system is a collision of epic disproportion."[46] This is counterbalanced by the presumption of innocence and the lawyer for the defence. According to Greenspan, the lawyer for the defence is "the one person in the entire world, apart from the accused person's mother, who *starts* with the assumption that the authorities must be mistaken."[47]

A criminal defence lawyer has a duty of resolute advocacy – what Americans call "zealous advocacy."[48] This duty requires the lawyer "to raise fearlessly every issue, advance every argument and ask every question, however distasteful, that the lawyer thinks will help the client's case and to endeavour to obtain for the client the benefit of every remedy and defence authorized by law."[49]

The Duty of Confidentiality and Solicitor-Client Privilege

The duty of confidentiality derives from the lawyer's duty of loyalty to the client.[50] The public safety exception created in *Smith v. Jones* directly challenges both duties. Thus, a lawyer such as Mackoff finds himself caught between his legal duty to his client and his moral responsibility to his society. The twin doctrines of confidentiality and solicitor-client privilege generally hold that the dilemma should be resolved in favour of keeping quiet. The public safety exception gives lawyers a choice between confidentiality and candour, a choice that they rarely have because of the stringent nature of confidentiality and solicitor-client privilege.[51]

The duty of confidentiality and solicitor-client privilege – what together Alice Woolley calls "lawyer-client trust and confidence"[52] – form a core part of lawyers' collective identity. In one of the most important cases about the practice of law, the Supreme Court stated that "[n]othing is more important to the preservation of this relationship than the confidentiality of information passing between a solicitor and his or her client. The legal profession has distinguished itself from other professions by the sanctity with which these communications are treated."[53]

The duty of confidentiality and solicitor-client privilege are intertwined and often confused.[54] The duty of confidentiality is an ethical duty imposed on lawyers by their regulatory bodies not to disclose any information learned about their clients during the course of the representation.[55] Solicitor-client privilege is the right to communicate in confidence with one's lawyer.[56] This right ensures protection against the voluntary or compelled disclosure by one's lawyer absent the client's consent or court order. It also includes protection against the client's being compelled to disclose information covered by the privilege. It can be invoked by the client or the lawyer on the client's behalf in the midst of or in the absence of court proceedings.[57] The privilege has thus become much more than an evidentiary privilege that can prevent testimony in court. It is now a substantive right with constitutional implications if not constitutional proportions. It is the strongest privilege protected by law.[58]

Because confidentiality is the *sine qua non* of privilege,[59] it is not surprising that the two doctrines "grew up together."[60] The privilege is the oldest of the recognized privileges for confidential communications – priest-penitent, doctor-patient, and lawyer-client. It dates back to the sixteenth century, when it was based on "the oath and honour of the solicitor, as a professional man and gentleman, to keep his client's secret. Thus, the early privilege belonged solely to the solicitor, and the client benefited from it only incidentally."[61] This basis for the privilege became known as the Honour Theory, the focal point of which was the status of the lawyer as a professional: "[I]t announced a broad value of high-mindedness and honor ostensibly inherent in the business of lawyering. The unseemliness of revealing an entrusted confidence necessarily required, it was thought, a regime of absolute privilege for the advocate."[62]

The Honour Theory has been relied on frequently by Canadian courts[63] and academic commentators[64] to explain the historical basis for the privilege. It is part of the historical narrative of the development of the privilege under Canadian law. Over time, however, this early rationale "gave way to the view that the privilege was necessary, not in order to maintain the solicitor's reputation, but for the protection of the client."[65] The Honour Theory is still an important part of solicitor-client privilege. It helps to explain why lawyers and judges treat the privilege as a matter of faith and often use religious terminology such as "sacred" or "sacrosanct" to describe its importance.[66]

By the early nineteenth century, the rationale for the privilege had shifted from the honour of the solicitor to more utilitarian justifications based on efficacy of the justice system. Although these justifications were developed in the nineteenth century,[67] they continue to resonate today. This passage from *Anderson v. Bank of British Columbia* (1876)[68] is often cited:[69]

> The object and meaning of the rule is this: that as, by reason of the complexity and difficulty of our law, litigation can only be properly conducted

by professional men, it is absolutely necessary that a man, in order to pros-
ecute his rights or to defend himself from an improper claim, should have
recourse to the assistance of professional lawyers, ... to use a vulgar phrase,
that he should be able to make a clean breast of it to the gentleman whom
he consults with a view to the prosecution of his claim, or the substantiat-
ing of his defence, ... that he should be able to place unrestricted and un-
bounded confidence in the professional agent, and that the communications
he so makes to him should be kept secret, unless with his consent (for it is
his privilege, and not the privilege of the confidential agent), that he should
be enabled properly to conduct his litigation.[70]

The privilege is said to be necessary in order to foster open communication between client and lawyer. This justification is often referred to as the
"full and frank disclosure" argument. Modern articulations of it can be found
throughout Canadian,[71] American,[72] and English cases.[73] This promise of
confidentiality is what allowed Leopold to confide in his lawyer, who promised Leopold the same confidentiality in confiding in Dr. O'Shaughnessy.

The utilitarian justifications for the privilege are closely linked to claims
about the well-functioning legal system. In short, it is asserted that the privilege "also serves to promote the adversarial process as an effective and just
means for resolving disputes within our society."[74] In the adversarial process,
"the client must look to a skilled lawyer to champion her cause against that
of her adversaries. The client justifiably demands the undivided loyalty of
her lawyer. Without client-solicitor privilege, the lawyer could not serve that
role and provide that undivided loyalty."[75] Leopold clearly looked to Mackoff
to defend his interests against the charges of the Crown.

That is perhaps the most important aspect of solicitor-client privilege
that is underappreciated: it allows all individuals – even people like Michael
Leopold – to participate in society and benefit from information and advice
from lawyers in order to exercise their rights.[76] There is a strong link between
the privilege and the exercise of one's rights.

Justice David Doherty of the Ontario Court of Appeal in *Chrusz* (1999)
saw solicitor-client privilege as "an expression of our commitment to both
personal autonomy and access to justice."[77] On the one hand, personal autonomy includes an individual's ability to control the release of personal
information and to maintain confidence. On the other, access to justice requires that individuals can obtain legal advice. One should not have to surrender her personal autonomy in order to get legal advice. Solicitor-client
privilege promotes both personal autonomy and access to justice.[78]

The tension between these interests and protection of the public lies at the core of the public safety exception. But before Mackoff was forced to confront these issues, he continued to seek the best possible resolution for his client.

Seeking a Plea Agreement

Les Mackoff attempted to negotiate with the Crown the best deal that he could for his client. Michael Leopold was a first-time offender, but he faced up to life imprisonment on the charge of aggravated sexual assault. Realistically, he probably faced a sentence of between four and eight years if convicted on that charge.[79] Mackoff struck a deal with the Crown that, in retrospect, was clearly a good one for his client.

Under the terms of the plea agreement, Leopold would plead guilty to aggravated assault, a lesser offence that carries a maximum term of fourteen years in prison.[80] The Crown agreed to seek a sentence of two years less a day of incarceration (*i.e.*, in a provincial facility and not in a federal penitentiary) plus three years of probation. So, on September 24, 1997, Leopold pleaded guilty in the BC Provincial Court to aggravated assault. Sentencing was adjourned until November 18 for a pre-sentence report. That date was later pushed back to December 15. Under the terms of the plea agreement, Crown counsel would be released from it if "something surprising" was revealed in a pre-sentence report or a psychiatric assessment.[81]

After Leopold pleaded guilty but before he was sentenced, Dr. O'Shaughnessy contacted Mackoff to check on the status of the case and when he could expect to appear in court to testify about Leopold's dangerousness. Mackoff informed Dr. O'Shaughnessy that he did not intend to communicate the doctor's opinions and concerns to the sentencing judge. Dr. O'Shaughnessy told Mackoff that he would seek legal advice.[82]

Mackoff must have been surprised. Dr. O'Shaughnessy was not following the rules of the legal game. Experts do not usually challenge lawyers, especially those who provide them with work and retain them. But Dr. O'Shaughnessy proved time and again that he was no ordinary expert witness. As the Head of Forensic Psychiatry at UBC Hospital, he would have known many lawyers. Moreover, Canadian doctors retain some of the most capable lawyers in the country through their insurer, the Canadian Medical Protective Agency (CMPA). That was how Dr. O'Shaughnessy came to retain one of the top lawyers in the province, Chris Hinkson, now the Chief Justice of the Supreme Court of British Columbia.

Launching Proceedings: *Smith v. Jones*

On behalf of Dr. O'Shaughnessy, Hinkson initiated an application in the Supreme Court of British Columbia seeking a declaration "as to whether or not [O'Shaughnessy] is required to make disclosure to the responsible authorities" regarding Leopold.[83] Hinkson and Mackoff agreed that, because of solicitor-client privilege, the identities of the parties could not be revealed because that would alert the Crown since proceedings against Leopold were pending. The two lawyers agreed that Dr. O'Shaughnessy would be known as "John Smith" and that Leopold would become "James Jones." At the request of the parties, the Court agreed to seal the file so that no one could access it and to impose a publication ban so that the media could not report on the case. That publication ban held up, except for the Supreme Court's inadvertent release of information about the case that tipped off journalist Stephen Bindman.[84]

In the Supreme Court of British Columbia, the judge decided the case based on both doctor-patient confidentiality and solicitor-client privilege. He held that Dr. O'Shaughnessy's duty of confidentiality is displaced when information exists to satisfy the doctor "that the patient is likely to kill or cause serious bodily harm to a member of the public and that the danger is imminent."[85] Noting the rarity of such an occurrence, the judge further stated that it would not suffice that the patient threatens to commit a criminal offence, even a serious one. Rather, the danger must be "clear, serious and imminent."[86] The judge further concluded that solicitor-client privilege is also displaced when "a lawyer receives information which satisfies him or her that a client is likely to kill or cause serious bodily harm to a member of the public, and that the danger is imminent."[87] The judge found that disclosure was mandatory, stating that no circumstances existed that could justify the exercise of discretion against disclosure.[88] He ordered Dr. O'Shaughnessy to disclose portions of his affidavit to the Crown and the police.[89] Mackoff appealed this order, and it was stayed or frozen, pending determination of the appeal.

Round Two: The British Columbia Court of Appeal

The British Columbia Court of Appeal heard an expedited appeal within a few weeks. This time the Court focused squarely on solicitor-client privilege. It held that Leopold's communications with Dr. O'Shaughnessy as well as the latter's opinion were protected by solicitor-client privilege and could not be revealed. It agreed with the trial court that the privilege was overridden by the public safety exception but held that disclosure was not mandatory, only permissible.[90]

Mackoff had one final hope for his client: the Supreme Court of Canada.

Round Three: The Supreme Court of Canada

Mackoff sought leave to appeal the Court of Appeal's decision. By 1998, the Supreme Court had abandoned the long-held practice of hearing applications for leave to appeal orally. The process had become entirely written. However, in rare circumstances, the Court would order an oral hearing on an application for leave. It did so in this case.

Thus, Les Mackoff and Chris Hinkson travelled to Ottawa at the end of May 1998 for their hearing on June 1. They were joined at the Court by Paul Schabas, representing Southam News, which had got wind of the case through its inquisitive justice reporter, Stephen Bindman.

When lawyers come to the Supreme Court to participate in a case, they must check in with the Court Registry, where staff help to orient them. Some lawyers, such as Hinkson and Schabas, had appeared in the Supreme Court before, but most were like Mackoff, who had never been there (and it would be his only appearance there). The Court Registry told the three lawyers that the Chief Justice wanted to see them before the hearing in his private chambers, a highly unusual occurrence that Schabas described as "extraordinary."[91] They were escorted up to the Court's third floor, through the secure corridor that housed the judges' private offices. Mackoff, Hinkson, and Schabas must have been nervous as they passed the stern portraits of Chief Justices past and waited in the antechamber of the august offices of the Chief Justice of Canada, the Right Honourable Antonio Lamer.[92]

After waiting for a few minutes, the three lawyers were ushered into the office, where Lamer was sitting with the Court's Executive Legal Officer, James O'Reilly, who served as his top adviser. There was no stenographer present, and there is no record of what was said beyond the recollection of Schabas.[93] Lamer told the lawyers that all nine judges would hear the leave application and Southam's motion, another highly unusual decision because almost all leave applications were decided in writing by panels of three judges. He also told the lawyers that they would make their arguments in open court but that nothing they said could be repeated or published. The Court would deal with the leave application first and then Southam's application to lift the publication ban.

Both Mackoff and Hinkson argued cryptically about the case. Lamer stopped the proceedings twice while members of the public entered and left the courtroom and admonished them not to speak about what they heard there.[94] Schabas was able to figure out that the case had something to do with public safety, solicitor-client privilege, and an expert. The judges seemed somewhat surprised that Hinkson did not contest that the issue was one of national importance. They granted Mackoff's motion for leave to appeal and then turned to Schabas.

For nearly half an hour, Schabas tried to convince the Court to lift the veil of secrecy over the case, to no avail. Even the identities of Mackoff and Hinkson had to be kept secret because, if people found out that they were on a case together, they might be able to figure out the identities of Smith and Jones. The Court denied the motion to lift the publication ban but allowed publication of the decision that leave to appeal was granted and that the issue pertained to an expert opinion as an exception to solicitor-client privilege.[95]

Smith v. Jones and the Public Safety Exception: The Court's Decision

The appeal was heard on October 8, 1998, and the Supreme Court released its decision on March 25, 1999, a little over five months later. In Supreme Court terms, this was a relatively quick decision.

The Supreme Court unanimously confirmed the existence of a public safety exception to solicitor-client privilege. Writing for the majority, Justice Peter Cory stated that there are certain circumstances "when the safety of the public is at risk [and] the solicitor-client privilege may be set aside."[96] The privilege can be set aside when there is a clear, serious, and imminent danger. First, there has to be a clear risk to an identifiable person or group of persons. Second, the risk has to be of serious bodily harm (including serious psychological harm) or death. And third, the danger has to be imminent.

In defining clear risk, the Court offered a number of criteria:

> Is there evidence of long range planning? Has a method for effecting the specific attack been suggested? Is there a prior history of violence or threats of violence? Are the prior assaults or threats of violence similar to that which was planned? If there is a history of violence, has the violence increased in severity? Is the violence directed to an identifiable person or group of persons?[97]

The Court emphasized the requirement that a group or person be ascertainable.[98] Regarding the seriousness of the risk, the Court held that the intended victim must be in danger of being killed or of suffering serious bodily harm (including psychological harm).[99] The third prong of the test requires imminence: "The nature of the threat must be such that it creates a sense of urgency. This sense of urgency may be applicable to some time in the future."[100] The questions seemed to be composed based on the facts before the Court in *Smith v. Jones*. Each of the criteria has to be defined in the context of each particular case, and different weights can be given to each factor in any particular case. The hardest factor to nail down is imminence.[101]

Given the weight accorded by the Court to public safety, it is not readily apparent why a threat judged to constitute a serious risk of bodily harm or death to an identifiable person or group need also be imminent. If public safety is an overriding concern, no apparent benefit exists in waiting until the threat is near its execution before permitting its revelation. Such a policy risks waiting until it is too late to prevent the harm. Perhaps cognizant of this problem, the Court embraced a watered-down notion of imminence in which "a sense of urgency" can extend indefinitely into the future.[102] The result is a criterion problematic in application[103] and unnecessary given the detailed exposition of the clarity factor, which addresses concerns about what most people would consider imminence: "Is there evidence of long range planning? [And h]as a method for effecting the specific attack been suggested?"[104]

Not surprisingly, the Supreme Court found that the public safety exception applied in the case of "Mr. Jones." The specific victim group (skid row prostitutes) was identified, as were specificity of method (forcing a prostitute to become his "sex slave" before killing her), evidence of planning (arranging for vacation time, modifying his basement apartment, taking rope and duct tape, and intending to shoot the victim to obliterate her identity), and prior attempted or actual acts that mirrored the potential act of threatened future harm (Leopold termed the initial assault to which he pleaded guilty a "trial run").[105] With regard to seriousness, the Court found that the intended sexually sadistic murder obviously sufficed.[106] Recognizing that imminence was the most difficult factor in this case, the Court acknowledged that no evidence had been presented on whether "Dr. Smith" considered a future attack to be imminent.[107] The Court balanced the failure of Dr. O'Shaughnessy to take any action for three months and the lack of evidence that he believed Leopold would commit a serious attack in the near future with Dr. O'Shaughnessy's actions in contacting Mackoff and initiating these proceedings.

The Court was divided on the important question of how much Dr. O'Shaughnessy could disclose. The majority sanctioned the scope of disclosure in the trial judge's order,[108] including Leopold's complete confession to Dr. O'Shaughnessy as well as the details of his plans to commit future attacks.[109] On this issue, Justice Major dissented (with Chief Justice Lamer and Justice Binnie), expressing the concern that, if the privilege is overridden to the extent of allowing disclosure of self-incriminating evidence, the result might endanger members of the public more than the public safety exception would protect them.[110] Major emphasized the "chilling effect of completely breaching the privilege," claiming that it would produce the undesired effect of discouraging individuals in need of treatment for serious and dangerous conditions from consulting professional help.[111]

The partial dissent raised serious self-incrimination concerns that result from using evidence against an accused obtained through privileged communication. Justice Major stated that "[o]ur jurisprudence does not allow the conscription of an accused's own words against him."[112] It is one thing to use the words of the accused to thwart his pending crimes and prevent serious harm; it is quite another matter to use his confession, made in a confidential and privileged setting, to convict him.

What Is a Lawyer to Do?

The Supreme Court did not establish guidelines for a lawyer faced with a client who might pose a threat to public safety. The best reading of *Smith v. Jones* – as evidenced by the discretionary rules enacted by law societies following the Supreme Court's decision – is that the lawyer (or her agent) has a discretion, not a duty, to disclose information determined to be a clear, serious, and imminent threat to public safety. But who determines that? Law society rules establish that again it is the lawyer's reasonable belief.

Thus, a lawyer can choose not to disclose such information. For the reasons explained above, that is what Mackoff did and what most criminal defence lawyers would likely do. However, lawyers faced with such a dilemma would likely speak to a colleague or law society. Since *Smith v. Jones*, there has been much more discussion about it than application of it.[113]

Revelation of Solicitor-Client Confidences

The Supreme Court of Canada allowed Dr. O'Shaughnessy to disclose the information, unsealed the file, and lifted the publication ban.[114] Leopold's sentencing was put on hold while the secret case was making its way to the Supreme Court. Once the Court allowed Dr. O'Shaughnessy to make his views about Leopold known to the Crown, the plea agreement was off. Instead, the Crown applied to the Court to have Leopold remanded for assessment as a dangerous offender under provisions of the *Criminal Code* that allowed for the imposition of an indeterminate sentence on those found to constitute a threat to the life, safety, or physical or mental well-being of other persons.[115]

A three-day dangerous offender hearing was held in July 2000 at which Dr. O'Shaughnessy was the key witness. Another psychiatrist who had prepared a court-ordered assessment also testified. Dr. O'Shaughnessy testified that he thought Leopold was at the severe end of the scale of sexual sadism and recommended chemical treatment for him. The other psychiatrist agreed that Leopold suffered from sexual sadism, but he thought that therapeutic treatment should be attempted before chemical treatment. He thought that with treatment Leopold could be reduced from high-moderate to high risk to reoffend in a sexually violent way to low-moderate risk.[116]

The sentencing judge was doubtful that, even with treatment, Leopold would cease to be a sexual sadist. However, he refused to focus on a prediction of Leopold's future behaviour. He refused to designate Leopold as a dangerous offender and instead sentenced him to eleven years at the age of thirty-eight,[117] nearly six times the length of the original sentence to which he had agreed before his solicitor-client privilege was overridden. The Crown appealed the length of the sentence.

The BC Court of Appeal allowed the appeal and designated Leopold as a dangerous offender. In so doing, it relied heavily on the testimony of Dr. O'Shaughnessy.[118] The Supreme Court of Canada turned down Leopold's application for leave to appeal and a chance to consider his case a second time. There were no more legal avenues for Mackoff to pursue for his client; he had done all that he could for him. Leopold began serving his indeterminate sentence as a dangerous offender.

Conclusion

As of November 2015, Michael Leopold, aka "James Jones," remains incarcerated as a dangerous offender. He remains the only known person sentenced on the basis of solicitor-client communications used against him. Dr. O'Shaughnessy, aka "John Smith," still practises forensic psychiatry in Vancouver. Chris Hinkson was appointed a judge of the Supreme Court of British Columbia in 2007. Three years later he was elevated to the BC Court of Appeal. On November 7, 2013, the Prime Minister named Hinkson Chief Justice of the Supreme Court of British Columbia. Justice Peter Cory, who wrote the majority decision in *Smith v. Jones*, retired on June 1, 1999. *Smith v. Jones* was one of his last decisions. It has become one of the leading cases on solicitor-client privilege in Canada and in the common law world, cited over 240 times by courts in Canada and many times by courts in other common law countries.

Stephen Bindman, the journalist who discovered the secret case and got Southam News to retain Paul Schabas, left Southam before the Supreme Court of Canada decided *Smith v. Jones* and now works for the Department of Justice as a Special Adviser on Wrongful Convictions. Southam ceased to exist after it was purchased by Hollinger and then Canwest. There are very few legal affairs correspondents like Bindman left in Canada. Schabas continues to work at Blakes in Toronto and still represents media clients. He called the day that he went to Ottawa to participate in the leave to appeal motion in *Smith v. Jones* "an extraordinary day" that he will never forget.[119]

Les Mackoff still practises criminal defence law in downtown Vancouver. When I interviewed him at his office in October 2013, it was clear that *Smith v. Jones* was one of the most memorable cases of his career. He was still somewhat troubled by the way that the Supreme Court had defined the public safety exception, specifically the imminence factor. He said that the case was far from clear-cut to him, and he still believes that he did the right thing. To Mackoff, the duty of loyalty to his client Leopold did not allow him to override the duty of confidentiality and his client's rights: "It was not my place to unilaterally displace solicitor-client privilege."[120]

Postscript

I faced my own ethical dilemma in this case. Between 1999 and 2001, I wrote several articles about *Smith v. Jones*.[121] In researching the articles, I had met both Les Mackoff and Chris Hinkson and continued to follow Leopold's case. After the Supreme Court refused to hear an appeal of the case and Leopold began to serve his indeterminate sentence as a dangerous offender, the Supreme Court decided another case in a series of solicitor-client privilege cases: *R. v. Brown*.[122] In it, the Supreme Court recognized a right to immunity under section 7 of the *Charter of Rights and Freedoms* for the holder of the privilege who has information disclosed pursuant to the innocence at stake exception to solicitor-client privilege.[123] Although the Supreme Court did not say so, it appeared to me that this rule should also apply to the public safety exception, and indeed I had argued as much in a previous article.[124]

As a junior lawyer and an aspiring academic practising in a Bay Street law firm, I was as far away from the criminal law trenches as I could be. Academics and lawyers in large firms seldom face the moral dilemmas that criminal lawyers such as Les Mackoff do. I thought that, as a matter of principle, solicitor-client communications should not be used against the holder of the privilege. I decided, as a matter of practice, to put my money where my mouth was, so to speak. I informed Mackoff about the new case in the Supreme Court and suggested that he apply to the Court for a reconsideration of Leopold's leave to appeal application in light of *R. v. Brown,* a long shot at best. Mackoff got instructions from Leopold to proceed and asked me to assist him as co-counsel on the case. I got permission from my firm to participate as *pro bono* counsel and drafted the motion materials with Mackoff. I knew that the motion was a long shot, but I honestly believed that we were right and that Leopold should get a further hearing in light of *R. v. Brown.* The Supreme Court did not agree and dismissed the motion for reconsideration.[125] That remains the one and only criminal case that I ever worked on as counsel.

Notes

Thanks to Stephen Bindman and David Tanovich for reading earlier drafts of this chapter and providing helpful comments and to Les Mackoff and Paul Schabas for agreeing to be interviewed for this project.

1 See Affidavit of Stephen Bindman, sworn May 28, 1998, in Intervener's Motion Record, filed May 28, 1998, Court File No. 26500; and Interview with Paul Schabas, October 31, 2013.

2 Schabas and his firm Blake Cassels & Graydon LLP regularly acted (and continue to act) for the *Toronto Star.* Although the motion on June 1, 1998, was instigated by Southam (specifically Bindman), Schabas got instructions from the *Toronto Star,* the *Globe and Mail,* and the Canadian Newspapers Association to represent them as well on the motion.

3 Stephen Bindman, "Supreme Court Violates Its Own Gag Order," Southam Newspapers (March 31, 1998), Exhibit F to Bindman, *supra* note 1.

4 Anne Roland to David W. Scott, Scott & Aylen, March 31, 1998, Exhibit E to Bindman, *supra* note 1.

5 Bindman, *supra* note 3.

6 Schabas, *supra* note 1.

7 *Ibid.*

8 Interview with Leslie Mackoff, October 11, 2013.

9 Online: Mackoff & Company, http://www.mackoff.ca.

10 *Smith v. Jones* (1998), 62 B.C.L.R. (3d) 198 at 200, [1998] B.C.J. No. 318 at para. 5 (B.C.C.A).

11 *Criminal Code of Canada*, R.S.C. 1985, c. C-46, s. 273.

12 *Smith v. Jones* (1998), 62 B.C.L.R. (3d) 198 at 200, [1998] B.C.J. No. 318 at para. 5 (B.C.C.A.).

13 See *R. v. Stinchcome*, [1991] 3 S.C.R. 326, [1991] S.C.J. No. 83.

14 There are three exceptions to this general rule absolving the defence of any duty to disclose. An alibi must be disclosed in sufficient time to allow the Crown to properly investigate it; see *R. v. Cleghorn*, [1995] S.C.J. No. 73. Similarly, a psychiatric defence must be disclosed with sufficient time to permit a Crown psychiatrist to examine the defendant; see *R. v. Worth*, [1995] O.J. No. 1063. Finally, any expert opinion evidence that the defendant will rely on should be disclosed thirty days before trial; see *Criminal Code of Canada*, R.S.C. 1985, c. C-46, s. 657.3. See, generally, Alice Woolley, Richard Devlin, Brent Cotter, and John M. Law, eds., *Lawyers' Ethics and Professional Regulation*, 2d ed. (Toronto: LexisNexis, 2012) at 469–70.

15 *Smith v. Jones*, [1999] 1 S.C.R. 455 at para. 36.

16 *Ibid.*

17 *Smith v. Jones*, [1998] B.C.J. No. 3182, 62 B.C.L.R. (3d) 198 at para. 7 (C.A.).

18 This description is largely rewritten from my case comment, Adam M. Dodek, "*Smith v. Jones:* The Public Safety Exception to Solicitor-Client Privilege" (2000) 34 U.B.C. Law Review 293 at 295.

19 The court of first instance that heard this case noted that Leopold was a gunsmith who collected firearms. See *Smith v. Jones*, [1997] B.C.J. No. 3136 at para. 6 (S.C.).

20 *Ibid.* at para. 7.

21 *Ibid.*

22 *Ibid.* at para. 8.

23 *Ibid.*

24 *Ibid.*

25 *Smith v. Jones* (1998), 62 B.C.L.R. (3d) 198 at 200, [1998] B.C.J. No. 318 at para. 8 (B.C.C.A.).

26 The clinical term for deviant sexual behaviours is "paraphilia": "Paraphilias are sexual disorders characterized by specialized sexual fantasies and intense sexual urges and practices that are usually repetitive and distressing to the person." H.I. Kaplan, B.J. Sadock, and J.A. Grebb, *Kaplan and Sadock's Synopsis of Psychiatry: Behavioral Sciences Clinical Psychiatry*, 7th ed. (Baltimore: Williams and Wilkins, 1994) at 674.

27 *Smith v. Jones* (1998), 62 B.C.L.R. (3d) 198 at 201; see also *Smith v. Jones*, [1997] B.C.J. No. 3136 at para. 13 (S.C.).

28 *Smith v. Jones* (1998), 62 B.C.L.R. (3d) 198 at 202.

29 On the extension of solicitor-client privilege to experts, see Adam Dodek, *Solicitor-Client Privilege* (Toronto: LexisNexis, 2014) at c. 5.

30 Interview with Leslie Mackoff, October 11, 2013.

31 Thanks to Ottawa criminal defence lawyer Anne-Marie McElroy for schooling me on "rounders" and many aspects of criminal defence.

32 Nor are lawyers likely to be particularly good at predicting future dangerousness, since it is a challenge even for psychiatrists. See, for example, Alan A. Stone, "The *Tarasoff* Decision: Suing Psychotherapists to Safeguard Society" (1976) 90 Harvard Law Review 358.

33 *R. v. Boucher*, [1955] S.C.R. 16.

34 *Ibid.* at 24.

35 *Ibid.*

36 Federation of Law Societies of Canada, *Model Code of Professional Conduct,* Rule 5.1–3.

37 *Ibid.,* comment 1.

38 *Ibid.*

39 *R. v. Boucher,* [1955] S.C.R. 16 at 24.

40 *R. v. Neil,* 2002 S.C.C. 70, [2002] 3 S.C.R. 631, [2002] S.C.J. No. 72.

41 *Trial of Queen Caroline* (1821), by J. Nightingale, vol. 2, "The Defence," part 1, at 8, quoted in *R. v. Neil,* 2002 S.C.C. 70 at para. 12.

42 See Jane Robins, *The Trial of Queen Caroline: The Scandalous Affair that Nearly Ended a Monarchy* (New York: Free Press, 2006).

43 See Trevor C.W. Farrow, "Sustainable Professionalism" (2008) 46 Osgoode Hall Law Journal 51 at 63–64.

44 Edward L. Greenspan and George Jonas, *Greenspan: For the Defence* (Toronto: Macmillan, 1987) at 51.

45 See Federation of Law Societies of Canada, *Model Code of Professional Conduct,* Rule 5.2–1.

46 Greenspan and Jonas, *supra* note 44 at 262.

47 *Ibid.* at 263.

48 On the difference between American and Canadian conceptions of "zealousness," see Alice Woolley, "Integrity in Zealousness: Comparing the Standard Conceptions of the Canadian and American Lawyer" (1996) 9 Canadian Journal of Law and Jurisprudence 61.

49 Federation of Law Societies of Canada, *Model Code of Professional Conduct,* Rule 5.1–1, comment 1.

50 *R. v. Neil,* 2002 S.C.C. 70 at paras. 17–18.

51 See, generally, Dodek, *supra* note 29 at c. 8.

52 See Alice C. Woolley, *Understanding Lawyers' Ethics in Canada* (Toronto: LexisNexis, 2011) at 107.

53 *MacDonald Estate v. Martin,* [1990] 3 S.C.R. 1235 at para. 15, per Sopinka J.

54 See David Layton, "The Public Safety Exception: Confusing Confidentiality, Privilege, and Ethics" (2002) 6 Canadian Criminal Law Review 209.

55 See Federation of Law Societies of Canada, *Model Code of Professional Conduct,* Rule 3.3–1.

56 See, generally, Dodek, *supra* note 29.

57 *Descôteaux v. Mierzwinski,* [1982] 1 S.C.R. 860 at 875.

58 See *Smith v. Jones,* [1999] 1 S.C.R. 455 at para. 44.

59 *Blank v. Canada (Minister of Justice),* 2006 S.C.C. 39, [2006] 2 S.C.R. 319 at para. 32 (per Fish J.).

60 Woolley, *supra* note 52 at 107.

61 Alan W. Bryant, Sidney N. Lederman, and Michelle K. Fuerst, *The Law of Evidence in Canada,* 3d ed. (Toronto: LexisNexis, 2009) at 728 [citations omitted].

62 "The Attorney-Client Privilege: Fixed Rules, Balancing, and Constitutional Entitlement" (1977) 91 Harvard Law Review 464 at 465, citing John H. Wigmore, *Evidence,* McNaughton, rev. ed. (Boston: Little, Brown, and Company, 1961) vol. 8 at s. 2290.

63 See, for example, *R. v. McClure,* 2001 S.C.C. 14, [2001] 1 S.C.R. 445 at paras. 17–21.
64 See, for example, Bryant, Lederman, and Fuerst, *supra* note 61; and Ronald Manes and Michael P. Silver, *Solicitor-Client Privilege in Canadian Law* (Toronto: Butterworths, 1993). The Honour Theory is frequently referenced in American legal literature; see, for example, "The Attorney-Client Privilege," *supra* note 62 at 465.
65 Bryant, Lederman, and Fuerst, *supra* note 61 at 728.
66 See, for example, *MacDonald Estate v. Martin,* [1990] 3 S.C.R. 1235 at para. 15, per Sopinka J. ("Nothing is more important to the preservation of this relationship than the confidentiality of information passing between a solicitor and his or her client. The legal profession has distinguished itself from other professions by the *sanctity* with which these communications are treated. The law, too, perhaps unduly, has protected solicitor and client exchanges while denying the same protection to others."); *Bre-X Ministers Ltd. (Trustee of) v. Verchere,* [2001] A.J. No. 1264 at para. 15 (C.A.) ("Solicitor-client privilege, one of the oldest forms of common law privilege, protects the *sanctity* of the confidence between client and lawyer"); *R. v. Comeau,* [2001] O.J. No. 3036 at para. 40 (S.C.J.) ("There was a breach of solicitor/ client privilege which our justice system holds *sacred*"); *Transcon Recycling Inc. v. London Assurance,* [1997] O.J. No. 2878 at para.15 (Ont. C.J. (Gen. Div.)) ("It is an undisputed and fundamental right, grounded in tradition, the adversarial nature of the legal process, and simple fairness and justice, *sacrosanct* the communications between solicitor and client"); and *474562 Alberta Ltd. v. J.M. Nelson Holdings Ltd.,* [1998] A.J. No. 1331 at para. 12 (Q.B.) ("Solicitor-client privilege is *sacrosanct* and should only be pierced in exceptional circumstances"). It is ironic, of course, that the privilege is accorded greater protection than communications with one's religious or spiritual adviser. See *R. v. Gruenke* [1991] 3 S.C.R. 263 (refusing to recognize a class privilege for confidential communications with a religious adviser on par with solicitor-client privilege).
67 See *Greenough v. Gaskell* (1833), 39 E.R. 618 at 620–21 (Ch. Div.).
68 *Anderson v. Bank of British Columbia* (1876), 2 Ch. D. 644 (C.A.).
69 See *Smith v. Jones,* [1999] 1 S.C.R. 455 at para. 45; and *R. v. McClure,* 2001 S.C.C. 14, [2001] 1 S.C.R. 445 at para. 32.
70 *Anderson v. Bank of British Columbia* (1876), 2 Ch. D. 644 at 649 (C.A.).
71 *R. v. McClure,* 2001 S.C.C. 14, [2001] 1 S.C.R. 445 at para. 33. See also *Smith v. Jones,* [1999] 1 S.C.R. 455 at para. 45; *R. v. Brown,* 2002 S.C.C. 32, [2002] 2 S.C.R. 185 at paras. 27, 89; and *Lavallee, Rackel & Heintz v. Canada (Attorney General); White, Ottenheimer & Baker v. Canada (Attorney General); R. v. Fink,* 2002 S.C.C. 61, [2002] 3 S.C.R. 209 at para. 36.
72 See, for example, *Upjohn Co. v. United States,* 449 U.S. 383 at 389, 101 S. Ct. 677 at 682, 66 L. Ed. 2d 584 at 590 (1981) (stating that the purpose of the attorney-client privilege is "to encourage full and frank communications between attorneys and their clients and thereby promote broader public interests in the observance of law and administration of justice. The privilege recognizes that sound legal advice or advocacy serves public ends and that such advice or advocacy depends upon the lawyer's being fully informed by the client").
73 See, for example, *R. v. Derby Magistrates' Court,* [1995] 4 All E.R. 526 (H.L.).

74 *General Accident Assurance Co. v. Chrusz* (1999), 45 O.R. (3d) 321, 1999 CanLII 7320 (Ont. C.A.), at para. 93.

75 *Ibid.,* quoting *McCormick on Evidence,* J.W. Strong, ed. (St. Paul, Minn.: West Publishing Co., 1992), vol. 1, at 316–17.

76 *Maranda v. Richer,* [2003] 3 S.C.R. 193, 2003 S.C.C. 67 at para. 40, per Deschamps J.

77 *General Accident Assurance Co. v. Chrusz* (1999), 45 O.R. (3d) 321, 1999 CanLII 7320 (Ont. C.A.), at para. 92 [citations omitted].

78 *Ibid.* Elsewhere I have attempted to develop a fuller rights-based theory of solicitor-client privilege. See Adam M. Dodek, "Reconceiving Solicitor-Client Privilege" (2010) 35 Queen's Law Journal 493.

79 See Clayton C. Ruby, *Sentencing,* 5th ed. (Toronto: Butterworths, 1999) at para. 22.199 (describing the range of sentences for aggravated sexual assault).

80 *Criminal Code of Canada,* R.S.C. 1985, c. C-46, s. 268.

81 *R. v. Leopold,* 2001 B.C.C.A. 396, [2001] B.C.J. No. 1209 at para. 4.

82 Dodek, *supra* note 18 at 297.

83 *Smith v. Jones* (1998), 62 B.C.L.R. (3d) 198 at 200, [1998] B.C.J. No. 318 at para. 9 (B.C.C.A).

84 Bindman, *supra* note 3.

85 *Smith v. Jones,* [1997] B.C.J. No. 3136 at para. 16 (B.C.S.C.).

86 *Ibid.* at para. 24.

87 *Ibid.* at para. 32.

88 *Ibid.* at para. 35.

89 *Ibid.* at para. 37.

90 *Smith v. Jones* (1998), 62 B.C.L.R. (3d) 198, [1998] B.C.J. No. 3182 (B.C.C.A).

91 Interview with Paul Schabas, Toronto, October 31, 2013.

92 *Ibid.*

93 This account is taken from my interview with Schabas, *ibid.* Chief Justice Lamer confirmed that the in-chamber meeting took place and revealed some of its discussions in open court in the oral hearing on leave to appeal. See Transcript of June 1, 1998, Hearing, Court File No. 26500, at 1.

94 Transcript of June 1, 1998, Hearing, Court File 26500, at 1, 9, 19.

95 Court File 26500, 1998-06-01. There was a motion brought by Leopold (aka James Jones) to have the appeal held *in camera* (*i.e.,* completely closed to the public). It was denied, again by all nine members of the Court. Southam's motion for access to the Court file was also denied. Southam was allowed to intervene in the hearing. See Court File 26500, 1998-10-05.

96 *Smith v. Jones,* [1999] 1 S.C.R. 455 at 478.

97 *Ibid.* at 487.

98 *Ibid.*

99 *Ibid.* at 488.

100 *Ibid.*

101 See, generally, Dodek, *supra* note 18.

102 See *Smith v. Jones,* [1999] 1 S.C.R. 455 at 467, per Cory J.

103 See Dodek, *supra* note 18 at 307–8.

104 *Smith v. Jones,* [1999] 1 S.C.R. 455 at 489.

105 *Ibid.* at 491.

106 *Ibid.* at 492.

107 Dr. O'Shaughnessy stated in his affidavit that he "considered [Leopold] to be a dangerous individual in that he would be more likely than not ... [to] act on these fantasies unless he had sufficient treatment." Affidavit of Dr. Smith at para. 32, *Smith v. Jones,* Vancouver Registry No. C976491.

108 *Smith v. Jones,* [1999] 1 S.C.R. 455 at 491.

109 Although the Supreme Court did not mention it, Leopold disputed the allegation that he had informed Dr. O'Shaughnessy of his future plans: "[A]t no time did I inform Dr. Smith that I had planned any similar act since my arrest approximately fifteen months ago." Affidavit of James Jones, *Smith v. Jones,* Vancouver Registry No. C9764691 (10 December 1997).

110 *Smith v. Jones,* [1999] 1 S.C.R. 455 at 466, per Major J. (dissenting in part).

111 *Ibid.*

112 *Ibid.* at 468–69, citing *R. v. Jones,* [1994] 2 S.C.R. 229.

113 One of the rare instances in which the public safety exception has arisen was *R. v. Butt,* 2012 O.N.S.C. 4326, [2012] O.J. No. 3553. The defendant pleaded guilty to one count of sexual interference involving luring a twelve-year-old boy off the street into his apartment, where he performed sexual acts on the boy. The Crown appealed the sentence, but before the appeal was heard counsel for the respondent-defendant sought an adjournment to investigate an ethical issue that had arisen. One week later counsel for the defendant advised the Court and the Crown in writing that her client had been diagnosed as HIV positive earlier that year. Counsel for the defendant assumed that the Crown would want to contact the family of the boy. The judge presiding over the sentence appeal, the Honourable Michael Code of the Ontario Superior Court of Justice, stated that counsel "is to be commended for her appreciation of her ethical obligations in this difficult matter. The 'public safety' or 'future harm' exception to solicitor and client privilege, and any reporting duties that arise from that exception, are not easy areas of law to apply. [Counsel] deserves great credit for the approach she took and, fortunately, no harm has been done to the victim." *Ibid.* For more discussion, see Dodek, *supra* note 29 at c. 8.

114 See *Smith v. Jones,* [1999] 1 S.C.R. 455 at para. 105; Kirk Makin, "Top Court Lifts Lawyer-Client Confidentiality; Public Safety More Important than Privacy in Case of Man Planning to Kill Prostitutes" *Globe and Mail* (26 March 1999) A3; and Tonda MacCharles, "High Court Lifts Veil on Sadistic Sex Assault Case" *Toronto Star* (26 March 1999).

115 Leopold attempted to withdraw his guilty plea but was denied by the Court on 11 June 1999. See *R. v. Leopold,* 2001 B.C.C.A. 396, [2001] B.C.J. No. 1209 at para. 7.

116 *Ibid.* at para. 13.

117 *Ibid.* at para. 35.

118 *Ibid.*

119 Interview with Paul Schabas, Toronto, October 31, 2013.

120 Interview with Les Mackoff, Vancouver, October 11, 2013.

121 Dodek, *supra* note 18; Adam M. Dodek, "Doing Our Duty: The Case for a Duty of Disclosure to Prevent Death or Serious Harm" (2001) 50 U.N.B.L.J. 215.

122 *R. v. Brown,* [2002] 2 S.C.R. 185, 2002 S.C.C. 32.

123 Strictly speaking, such a pronouncement was *obiter* because the Court in *Brown* found that the *McClure* test was again not satisfied and therefore was not required to address the issue of immunity.

124 Dodek, *supra* note 121 at 226–27.

125 *R. v. Leopold*, [2001] S.C.C.A. No. 551.

2

Putting Up a Defence

Sex, Murder, and Videotapes

ALLAN C. HUTCHINSON

The legal profession is not the most beloved of vocations. From Plato through Shakespeare and Dickens to Tom Wolfe and Lynda La Plante, literature attests to its impugned status. Matters are not much different in real life. In the public's mind, lawyers are not only adept at the dubious arts of manipulation and double dealing, but also moral hypocrites because they defend these practices in the brazen name of "professional ethics." Along with used car dealers and telemarketers, lawyers are considered to be among the least trustworthy and least respected of all professionals. Lord Bolingbroke's assessment of the legal profession several centuries ago remains true today: "[T]he profession of law, in its nature the noblest and most beneficial to mankind, is in its abuse an abasement of the most sordid and pernicious kind."[1]

If the legal profession at large suffers from bad press, the criminal defence bar is the butt of the most insistent criticism. The history of criminal defence lawyering is populated by a cast of colourful characters – from the noble image of Clarence Darrow to the more dubious persona of Johnnie Cochrane. People tend to identify defence lawyers with their unsavoury clients and their unforgivable deeds. However, when individuals are in trouble, they want the best and most dogged lawyers on their side and their side alone; they need to be assured about the unquestioned loyalty of their lawyers to their causes. Whatever the rap against the legal profession generally, accused persons want their lawyers to do all that they can to raise every issue and argument in an uncompromising way that affords them every chance of acquittal.

This puts criminal defence lawyers in an ethical and professional bind. They have to juggle competing obligations to their clients, the courts, the legal profession, and the public interest. And that is no mean feat. Often misunderstood in their actions and motivations, criminal defence lawyers are there to defend their clients – not to judge them. Indeed, the mantra of the defence bar is that these lawyers "lend their exertions to all, and themselves to none."[2] Because accused persons are presumed to be innocent and entitled to a fair trial, the lawyer is required to challenge the Crown's case in the most vigorous and partial way. Against such a backdrop, criminal defence lawyers have to tread a very thin line between zealous advocacy and unethical conduct. Of course, it is not at all surprising that some have overstepped that line.

Two decades ago there was a notorious Canadian case that put the ethical practice of criminal defence lawyers under official and public scrutiny.[3] So difficult and sordid were its circumstances that it divided the profession over what lawyers can and should do in mounting defences for their clients. In a case about sex, murder, and videotapes, a lawyer was placed in the invidious position of having to decide how to handle his competing duties to the private interests of his client and the public interests of justice. How far can a lawyer go in defending his client without obstructing the pursuit of justice? The fact that lawyers still disagree over what they should do in such circumstances only adds to the significance and status of the case in the legal canon.

A Sordid Tale

In February 1993, Kenneth Murray received a collect call from Paul Bernardo, who sought his legal assistance. Bernardo had been given Murray's name by a family member and a friend. Murray was a sole practitioner in Newmarket, a small Ontario town close to Toronto. He had been in practice for about ten years and was certified as a specialist in criminal litigation. Although he had extensive experience in criminal courts, he mostly did run-of-the-mill legal aid work. In agreeing to act for Bernardo, Murray became involved in a series of events that made grisly headlines in the popular and professional press for several years. Bernardo was ultimately convicted of both rape and murder, and Murray himself was charged with "obstructing justice."[4]

When Bernardo made that initial call to Murray, he was in serious trouble. He had been arrested for a series of rapes in Scarborough, a Toronto suburb. He was also under suspicion for at least two murders that had occurred earlier in St. Catharines, a small city about fifty kilometres from Toronto, where he and his wife, Karla Homolka, lived. The circumstances of those criminal charges provided a nauseating and dreadful backdrop against which Murray's professional integrity and judgment would be severely questioned. Regretfully, Murray assumed an important and detrimental role in this sordid drama.

Bernardo was no ordinary criminal. Not only did he participate in some particularly gruesome rapes and murders, but also he did not fit what many considered to be the image of a sadistic killer. With boyish charm and good looks, he was a trainee accountant who presented as a likable boy next door. However, behind that face was a tormented young man who had been brought up in a highly dysfunctional family and abused by his stepfather. Although Bernardo had a reputation as "a ladies' man," his relations with women were far from pleasant or straightforward. Once he connected with Homolka, he found a kindred perverse spirit with whom he could fulfill his darkest fantasies.

In October 1987, twenty-three-year-old Bernardo met seventeen-year-old Homolka in a hotel coffee shop and instantly bonded with her. Whether Homolka knew it or not, Bernardo had already raped several women. They were soon engaged to be married; they presented as an enviable Ken and Barbie couple. However, Bernardo was still troubled that Homolka was not a virgin when they first met. So, on Christmas Eve 1990, by way of recompense, she offered up her virgin fifteen-year-old sister, Tammy, as a peace offering and early Christmas present. Homolka drugged her sister, and Bernardo raped her while she was unconscious. As cruel fate would have it, Tammy choked on her own vomit and died. After an elaborate cover-up, the death was ultimately ruled accidental. However, as part of their nefarious scheme, they had videotaped the whole affair. It was this act of vicious and voyeuristic vanity that would prove to be their and, as circumstances would have it, Ken Murray's undoing.

A fortnight before their wedding in June 1991, Bernardo and Homolka escalated their sadistic activities by abducting a fourteen-year-old girl, Leslie Mahaffy. She was tortured, raped, and then killed. Again they videotaped the degradation. Later that month, her concrete-encased body was found in a nearby lake. About nine months later, in April 1992, the couple kidnapped fifteen-year-old Kristen French at gunpoint in a local church parking lot. She was held for three days during which she was also tortured, raped, and then killed. Again the acts were videotaped by Bernardo and

Homolka. French's body was found two weeks later in a ditch. One other woman – known to this day only by the pseudonym "Jane Doe" – was abducted, but she managed to escape.

By this time, the police were closing in on Bernardo. But the case against him was far from made. However, after a three-year investigation, the police had enough evidence to arrest him for the Scarborough rapes. While he was in custody, he retained Murray as his lawyer. At the same time, the police obtained a warrant to search the home of Bernardo and Homolka, the prime suspects in the murders of Mahaffy and French. It was at this stage that Murray found himself faced with a dilemma that would haunt him and the legal profession to this day.

In May 1993, after a ten-week search of the house during which no tapes were located, the police contacted Murray to ask him if his client wanted any personal belongings from the house. On May 6, Murray went to the house with Carolyn MacDonald (a young lawyer with whom Murray shared office space and, on occasion, files, now including the Bernardo one) and Kim Doyle (his office manager and law clerk). He had received written instructions from Bernardo to retrieve the videotapes, which had been hidden in the bathroom ceiling above a light fixture. Although it is unclear whether Murray and Bernardo spoke by cell phone while Murray was in the house, Murray did locate the six 8mm videotapes. Excited that he had found "a bonanza" and "a gold mine,"[5] he followed Bernardo's instructions and made the fateful decision to take the tapes with him. However, though he made copies of the tapes, he did not view them immediately. Instead, he stashed them in his office safe, where he kept them for the next seventeen months.[6]

By this time, the police were convinced that Bernardo and Homolka were responsible for the murders of Mahaffy and French. However, lacking any definitive evidence against them, the police thought that they had little choice but to make a plea bargain with Homolka, who had become disaffected with Bernardo after he had seriously assaulted her. So, on May 14, a week after Murray had located the tapes, Homolka signed an agreement whereby, in return for giving extensive and damning evidence against Bernardo, she would plead guilty to manslaughter for the deaths of French and Mahaffy, and the Crown would only seek a sentence of twelve years of imprisonment. No deal would have been made if the tapes had been available to the police or prosecutors. That such a deal was made led to its being termed "the deal with the devil."[7]

Although Murray did not know that such a plea bargain was in the immediate works, he realized that such a deal had been made when, in the following week on May 18, Bernardo was charged with two counts of first-degree murder. As a result, Bernardo continued to retain Murray to cover these new charges. At this pivotal moment, Bernardo instructed Murray to view the tapes and use them as best he could to defend him. Two of the six tapes offered graphic evidence of the rape and torture of Mahaffy and French by Bernardo and Homolka. However, there was no direct depiction of the killings themselves.

Thus educated and with Bernardo's initial supporting instructions, Murray determined that it might be possible to use the tapes to defend Bernardo. His plan, apparently, was to contend that, though Bernardo was guilty of the rapes, he was not the exclusive or leading perpetrator of the murders – that was the prime responsibility of the duplicitous Homolka, less the abused spouse and more the leading malefactor. This seemed to be an odd strategy because, among other things, Murray did nothing to intervene in her hearing in July 1993 when she pleaded guilty to two counts of manslaughter and received a twelve-year jail term. If he had revealed his custody of the tapes, the deal might not have gone through, and Homolka would have been less able to downplay her role in the deaths of Mahaffy and French.

Nevertheless, Murray held on to the tapes through the remainder of 1993 and into 1994. During this time, Bernardo flip-flopped on what his defence should be and how the tapes should be handled. However, when he instructed Murray that he would deny any involvement in the abduction, let alone the murder of Mahaffy and French, and that the tapes should remain concealed indefinitely from the police or anyone else, Murray decided that he should no longer continue as Bernardo's lawyer. He believed that he could not provide a full and vigorous defence since professional integrity demanded that, once he knew beyond doubt that Bernardo had been involved in the rapes and murders, he withdraw his services. His decision was reinforced in July when he received test results from a sample of vomit on a piece of Bernardo's clothing that showed a DNA match with French.

Accordingly, in August 1994, Murray asked John Rosen, a very experienced criminal defence lawyer, to take on the case. Although Rosen agreed to take it on, Murray did not initially inform him that he still had the "lost tapes" in his possession.[8] What he did do was retain another lawyer, Austin Copper, as his own counsel and sought his confidential advice on what to do with the tapes. After consultations with the Law Society of Upper Canada (Ontario's governing body), it was decided that the tapes should be handed over to Rosen as Bernardo's new counsel. After viewing them and making unsuccessful efforts to cut a plea bargain for Bernardo, Rosen delivered the tapes to the police on September 22, 1994.

In the summer of 1995, Bernardo was tried and convicted for the murders of Mahaffy and French. On September 1, he was sentenced to life without parole for twenty-five years. The tapes were used at the trial, and Homolka gave strong evidence against Bernardo as the guilty party in both orchestrating the entire wretched saga and murdering the victims. Despite concerted efforts to overturn Homolka's plea bargain and relatively light sentence, the deal remained in place. Although Murray had not been part of the action for many months, he was far from done with the whole Bernardo-Homolka affair.

Duties of the Criminal Defence Lawyer

In the process of criminal defence, the basic thrust of professional ethics is that, though prosecutors have a duty to ensure that the truth is exposed in court, defence counsel have no such duty. The responsibility of defence lawyers is specific and specialized – they must take all possible steps to raise a reasonable doubt about a client's innocence, not to prove his or her innocence. Many rights are given to the accused, and it is the role of defence lawyers to ensure that those rights are respected. Although there might be general public concern with whether the accused "did it," the focus of defence lawyers is limited to challenging the legal guilt of their accused clients. In an adversarial system, each accused person is entitled to have his or her own champion whose loyalty is to the cause of the accused and to no one else. Criminal defence lawyers are in the business of advocacy, not judgment. Nevertheless, the fact that an accused person is entitled to as strong a defence as possible does not translate into an invitation to counsel to do anything and everything to avoid conviction. The critical challenge is to establish the ethical limits on the methods and strategies used to achieve that goal.

In being the "zealous advocates" of their clients, criminal defence lawyers must do all that they can to seek acquittals for their clients by "fair and honourable means" and "without illegality":[9] nothing that lawyers do becomes lawful by that fact alone. But, in doing so, they must also treat the court with "candour, fairness, courtesy and respect."[10] This general injunction pulls in a number of different directions and places a considerable burden on defence counsel to juggle the competing obligations to clients, courts, and society in general. That said, the dominant duty, to which the others function as limits, was well expressed by an English judge who said that advocates are expected "fearlessly to raise every issue, advance every argument, and ask every question ... which will help [their clients'] case[s] and to obtain for clients the benefit of any and every remedy and defence which is authorized by law."[11]

A major source of difficulty for criminal defence lawyers flows from their general duty of confidentiality to clients.[12] Except where future serious harm to another is about to occur,[13] lawyers must not divulge any communications between themselves and their clients. When this duty is combined with the fact that defence lawyers are generally under no obligation to assist the prosecution in making its case by making available incriminating evidence otherwise unknown to the prosecution, the difficulties are further increased. A prominent commentator has suggested that it creates "the lawyer's trilemma": the lawyer has a duty to know everything, to keep it in strict confidence, and to reveal it to the court.[14] Nevertheless, though some disagree, the traditional wisdom is that, though lawyers are free and often obliged to challenge all of the prosecution's evidence (even if they think that it is likely true), they cannot put forward affirmative defences (*e.g.*, alibis, duress, *etc.*) if they have no reasonable basis in fact or allow their clients to offer perjured evidence.[15] Even if lawyers withdraw from the cases, they must maintain their clients' confidences.[16]

This competition among duties of zealous advocacy, client confidentiality, and court candour is particularly acute in regard to physical evidence (*e.g.*, murder weapon, clothing, *etc.*). Because confidentiality attaches only to communications between lawyers and clients, it does not extend to the physical evidence itself. If lawyers come into possession of articles that they know are incriminating and will be beneficial to the prosecution, they cannot destroy or conceal them. Such evidence must be handed over to the police or the appropriate authorities. However, lawyers are obliged to make all efforts to keep confidential the source of the evidence turned over to the police or another authority. To preserve confidentiality as best as possible in such circumstances, the most desirable course is to turn over the physical evidence to an intermediary (*e.g.*, another lawyer or the law society), which can then pass it on without revealing its source. Nevertheless, this duty to disclose confidential information has been traditionally interpreted narrowly to apply only to physical evidence that can reasonably be considered the instruments of crime (*e.g.*, weapons or equipment) or the proceeds of crime (*e.g.*, stolen money or property). Although criminal defence lawyers must advise their clients not to destroy or conceal evidence themselves, they cannot disclose such communications to anyone about the fact of destruction or the location of concealment.

All of these matters came into play in Murray's defence of Bernardo. The main fact, of course, was that Murray had kept the incriminating tapes hidden for seventeen months. However, several factors took this case out of the ordinary: Murray was following his client's confidential instructions; the tapes were not instruments of the crimes; he came across them after being invited to his client's house by the police and after an extensive search by them; they were possibly seen as being both inculpatory and exculpatory in content; and he always intended to hand them over. Taken together, these facts muddy what are already very murky ethical and professional waters.

In January 1997, eighteen months after Bernardo was convicted, charges were brought against both Ken Murray and his co-counsel, Carolyn MacDonald. The gist of the indictment was that, by viewing the tapes and keeping their whereabouts secret, they had committed the crimes of obstructing justice and possessing child pornography.[17] As well, Murray became the subject of complaints to the Law Society of Upper Canada. As a result, the Law Society decided to pursue charges of professional misconduct against him. Although the criminal charges against MacDonald were later dropped as well as most of the criminal charges against Murray, the authorities refused to set aside the charge of obstruction of justice against him.

It was not until June 2000 that Murray went on trial and offered the courts the opportunity to clear up matters. Pleading "not guilty," he realized that he was in for the fight of his professional life and reputation. The proceedings took place before Justice Patrick Gravely, a seasoned judge coming to the end of a long and pioneering judicial career, in the Ontario Superior Court in Toronto. Murray was charged under section 139(2) of the *Criminal Code*. It states that "everyone who willfully attempts ... to obstruct, pervert or defeat the course of justice is guilty of an indictable offence and liable to imprisonment for a term not exceeding ten years."[18] After hearing arguments and giving careful consideration, Gravely was insistent that he was concerned only with the criminal status of Murray's action: "I want to make clear that my function in this case is limited to deciding if Murray has committed the crime of attempting to obstruct justice, not to judge his ethics."[19]

Justice Gravely took the view that Murray's concealment of the tapes for seventeen months constituted an improper and continuing interference with the operation of justice. However, he was not convinced that the Crown had demonstrated beyond a reasonable doubt that Murray had done so "willfully," as was required to turn this troubling action into a criminal offence.[20] In legal parlance, he had committed the *actus reus* (*i.e.*, "guilty act") but had not exhibited the necessary *mens rea* (*i.e.,* "guilty mind"). Accordingly, Murray was acquitted. In reaching this decision, Gravely made several important findings that not only explicated the crime of obstructing justice but also touched on the ethical obligations of legal counsel. Indeed, he firmly thought that, though Murray had not acted in line with the ethical expectations of the legal profession, he had been sufficiently, if wrongly confused about his ethical and legal obligations that he should not be subject to criminal sanctions.

For Justice Gravely, it was crucial that a distinction be drawn between conversations about the tapes and handling of the tapes. All communications between Bernardo and Murray fell under the umbrella of solicitor-client privilege and could not be divulged by Murray; this included any discussion of the tapes and their use. Nonetheless, the concealed location of the tapes raised a very different set of issues. Although defence counsel are under no obligation to assist the police in their investigations, Gravely opined that they cannot and must not take steps to keep so-called real or physical evidence out of the police's hands. However, the professional rules are far from clear in intent and scope. Moreover, Gravely accepted that Murray did intend to reveal the tapes and their contents at trial in order to cross-examine Homolka and/or raise a reasonable doubt about whether Bernardo had actually killed the victims. As Gravely concluded, "[w]hile Murray made only a token effort to find out what his obligations were, had he done careful research he might have remained confused. The weight of legal opinion ... is to the effect that lawyers may not conceal material physical evidence of crime, but how this rule applies to particular facts has been the subject of extensive discussion."[21]

The response to Justice Gravely's decision was cool. A common observation was that Gravely gave lawyers too much leeway in that he allowed Murray to rely on ignorance of the law; this defence is not available to most accused persons, and only a mistake of fact can be relied on as a valid excuse for what would otherwise be criminal conduct. This error was compounded by the fact that Murray had made no genuine effort to research the legal and professional expectations in regard to concealment of the tapes. Also, the fact that the Crown did not appeal the decision on a point of law suggested to some that the legal community accepted a decision that seemed to extend special protections to lawyers from obstruction of justice charges. All in all, therefore, the decision did little to assuage public opinion about the performance of lawyers in the Bernardo-Homolka saga.

Continued Confusion

As if the challenges facing criminal defence lawyers were not difficult enough, the confusion surrounding the circumstances of when and how they should hand over incriminating evidence to the police or prosecution makes their task doubly hard. Ensuring that lawyers act properly not only is a matter of professional propriety but also can directly and decisively affect the fates of persons accused of crimes. The dilemma is this: if lawyers fail to disclose to the investigating authorities inculpatory material evidence against their clients, they risk professional and criminal sanctions; if lawyers do hand over such incriminating evidence, they might also sell their clients down the proverbial river and face professional discipline for doing so. Although being able to draw a line between the two options seems to be a necessary and desirable condition for criminal defence work, that task calls into play foundational understandings of lawyers' ethical duties. Yet its satisfactory fulfillment has eluded many law societies and professional organizations.

Accordingly, while the trial determined Murray's criminal responsibility, little was clarified about the professional and ethical qualities of his actions. Despite the implicit plea by Justice Gravely for greater clarity of the relevant professional rules of ethical conduct, the Law Society decided six months later to withdraw any charge of professional misconduct against Murray; a working group was established, but its recommendations were ignored by the society's governing body. This left something of an ethical black hole into which criminal defence lawyers could fall. Although they all agree that they must not take active steps to conceal physical evidence from the investigating authorities, there remains a wide division of professional opinion over the precise operation and parameters of this directive. In short, Gravely had set the ethical stage, but he had not scripted the dramatic action: both lawyers and, as importantly, accused persons remained in the dark about their rights and responsibilities.

Of course, other jurisdictions have grappled with this professional quandary of legal ethics. Although most adopt a similar core of solutions and values, there is an important division of opinion over some of the more tricky issues. The leading American authority is the Washington state case of *Olwell* in 1964. A lawyer was given a gun by his client, likely the weapon used by his client in a murder. The lawyer claimed that he was under no obligation to hand over the gun to the police. The court decided that the lawyer-client privilege did not apply and that he should not hold on to the weapon:

The attorney should not be a depository for criminal evidence (such as a knife, other weapons, stolen property, etc.), which in itself has little, if any, material value for the purposes of aiding counsel in the preparation of the defence of his client's case. Such evidence given [to] the attorney during legal consultation for information purposes and used by the attorney in preparing the defence of his client's case, whether or not the case ever goes to trial, could clearly be withheld for a reasonable period, should, as an officer of the court, on his own motion turn the same over to the prosecution.[22]

However, in the 1981 California case of *Meredith*,[23] which has some close parallels with Murray's dilemma, a client told his lawyer that the victim's wallet in a murder case had been thrown away behind the client's home. The lawyer hired someone to recover the wallet and bring it to his office. After examining the wallet, the lawyer handed it over to the police. At trial, the police sought to call the person who had retrieved the wallet and have him testify about its location. The lawyer contended that, though the prosecution could enter the wallet as evidence, it could not reveal where it was found since the source of that information was a privileged communication from the accused client. The court rejected that claim since the lawyer had interfered with the wallet and prevented the police from locating it themselves. The wallet and its location were used to obtain a conviction.

All of this suggests several things about what Murray should have done. First, he should have realized at an early stage that he was out of his depth; he had little experience dealing with high-profile and complicated murder cases. His ethical duty was to withdraw from the case so that Bernardo could obtain a more competent counsel. The fact that he came to this realization eighteen months into the case when he decided to pull out and hand it over to John Rosen merely confirms his failing; Murray did no favour to his client, himself, or the legal profession generally.

Second, a rudimentary sense of the professional rules and prevailing wisdom would have warned Murray about the danger of going to Bernardo's house and locating the tapes. Simply because he received instructions from Bernardo to do so does not validate or justify his actions. The most appropriate and ethical course would have been for Murray to inform Bernardo that, if he retrieved the tapes, he would likely be under an obligation to hand them over to the police. Consequently, he should have advised his client that, all things considered, the most beneficial action would be to let sleeping dogs lie. After all, Murray was obliged not to reveal any communications with Bernardo about the whereabouts of the tapes, and the police had indicated that they would demolish the house after Murray's visit (which they did). In this way, the tapes would never have been found, and Murray would not have been implicated in their concealment or destruction. Although this course of action might not have endeared Murray to the public, it would have been the best possible way of satisfying the competing demands placed on him.

Third, Murray could have acted with professional integrity even after removing the tapes from Bernardo's house. He could have held them for a short time, viewed them, and then handed them over to the police or Crown; holding them for eighteen months, not retrieving them, was his downfall. In this way, Murray would have been able to satisfy himself that there was or was not something exculpatory about the tapes' contents and prepare a defence of Bernardo accordingly. If Bernardo had instructed Murray not to view them, Murray would have been obliged to hand them over immediately without viewing them. However, the one fly in the ointment was that, in the days following retrieval of the tapes, Homolka made her plea bargain with the police. Assuming, as Murray claimed, that he did not hear of that deal until later, he could have handed the tapes over in short order and certainly before Homolka's sentencing a couple of months later.

However, what remains contested is whether Murray was entitled to visit the house, locate the tapes, verify to Bernardo that they were still there, and leave them where they were. Although it is clear that Murray had to keep confidential any communications with Bernardo about the tapes, it is unclear whether his actions of visiting the house and actually seeing the tapes, even touching them, put him in a different position. Was he under any obligation to report the location of the tapes to the police?

A similar situation arose in New York in the case of *Belge* in 1975, known generally as the Buried Bodies case.[24] A lawyer was told by his client about the location of bodies of people whom he had murdered and buried. The lawyer visited the site, saw the bodies, and took photographs of them but did not reveal this information or the photographs to anyone. At the trial, he used this knowledge to support his defence that his client was insane. Following a public outcry, he was charged with failing to provide a decent burial for a dead person. His defence was that, because he had not disturbed or relocated the bodies and made it more difficult for the police to locate them, he had acted professionally; he was under an ethical obligation both not to reveal this privileged information and not to do something that would incriminate his client. The trial court accepted this argument and held that the lawyer had "conducted himself as an officer of the court with all the zeal at his command to protect the constitutional rights of his client ... and the interests of justice."[25]

Therefore, a strong argument can be made that Murray would not have been in breach of his professional duties if he had located the tapes and left them where they were. In so doing, he would not have obstructed justice but simply failed to come forward with information. Whether he (or anyone, including non-lawyers) was expected to volunteer such information is a moot point. Some lawyers insist that, once they move outside the realm of privileged communications, they might actually have greater responsibility in such circumstances than ordinary citizens. But this is far from a settled or majority position. Certainly, had Murray acted in this way, he would still have been the target of public condemnation for failing to do what was considered the right thing. Yet this speaks as much to the gap between lawyers' understanding and citizens' understanding of the expectations of lawyers' professional and ethical commitments.

The *Murray* case highlights the fact that the challenges to the criminal defence bar in meeting its ethical and professional responsibilities are difficult and many. It is relatively easy for counsel, as Murray did, to drift into a professional stance that shirks questions of ethical significance and simply muddles through. However, criminal defence lawyers can and should do a vigorous and committed job for their accused clients without fear that they are acting unethically. If there is one area of the law where lawyers must court considerable ethical risks in the name of greater professional and social values, it is in the process of dealing with those accused of having committed criminal acts. Although it might not be acceptable that "a man should, with a wig on his head, and a band round his neck, do for a guinea what, without those appendages, he would think it wicked and infamous to do for an empire," it might be that, "not merely believing but knowing a statement to be true, he should do all that can be done by sophistry, by rhetoric, by solemn asseveration, by indignant exclamation, by gesture, by play of features, by terrifying one honest witness, by perplexing another, to cause a jury to think that statement false."[26] Thomas Macaulay saw the ethical opaqueness in all of this. Perhaps we should too.

Conclusion

As might be expected, there is no happy ending to a sordid saga like this one. The infamous tapes were destroyed in December 2001, though there are lingering suggestions that a copy of them remains. Ken Murray quickly returned to the relative obscurity of small-town criminal law practice; his brush with celebrity status was chastening, to say the least. Paul Bernardo remains locked up in a small segregated cell from which he is released for an hour of exercise each day. Initially locked up in the old Kingston Penitentiary, he is now at the high-security Millhaven Institution in Bath, Ontario, and is eligible for a faint-hope parole hearing in 2020. As for Karla Homolka, she was released from prison on July 4, 2005. She has since remarried, had three children with Thierry Bordelais, the brother of her Quebec lawyer, and changed her name to Leanne. She is reportedly living in the Caribbean.

The Bernardo-Homolka case stands out as one of the most gruesome in Canada's criminal annals; its facts have been used as storylines in various TV dramas, including *Law and Order, Close to Home,* and *Inspector Linley Mysteries.* There was also a movie, titled *Karla,* that received limited release in Canada in the mid-2000s. Ontario's premier, Dalton McGuinty, encouraged a boycott of the movie, and it fared poorly. Nonetheless, a year does not pass in which mention is not made of the case and its traumatic effect on the Canadian public imagination. However, despite all of this and many promises to the contrary, the Law Society of Upper Canada never lived up to its promise to amend its rule and clarify the responsibilities of criminal defence lawyers in regard to physical evidence. When and how should they deal with physical evidence that comes to their attention or into their possession? This omission is a cheerless and unnecessary footnote to a thoroughly nauseating story of sex, lies, and videotapes.

Notes

1 Lord Bolingbroke, *On the Study and Use of History,* Letter 5 (London: T. Cadell, 1739).
2 *Giannarelli v. Wraith* (1988), 165 C.L.R. 543.
3 See *R. v. Murray* (2000), 48 O.R. (3d) 544; 186 D.L.R. (4th) 124; 144 C.C.C. (3d) 289; 34 C.R. (5th) 290; [2000] O.J. No. 2182 (S.C.J.).
4 *Ibid.*
5 *Ibid.* at para. 11.
6 *Ibid.*
7 See Stephen Williams, *Karla: A Pact with the Devil* (Toronto: Random House, 2003).
8 *R. v. Murray* (2000), 48 O.R. (3d) 544; 186 D.L.R. (4th) 124; 144 C.C.C. (3d) 289; 34 C.R. (5th) 290; [2000] O.J. No. 2182 (S.C.J.).
9 See Federation of Law Societies of Canada, *Model Code of Professional Conduct* (2012), http://flsc.ca/wp-content/uploads/2014/12/conduct1.pdf.
10 *Ibid.*
11 *Rondel v. Worsley,* [1967] 3 W.L.R. 1666 (H.L.), per Lord Reid.
12 See Federation of Law Societies of Canada, *supra* note 9 at Rule 3.3.

13 See *ibid.*, Rule 3.3-3 to Rule 3.3-6. See, generally, the chapter by Adam Dodek in this volume.

14 Monroe H. Freedman, "Perjury: The Lawyer's Trilemma" (1975) 1(1) Litigation 26.

15 See the excellent discussion in Michel Proulx and David Layton, *Ethics and Canadian Criminal Law* (Toronto: Irwin Law, 2001).

16 Federation of Law Societies of Canada, *supra* note 9 at Rule 3.3-1, commentary 3.

17 *R. v. Murray* (2000), 48 O.R. (3d) 544; 186 D.L.R. (4th) 124; 144 C.C.C. (3d) 289; 34 C.R. (5th) 290; [2000] O.J. No. 2182 (S.C.J.).

18 *Criminal Code of Canada*, R.S.C. 1985, c. C-46, s. 139(2).

19 *R. v. Murray* (2000), 48 O.R. (3d) 544; 186 D.L.R. (4th) 124; 144 C.C.C. (3d) 289; 34 C.R. (5th) 290; [2000] O.J. No. 2182 (S.C.J.) at para. 87.

20 *Ibid.*

21 *Ibid.* at para. 149.

22 *State Ex. Rel. Sowers v. Olwell*, 394 P.2d 681 (Wa. 1964).

23 *People v. Meredith*, 29 Cal.3d 682 (1981).

24 *People v. Belge*, 83 Misc.2d 186 (N.Y. 1975).

25 *Ibid.*, 191.

26 Thomas Babington Macaulay, "Francis Bacon" (1926) 2 Critical and Historical Essays 290 at 314.

3

"No One's Interested in Something You Didn't Do"

———— Freeing David Milgaard the Ugly Way

DAVID ASPER

On December 14, 1968, the Saskatoon *Star-Phoenix* newspaper published a warning that had been issued by the police. Under the headline "Women Given Warning," the article described two alleged rapes and one assault brought to the attention of the newspaper. The article concluded by paraphrasing the police: "They said the alleged assailant first talks to women and then takes them into alleys."[1]

Six weeks later, on January 31, 1969, Gail Miller was found murdered and sexually assaulted in an alley in the same area where the reported attacks had happened. A few days after the murder, the Regina *Leader-Post* carried a story under the headline "Killer Possible Rapist," which reported that the police were investigating the possibility that the killer was the same person who had previously attacked three women in Saskatoon.[2]

But on January 31, 1970, David Milgaard, sixteen years old at the time, who had never been suspected or accused of any similar assault, was convicted of the crime and sent to prison for life. His appeals were unsuccessful.[3]

Always believing in the innocence of her son, Joyce Milgaard distributed flyers in Saskatoon in 1980 and offered a $10,000 reward for information related to the murder of Miller. That year Linda Fisher attempted to contact the Saskatoon City Police to tell them about her suspicions of her husband, Larry.[4]

In 1983, a journalist named Peter Carlyle-Gordge, working with the Milgaards, discovered that Fisher had lived in the basement of the home that Milgaard had visited on the morning of the murder and that, according to a source, he might be a convicted rapist. Carlyle-Gordge placed an ad in the *Star-Phoenix* in 1983 looking for Linda Fisher. Both she and her then common-law husband, Bryan Wright, responded by mail, indicating that they would talk to Carlyle-Gordge, but by then he had gone to England to pursue other endeavours.[5] Tragically, nothing came of this information for a long time.

Milgaard spent twenty-three years in prison. He was released only after the exercise of extraordinary powers given to the Minister of Justice in the *Criminal Code of Canada*[6] and a reference hearing before the Supreme Court of Canada in 1992.[7] The Supreme Court ordered a new trial, but the government of Saskatchewan decided not to pursue the case and entered a stay of proceedings.

In 1997, David Milgaard was completely exonerated. Advanced DNA testing led to the identification and conviction of the real killer of Gail Miller, Larry Fisher, who died in prison. Milgaard received $10 million in compensation for what he had suffered. I was one of his lawyers from 1986 to 1992 and played a lead role in getting his conviction overturned. I had the tainted pleasure of being by his side as we walked him out of Stony Mountain Penitentiary as a free person.

The complete story of how we achieved this result cannot be told here. However, in a careful-what-you-wish-for way, we had called for an inquiry into the wrongful conviction of Milgaard, and eventually we got it. In this chapter, I tell the heart of the story of his exoneration and my role in it, and I identify some of the lawyering issues that arose during the inquiry about how we accomplished our objective.

The start of this story is the end, the Commission of Inquiry into the Wrongful Conviction of David Milgaard in 2006. How I perceive what happened before and my assessment of our conduct and that of other lawyers are informed by the inquiry, my experience appearing before it, and my reflections on what occurred after its report was issued.

When I was first called to testify at the inquiry, it felt Kafkaesque. Confronted by many lawyers representing parties who had been affected by the reopening of the Milgaard case, his exoneration, and the eventual conviction of the true killer, I found myself incredulously defending or answering for our efforts to free him. The process had turned into an inquiry about a wrongful liberation and not a wrongful conviction.

I think that counsel for the Crown, police, and government whom we had taken on in our fight relished the opportunity to have at me. Perhaps it was their duty to do so. They were doing for their clients what I had done for mine, and, in fairness, it set the record straight in a number of ways sometimes difficult to admit. As one who continues to take an interest in how our criminal justice system operates, and the roles played by its various actors (lawyers, police, judges, witnesses), I found some value in looking back. Various lawyers at the inquiry tried like mad to get me to admit that we had made mistakes during our representation of Milgaard and to have me apologize to their clients, whose reputations had ostensibly been smeared.

Yet in the end it was also my role to ensure that the real issue – Milgaard's wrongful conviction – remained at the forefront. It was their clients who had damned mine, their clients whose efforts had resulted in his wrongful conviction. None of their clients had served a sometimes harsh twenty-three years in prison. In the end, whatever hurt they had supposedly suffered was irrelevant – to me, to Milgaard, and certainly to the inquiry.

At one point in the proceedings, it was suggested to me that I suffered from "tunnel vision,"[8] a psychological phenomenon commonly known as a root cause of wrongful convictions. Police and prosecutors with tunnel vision become trapped in a single view of a case such that they ignore or reject evidence that runs counter to it.[9] In my response, I wondered whether it could be tunnel vision when we were right: Milgaard didn't do it. But this line of questioning illustrated to me how the whole inquiry had flipped into *Alice in Wonderland*.

Yet, as time passes, I still think about the complicated question that the inquiry raised: what role did each lawyer play in wrongfully convicting Milgaard, in allowing that conviction to persist, or in ensuring his exoneration?

On the one hand, whether or not you agree with what we did on Milgaard's behalf and how we did it, the Commission of Inquiry concluded that without our efforts Milgaard might never have been freed and the true killer of Gail Miller never prosecuted.[10] On the other hand, the police and Crown attorney did not deliberately set out to convict the wrong person and allow the true killer to go free. They might have worked hard to convict Milgaard and in so doing overlooked evidence that pointed away from him and toward a more obvious suspect. But nonetheless I came away from the inquiry firmly believing that there was no intentional evil at play. People made mistakes, and so did I. To some degree, the inquiry allowed for some reconciliation between me and those responsible for the investigation and prosecution of Milgaard. In many ways, each of us was simply trying to discharge the role that he or she had been assigned in the justice system. That rights or wrongs flowed from those roles was, in a sense, independent from the ethics of the people who occupied them.

The only part of the case about which I remain relatively critical is how the federal Department of Justice responded to the increasingly powerful case that Milgaard had been wrongfully convicted. To me, there remains a strong argument that his exoneration was improperly delayed. The remainder of the case, as the inquiry showed, indicates only that, even when people in the justice system try to do their best, great wrongs can occur. Our job as lawyers might be, as much as anything, to try to correct those wrongs when they become apparent.

Yet this chapter does not seek to justify what we did to free Milgaard. I think that the conclusion of the case speaks for itself. I remain extremely proud to have played a lead role in getting to that result. Undoubtedly, as I tell the story, and as you read it, each of us will have occasion to consider whether that end justified the means that we used to achieve it. Although there is no "true" answer to that question, for me the answer is certain: given what we achieved, what we did was worth it. What action could actually be considered illegitimate to win freedom for your wrongly imprisoned client? In hindsight, the one thing that I would have done differently was in a single crucial area. Like the Saskatoon police at the time of the murder of Miller, we completely missed the clues implicating Fisher. Had we pursued them with more vigour early on, my guess is that none of the rest would have happened. It's a tragedy that still sickens me.

And beyond the question of whether our actions were justified in any specific instance is the issue of living the ethical dilemmas of lawyering in real time in real situations, with a client's life and welfare at stake. In relation to that issue, what happened when we represented Milgaard and sought to exonerate him was not what we had expected and was miles apart from my view of how the justice system should operate.

Becoming a Criminal Lawyer

In 1986, I was an articling student in Winnipeg who had spent most of my time in law school focusing on corporate law courses and thriving in the advocacy and moot court programs. I had been rejected by every law school in Canada because of my low LSAT scores and had chosen to go to California Western School of Law in San Diego. One of the people there who made the biggest impression on me was my criminal law prof. His name was Arthur

Campbell, and, even though I never dreamed for a moment that I would be a criminal defence lawyer, he brought fire and brimstone to the classroom because of the liberty interests at stake in the criminal justice process. God help anyone who went to his class unprepared; in Professor Campbell's world, an unprepared student could lead to an unprepared lawyer, and an unprepared lawyer could lead to someone going to jail who ought not to be there. His passion for the law stuck with me and remains a testament to the value of great teachers.

When I came back to Canada, the Law Society of Manitoba required me to take a number of courses before articling. One of them was on criminal procedure, in which I first encountered the *Milgaard* decision for its interpretation of a provision of the *Canada Evidence Act*. The course was taught by Heather Leonoff, a partner in the criminal law firm in which I later worked. Heather wound up playing a role in drafting our application on behalf of Milgaard to the Minister of Justice.

Prior to that, however, I began articling at a firm founded by my father. My practice was limited mostly to solicitor's work. Soon after starting, and seeing what the real world of the corporate lawyer looked like, I began to go a bit stir crazy. To me, it was boring.

In Manitoba at the time, the bar admission classes were taught every Friday, and the whole articling class would gather at the law society offices to hear lectures on various topics. I sat at the back of the room and got to know a number of people whose lives and articling experiences seemed a lot more exciting than mine. They were the students doing criminal law. They were going to court, going into jails, drafting documents, meeting clients, and certainly not sitting at desks all day.

Increasingly disillusioned with my own articling experience, I decided to see if a change was possible. I sent out a few letters and resumés to leading criminal defence firms. One firm, Wolch Pinx Tapper Scurfield, responded almost immediately and wanted to set up an interview right away. This was around Christmas of 1985.

I went at the appointed time and, in a sort of amusing way, met with four people sitting around the end of a conference table. They were, in order, Hersh Wolch, QC, Sheldon Pinx, QC, Robert Tapper, and John Scurfield, just as on the letterhead (later on, at firm parties, and there were many, we used to love putting the name partners in order like that as though looking at Mount Rushmore). I recall them focusing the discussion on my moot court experience in law school and whether I felt ready to go to court. I told them what I thought they wanted to hear, and the conversation quickly turned to

"When can you start?" I applied for and was granted a transfer of articles, and on March 3, 1986, I formally made the fateful move in this new direction.

Meeting Joyce Milgaard

That first week of March 1986 was an eventful one for me at the firm. On the first day, I was given a copy of the *Criminal Code* and a book on judicial interim release. I was instructed to familiarize myself with bail, bail appeals, and a number of fairly minor offences, such as theft under $1,000, and I was expected to be ready the following week to attend court with my articling colleague, Michael Thomson (now Justice Thomson of the Manitoba Court of Queen's Bench).

By the end of that first week, I had met Joyce Milgaard, who claimed that her son was in prison for a crime that he hadn't committed. On another day, since I was the only person in the office while all others were in court, I had been called to the RCMP D Division offices to deal with a client who was in custody and had been charged with first-degree murder for killing a police officer.

This kind of action was exactly what had been missing in my career. A wrongful conviction and a first-degree murder charge – why waste time at base camp when you can go straight to the top of the mountain in the world of criminal law!

It was a remarkable week, and I'll never forget the professionalism of the RCMP officers who, under the most trying circumstances (two of their colleagues had been shot, and one was dead), recognized that I was a babe in the woods and properly guided me on what to do as the lawyer when they presented their prisoner. This experience drove home a very important lesson about knowing what you don't know and not being shy about stopping the world if it spins too fast. This can be a hard lesson for bright young lawyers who want to project confidence, and it's a lesson that I can now see might have been better applied to my involvement in the *Milgaard* case.

With that exciting start, I never would have predicted that the brief meeting with Mrs. Milgaard would turn into a six-year project that would leave me emotionally and intellectually spent, disgusted with the Canadian justice system, and leaving the practice of law. If the criminal trial – supposed to have a truth-seeking function – had produced a wrongful conviction of David Milgaard and ruined his life, then all I could hear was "When the truth is found to be lies, and all the joy within you dies."[11] Happily, the law and I made peace with each other when I was finally admitted to a Canadian law school in 2006 in the LLM program at the University of Toronto. Since graduating with an LLM, I have taught law for several wonderful years at the University of Manitoba, and recently I initiated an intensive course in wrongful convictions at Lakehead University's Bora Laskin School of Law.

When Hersh Wolch agreed to look into the *Milgaard* case, he assigned it to me. I was provided with a bunch of material that included transcripts of the trial evidence, notes, correspondence, and some details of investigative efforts undertaken by Joyce Milgaard and a journalist named Peter Carlyle-Gordge.

The prospect of freeing an innocent man was more than just a romantic fantasy. It struck at a core set of personal values driven into our family in a religious way during the Jewish holiday of Passover. We always began the annual celebration of the Exodus of the Jews from slavery in Egypt by reciting a prayer that contained a call to action: "May the problem of all who are downtrodden be our problem; may the concern of all who are afflicted be our concern; may the struggle for all who strive for liberty and equality be our struggle."

I took that to heart, and I'm certain that it was in my mind as we set out on the adventure of the *Milgaard* case. Undertaking this case flipped the usual criminal defence lawyer's dilemma on its head. Instead of answering for defending the guilty, we were ostensibly representing the innocent. This added a moral dimension to the religious lesson from the story of Exodus.

Representing the Guilty (or Innocent?)

My task was to look at the material and try to determine whether there was a basis for the Milgaards' contention that David was innocent. I largely ignored everything other than the trial evidence in order to fully understand the case against him. The conviction had been unsuccessfully appealed to the Saskatchewan Court of Appeal, and the Supreme Court of Canada had rejected leave to appeal. The usual systemic safeguards apparently hadn't uncovered any basis to intervene in the decision reached by the jury.

Without having been in the courtroom to assess the credibility and demeanour of the witnesses who had implicated Milgaard, reading the evidence suggested a pretty strong case against him. It put him near the scene of the crime, away from his friends, with blood on his pants, potentially in possession of what could have been the murder weapon, making what could be construed as inculpatory comments, and then seeming to want to leave town quickly. There was also evidence that several months later Milgaard had effectively admitted to the crime in front of several people during a party in a motel room.

There was some contradictory evidence from independent witnesses about the timing of events and about whether they had seen blood on Milgaard's pants. Scientific evidence regarding semen samples found four days after the murder at the crime scene did not implicate Milgaard. (I argue to this day that presenting that evidence at trial was at best confusing to the jury and at worst misconstrued as somehow connecting Milgaard to the crime. Even the Saskatchewan Court of Appeal didn't seem to understand the value or purpose of the evidence.[12] It sure left me wondering whether the semen was Milgaard's or not.)

After going through the transcripts many times, I found it hard to see how Milgaard *hadn't* done it. If his position was the truth, then a lot of people had either lied or been mistaken. Indeed, even though one of Milgaard's friends became a problematic witness at the trial, she had given the police a statement saying that she had actually witnessed Milgaard commit the murder.[13] It never occurred to me or anyone else in our office that, despite the accuracy of significant pieces of the police investigation and trial evidence, he was nevertheless innocent.

Finding My Own Identity as a Lawyer

While I was trying to digest the Milgaard file, I was also busy articling and then, after being called to the bar, building my practice. Our firm was extremely busy, and virtually every day was consumed with courtroom practice in Winnipeg as well as rural Manitoba towns and remote, fly-in, First Nations circuit courts. It was an exhilarating time serving as junior counsel on the big cases and on my own for the more manageable ones. I built excellent relationships with Crown attorneys that facilitated so much of the daily churning of files. In court, I tried to keep judges interested with fresh and engaging repartee on the nuts and bolts of the law. As a junior lawyer always relegated to the back of the line behind senior counsel, I knew that by the time I got my chance, ennui would have set in. This was a great opportunity to advance my client's interests by adding rhetorical colour and even a bit of collegial if not theatrical combativeness with Crown counsel, which I think interrupted the routine and got the court's attention. It was a ton of fun, and I worked hard to enliven each appearance. Where the law was overwhelmingly not on my client's side, sometimes reference to a Broadway musical or a sports metaphor had to suffice, and at times judges were barely able to contain their reactions.

Soon I started to emerge with my own identity both professionally and, with increasing frequency, in the media as my cases were covered in the daily court briefs. Having grown up with a famous father,[14] it was especially satisfying to start being known for what I did rather than for being the son of Izzy Asper. I think that this also played a role in my zeal for the *Milgaard* case. I knew full well that, if Milgaard was right, it would be a sensational and widely reported matter of public interest. I would be not only "Izzy's kid" but also, and even better, David Asper, the lawyer who got Milgaard out of jail.

Of course, the downside was that, as I became Milgaard's lawyer, I also became inextricably identified with my client. Most criminal defence lawyers don't want that to happen. In fact, the criminal defence lawyer *can't* allow that to happen because it blurs the role of the lawyer as a necessary actor in the system of justice. Lawyers are officers of the court and must be diligent in maintaining that status. Mine got blurred, and I can recall one senior Crown attorney always referring to me as David Milgaard Asper, which really bothered me. I think that it was part ego and part search for self-identity that added a driving element to what eventually unfolded.

Having essentially concluded from the trial evidence that David had probably committed the crime, I challenged him and his mother to explain to me how all of this damning evidence was wrong. The first session occurred at Stony Mountain Penitentiary. I used to ride a motorcycle, a Yamaha 650 Virago, and rode it to the prison that day. I walked into the visiting area carrying my beaten-up helmet, and David was focused more on the fact that I was a "biker" than on his case. He laughed at the state of my helmet and said that, if I got him out of prison, he'd buy me a new one. A lifetime later, after he got $10 million in compensation, David knew that I hadn't shared in the legal fees earned by the firm, so he bought me a beautiful Harley Davidson, and I got the licence plate DM2DA. It was sweet.

Discovering the Truth?

Both David and Joyce seemed to relish the challenge that I brought to them that day in the prison and on many subsequent occasions. I had a list of the witnesses who had testified against David at the trial and kept going through it with them, asking "What about this?" and "What about that?"

A lawyer has to be very careful about information provided by the client, and in the criminal law context there has to be a rigorous balance between acceptance and skepticism. Common sense suggests that convicted criminals have little to lose and can lie about what happened. I was very conscious of the enormity of what the Milgaards were saying about the case. As questions about the trial arose, I tried hard to be critical and sequester the concept of innocence from the idea that a new hearing might be warranted. There was a big difference in my mind. Either way a new trial might be required, but obtaining that trial for an innocent man went far beyond the ordinary duties of a criminal defence lawyer in maintaining the rule of law. Reversing an unfair trial rights one sort of injustice; reversing a wrongful conviction rights another that is far more significant and substantial.

The Milgaards were also highly paranoid about everyone in the system that had led to the conviction, including their own lawyer at the trial. This was understandable, but it created some significant issues in terms of how we proceeded and acted on instructions from our clients. We had to be wary of this paranoia, but I can't say that it didn't affect my thinking at times. This is a very dangerous path for a lawyer, who has to be able to work within the system and effectively with others, including opposing counsel.

At one point, Joyce mentioned to me that she and her daughters had once tried to make a rudimentary 8mm movie depicting the movements of the victim, Gail Miller, on the morning of her murder. This retracing turned out to be maybe the biggest thing that made me consider seriously the possibility that David might have been wrongly convicted. Joyce and her daughters had gone to where Gail had lived and walked the way that she would normally have gone on the morning of the murder. It surprised me how short the distance was from her house to the bus stop and how quickly she would have covered the distance, especially on a morning when it was minus forty degrees Celsius. Peter Carlyle-Gordge had also explained his analysis of the sequence of events that had led him to question the totality of the Crown's case against Milgaard.

As I thought about the moviemaking, and what it indicated about the murder, I started to coalesce all of the evidence as measured against the timelines established by independent witnesses for the morning of the murder. I started to think about the facts of the case as having a starting point and an ending point and to look down on them from a bird's-eye view. If we put everyone where they said they were at a certain time, and then set them all in motion until the next time marker, what would that look like?

Initially, I visualized this in my mind and then eventually went to Saskatoon and did a walk-through of the area in which the murder had occurred. For the reference at the Supreme Court, we commissioned a professional video production unit to illustrate our point. What I saw was that important and damning chunks of evidence did not add up and that it was impossible to believe everyone who had testified because, taken together, what everyone said couldn't have actually happened.

Some witnesses had to be mistaken or not telling the truth. But which ones? Which piece of the puzzle looked like it fit but didn't? For example, an independent witness put Milgaard and his friends at a motel on the out-skirts of Saskatoon at about 7 a.m. The caretaker of a church saw someone in the lane where the body was found at 7:10 a.m. Gail Miller normally left for work at 6:45 a.m. It was not possible for Milgaard to have committed the murder and be at the motel within this time frame. In addition, whereas his friends said that they saw blood on Milgaard's pants, independent wit-nesses who saw Milgaard at a time that would have been right after the mur-der said that they saw nothing. Miller was stabbed through her coat but not her dress, meaning that the coat had been taken off, the dress taken down, and then the coat put back on. It must have been a prolonged attack.

These questions swung me onside with the Milgaards that the trial evi-dence was very problematic. It was largely on that basis that Joyce and I met with Hersh to report on our work. We had hand-drawn diagrams of the area and placed all of the key players where they said they were and showed Hersh how it didn't make sense.

By this time, Hersh had started an informal dialogue with officials in Ottawa at the Department of Justice. He knew a number of senior people there and was warming them up to the fact that we were looking into the *Milgaard* case. The message from them was that for us to succeed we could not simply reargue the case at trial. There had to be some new and material evidence. But Hersh and other senior members of the firm who listened to our pitch agreed that things as presented at trial didn't seem to hold together under closer analysis.

However, there was nothing in the *Criminal Code* at the time that gave us any guidance on how to proceed or what we needed to do in order to persuade the Minister of Justice. We probably could have spent a bit more time researching the matter rather than operating informally on the basis that we had to find something new. In hindsight, that approach seems a bit crazy, but one of the good things to come out of the *Milgaard* case was that the government amended the former section 619 of the *Criminal Code* to make things a bit clearer to those who now seek the remedy.[15]

Among the material that Joyce brought with her for the first meeting when she retained our firm was correspondence with a producer and host of the CBC program *The Fifth Estate*. She had mentioned that CBC might be inter-ested in doing something on the case but so far had opted not to proceed.

Joyce strongly believed that people knew what really happened on the morning of January 31, 1969, when Gail Miller was murdered and that they were more likely to come forward with information if they knew that the case was still under review. In fact, as noted, she had been trying to raise public awareness since 1980, when she had put up posters in Saskatoon and offered a reward for information leading to the exoneration of her son. She truly believed that people who knew the truth of what had happened might come forward.

In a horrifying twist, we eventually learned that Linda Fisher, the wife of Larry Fisher, now convicted of the crime, had tried to communicate with the Saskatoon police in 1980.[16] Had the police paid attention then, David's stay in prison could have been much shorter, of course, and Fisher's subsequent victims might never have suffered so terribly.

I reached out to one of the producers of *The Fifth Estate* to get her impression of the case because she had spent a great deal of time researching its background. She thought that there was a story to be told but couldn't put her finger on where it began or ended. She also mentioned the name of a person, Deborah Hall, who had not testified at the trial but seemed to contradict powerful evidence that Milgaard had allegedly admitted to and re-enacted the crime at a party. Peter Carlyle-Gordge also thought that Hall's testimony might be a means of establishing new evidence. Around the same time, I met a reporter from the *Winnipeg Free Press* named Dan Lett and told him about the *Milgaard* case.

Lawyers have to be very careful with the media. On the one hand, we have an obligation to help the public understand what the justice system is all about, warts and all. We can play an important role in shoring up public perception of and confidence in the administration of justice. But media reporting isn't law reporting. It gets edited and parsed in ways that the lawyer cannot control, and it is done by people who aren't lawyers. It's generally understood, therefore, that when dealing with the media we have to situate what we're saying within the larger context of the role of the lawyer. What we say matters, and, as I will relate, we have to watch that we don't let our stories run away on us.

Although I was now convinced that there was something wrong with the case against Milgaard, I was a bit mortified about how bad that wrong would be if it were true. I thought that it might be valuable to have an investigative journalist look at the case and provide a contrary perspective. Since CBC wasn't interested, and Dan seemed to be, we began a relationship that I believe was seminal to why David is free today. The Milgaards were okay with this approach, and I thought that there was something good about their not seeming to have anything to hide. It was confirmation for me that we were on to something because, if David was guilty, he likely wouldn't have wanted a skilled journalist proving it yet again. I gave Dan the transcripts and our analysis of the facts.

I also started to look for Deborah Hall and, with some assistance, found her in Regina. I went to Regina and met with her over coffee, and she gave me her interpretation of the damning evidence used at the trial in which people had testified about Milgaard having admitted to and essentially re-enacted the murder while at a party. Her version was that Milgaard had made a bad joke and little more. I drafted an affidavit on her behalf and then did an especially dumb thing. I had her sign the affidavit, and then I signed it as a witness. In so doing, I put myself in jeopardy of becoming a witness if the matter ever went to court; if she were not to adopt the statement, then I could be called as a witness for the other side of the litigation. It was an elementary mistake that should never have happened, because in due course her evidence would change. When Hall was examined by a representative of the Department of Justice, her evidence was different and more damning than what she had given me.[17] My ethical dilemma deepened. However, when I got the original affidavit from her, it was something "new," and we considered it a significant development.

As Dan Lett progressed through his review of the case, he and I talked frequently, and he began to see problems with the evidence.

Joyce read an article somewhere about an emerging area of science related to DNA and the possibility of solving crimes through something called "genetic fingerprinting." She asked me if I knew about it and referred me to Dr. James Ferris, a forensic pathologist in Vancouver. I contacted him and asked him about the DNA research and whether it could assist us in the *Milgaard* case, since all of the trial exhibits had been preserved.

The fact that those exhibits had been stored in the Saskatoon courthouse for almost twenty years was a miracle, because under normal circumstances they would have been destroyed. As it turned out, with advanced DNA technology, those exhibits eventually exonerated David and identified the true killer. But the biggest miracle about those exhibits was that I didn't personally ruin their usefulness by doing an extremely foolhardy thing.

I went alone to the courthouse and asked to see them. A clerk wheeled the bags into the very room in which Milgaard's jurors had sealed his fate. Blindly and recklessly, I removed the items from the bags and lay them out across the long table. I was probably thinking that there might be a clue to be found but wasn't thinking about the risk of contamination. It was an unacceptable risk that could have seriously affected my client's interests. It never occurred to me that I could be offside with both the *Code of Conduct* and the *Criminal Code* by tampering with the evidence and potentially obstructing justice. Fortunately, I didn't open any of the bags of evidence later used for the DNA testing. Thank God.

However, it seemed clear that, if this new DNA technology were to be useful, there might be evidence remaining that could be analyzed. Dr. Ferris advised me that DNA research was in its early stages and that, given the age and size of the potential samples, it was unlikely that we could expect anything. However, he agreed to look at the case along with some of the exhibits and to provide us with his impressions. We got a report from Dr. Ferris confirming that semen found in the snow a few days after the murder did not implicate Milgaard as the perpetrator.[18] Dr. Ferris agreed with our assessment of the unlikelihood that David was the killer.

With that report and the affidavit of Deborah Hall, we determined to make a formal application to the Minister of Justice to have the case reviewed. It was filed in late December 1988. The application was made under a rarely used section of the *Criminal Code* allowing the Minister of Justice to intervene and take certain actions when there has been a miscarriage of justice. We didn't know what to put in the application, so we kind of made it up, prepared a summary of the case, and then wove the Hall and Ferris information into our narrative.

Dealing with the Department of Justice

Even though I had been cautioned by lawyers representing Donald Marshall Jr. that we should expect little from the government, I honestly thought that we could link arms with the Department of Justice and work collaboratively and with mutual interest in determining whether there had been a miscarriage of justice. Without specifically thinking about the principles found in *R v. Boucher*,[19] which situates the Crown attorney as a "Minister of Justice," I really thought that the Crown would be our ally. We had gone to Justice, and justice was what I expected to find.

More importantly, we had no resources to undertake an investigation of our own. Joyce had provided the firm with an initial retainer of $2,000, but that had been quickly spent. We decided to proceed with the case on a *pro bono* basis in the hope that the Department of Justice would take an interest and use its resources to look into the matter fully.

Some will have a contrary view, but mine is that what we expected didn't happen, and in the next three years we thought that we had to take matters into our own hands. We began the sometimes nasty process that truly led to winning Milgaard's freedom, an approach that, the Commission of Inquiry ultimately acknowledged, won the day.

This is a crucial point in the story, and in due course I will conclude with a vivid description of the mindset that we faced and had to overcome. It called for extraordinary measures. But the process was fraught with all kinds of problems, the most significant being that we took an approach with the media that in the end was obviously successful but once begun was out of our control. Once the media took an interest in the case, reporters not only drove to develop their own stories but also competed with each other to see who would get a better story by finding new angles. It created a situation in which, while in many regards the media were extremely helpful, every word that we uttered was capable of creating a story that we didn't necessarily want. And that happened on a few occasions.

Rather than feeling like we were working together with the Department of Justice, it felt like we were getting the cold shoulder or, worse, that the feds were more interested in preserving the conviction than in accepting our view that it might be flawed. All we wanted was an open mind.

We didn't get that, at least not from some key people at the Department of Justice. There were people who believed that we were on to something, but they were outnumbered. I would bet that a senior Justice official who compared those who believed in Milgaard's innocence with those who believed that Elvis was still alive[20] regrets saying it as much as I now regret allowing a reporter to believe and publish that Milgaard's original prosecutor hadn't disclosed something that he in fact had.[21]

We made the fact of our application to the Minister of Justice available to the media along with the Hall affidavit and the Ferris report. By early 1989, a number of media outlets were expressing interest in the story, but Dan Lett and his superiors at the *Winnipeg Free Press* had taken it on in a big way. In August 1989, about eight months after we had filed our application, he began publishing various stories, which piqued the interest of other media outlets, including the *Globe and Mail*, CBC, CTV, Global TV, and the *Toronto Star*, which, together with the *Winnipeg Free Press*, would provide the foundation for three objectives that we had set out to achieve:

- create pressure on the Department of Justice to undertake a proper investigation of the case;
- create public awareness to put political pressure on the Minister of Justice to reopen the case; and

• further promote public awareness of the case in the hope that those who knew what had really happened would come forward.

Although we had submitted our application to the Minister in December 1988, Justice officials didn't interview Deborah Hall until almost a year later, in November 1989. We had come to the conclusion that, if anything was going to happen, it needed a nudge, and to make that happen we would change both our tone and our level of contact with the media. Up to that point, we had been circumspect about our position by saying that the case had irregularities and needed a review. Our new approach, as I described at the inquiry, was to go to war. We created the narrative that a sentenced prisoner who raised legitimate doubts about his conviction because of the tireless efforts of his supportive mother was being ignored by an intransigent, uninterested Department of Justice.

And, if we were of a warmongering mind as 1989 wore on, the escalation went nuclear by the summer of 1990, when we were able to start thinking seriously about an answer to a crucial question: if Milgaard didn't do it, then who did? In late February 1990, Hersh Wolch got an anonymous phone call from someone who claimed that the true killer of Gail Miller was Larry Fisher.[22] Fisher was originally from North Battleford and was serving a sentence in a federal prison at the time.

Joyce Milgaard immediately recognized the name and went back to an early police report. Sure enough, a few days after the murder, the police had interviewed people at bus stops in the vicinity of the crime scene and had talked with someone named Fisher. Through a contact at the RCMP, I was able to get a search done discreetly on his criminal record. It showed convictions for a series of rapes and indecent assaults in Regina and Winnipeg.

However, I didn't look deeply enough into the Carlyle-Gordge files from his investigation in the early 1980s. Had I done so, I would have seen that he had notes from a witness suggesting that Fisher had been convicted of a number of rapes. I had missed this in the initial review of the files, and it pains me to this day because it was a clue that could have short-circuited the entire process. We immediately communicated the information to Justice officials, and they actually reacted quickly by assigning the information to a senior RCMP officer. However, before he could begin his work, Joyce Milgaard and a private investigator tracked down Linda Fisher, the wife of Larry, and went to interview her at her home in Saskatchewan.

I was in a very difficult position and later expressed my concerns to both Justice officials and the RCMP officer that Joyce wanted everything done immediately concerning the Fisher tip, and it would be hard to contain her, even though I completely understood her anxiety. Surely the whole ordeal could be ended quickly were we to identify the real killer. But this was also an extremely high-stakes turn of events, and managing its sensitivities was very difficult and sometimes created tension between Joyce and me.

Interestingly enough, when we eventually told David about the Fisher development, he was adamant that we not try Fisher in public and that we ensure he had what Milgaard claimed he never got – a fair process. But having engaged the media, that wasn't so easy. Even though I was trying to keep a lid on the RCMP investigation of Fisher, Joyce provided background information to a couple of local CBC producers who had agreed to do some research on her behalf. The problem, of course, was that, if it led them to a story, they were going to use it, and they did. In May 1990, the story arc that had developed in the case crystallized in a way that we couldn't have scripted better ourselves.

Arguing Our Case in the Media

In Canada, lawyers must try cases in the courts and not in the media. The problem in the *Milgaard* case was that we couldn't get to court. We were trying to get into the courtroom and were having no success, which put things in a different light. We were hammering away at an attitude in the Department of Justice toward our case that I think was encapsulated by the Lamer Commission as "Crown culture," in which the Crown adopts and supports the tunnel vision of the police investigation rather than casting an independent and critical eye on the case.[23] Faced with this culture, what else were we to do in order to advance the case on behalf of our client?

Then lightning struck. Joyce was really frustrated with the pace of the Justice investigation and decided to take her plight directly to Kim Campbell, then the Minister of Justice. In May 1990, Campbell was in Winnipeg, and, having tipped off all the local media, Joyce waited for her outside the elevators in a hotel. The doors opened, and Campbell emerged and was completely sandbagged. In front of all the cameras, she was surprised and basically blew off Joyce, who was left in the dust as Campbell was whisked away. Although Campbell didn't actually say anything that was wrong, the optics were terrible.

From our perspective, however, as Milgaard's counsel, the optics were perfect because they solidified the public perception that the Milgaards were not getting a fair shake. Campbell's reaction to Joyce angered many Canadians across the country. The event was prominently played in all news media and created a slingshot effect in terms of coverage of our efforts. People across Canada reached out to us and expressed their outrage; we knew that the story had connected with Canadians at a visceral level. I actually got letters from a few outraged Second World War veterans wondering what they had fought for in Europe if Milgaard couldn't get his day in court in Canada.

While the RCMP and CBC were quietly digging into the Fisher angle, we had basically given up on the Department of Justice looking into other aspects of the case. We asked for and received further independent forensic analysis that ultimately was not helpful but raised the sensational spectre that semen samples found in the snow at the crime scene might actually have been dog urine. But because it was not helpful to our case, I do wish that we'd been more careful about releasing that information. However, at the time, we were admittedly flailing a bit and throwing wild punches.

Then, through our private investigator, we were able to get the first major witness recantation in early June 1990 from Ron Wilson. His recantation and recollections became so scattered that he was cited for contempt during his testimony at the Supreme Court of Canada. In the end, Wilson was of little value other than that his evidence became of little value, and we argued as a consequence that an important evidentiary foundation had been removed from the case against Milgaard.

On top of that, we thought that we might be on to the real killer. By then, Larry Fisher had surfaced in the media as a possible suspect in the murder of Gail Miller. CBC had also discovered that the convictions in Regina on Fisher's criminal record were actually for offences in Saskatoon in 1968 and 1969. Fisher had pleaded guilty in Regina to the offences in Saskatoon, which is why the police record that I had received showing convictions in Regina was misleading.

Remember that newspaper clipping that I referred to at the beginning? The one about the police issuing a warning to women in December 1968? And the one about the killer being the rapist? It was now clear that a serial rapist had been on the loose in Saskatoon, attacking women in the vicinity in which Miller had been murdered. If you had to pick a suspect between that person and Milgaard, who didn't live in Saskatoon and was passing through on the morning of the murder, where would you look first? And, as it was later learned, several police officers in both the Saskatoon City Police and the RCMP had thought the killer and rapist might be the same person.

If I were to admit to any degree of my own tunnel vision, then the Fisher information was the turning point. As Dan Lett observed, it completed the story arc that I described earlier: the prisoner claiming innocence, his persistent mother, and now, with the information on Fisher, the real villain.

All of this information was sent to Ottawa as addenda to our application to the Minister of Justice. The RCMP and Justice officials interviewed Fisher in prison but didn't really get anywhere with him. We hoped that the information on him would lead to a complete analysis of his activities leading up to and after the murder of Miller. We hoped that they would do something more than merely ask Fisher whether or not he did it. But that didn't happen until we got *really* fed up with everyone.

By the late fall of 1990, all that Justice was going to do on the file was done, and Hersh and I were summoned to a meeting with officials in Ottawa. My recollection of that meeting was that the person who had primary oversight of the file was totally unconvinced that there was anything wrong with the Milgaard conviction. He was steadfast that there was no evidence linking Fisher to the crime and that one of Milgaard's friends had witnessed Milgaard committing the murder. We went through all of the information that had been filed in support of the application and were told that the Minister would make a decision in the near future.

On February 27, 1991, Kim Campbell formally turned down our application for a judicial review of the case. We were devastated. I felt that I had failed and apologized to David when I went to tell him the bad news. At the time, David, not always a model prisoner, was in "the hole" or what they otherwise call administrative segregation. Solitary confinement. There we were deep in the bowels of the prison, and it was David who wound up consoling me.

It took us a couple of weeks to recover; however, given that we had been publicizing the case, we decided to do so even more. I vividly recall a meeting with Joyce and our investigators in which I got a tub-thumper of a speech asserting that Fisher was the true killer and that we needed to stop sulking and make that case. We couldn't give up. Rather, we had to redouble our efforts, and whatever restraint I had left in me vanished.

Thus began an overt political campaign against Kim Campbell and the Department of Justice. It involved every Member of Parliament and Senator, and it included entreaties from the Speaker of the House, heated questions asked by local Manitoba MPs during Question Period, Joyce and me appearing on news and talk shows in electronic media across the country, and what I would generally describe as a complete circus. We had nothing to lose, and we held nothing back.

In retrospect, I didn't care as much as I should have about the collateral effects of bringing the circus to town. In my mind, Milgaard had been wronged again, especially with the Fisher information in hand, and by that point I was prepared to go to hell and back on the file. To the extent that it hadn't already happened, the niceties of what we would now call "civility" went out the window. I paid a high price for this when everyone who got caught in the crossfire had his or her lawyer hold me accountable during the Milgaard Inquiry. That was an unpleasant experience, but at the time my only focus was on my client and on righting the wrong that had been done to him. Collateral damage was incidental.

For example, we asserted that there were conflicts of interest with the federal Department of Justice collaborating with the Crown in Saskatchewan rather than treating that Crown as a witness just like all of the other witnesses. Since it was accusatory, and highlighted conflict between us and Ottawa, it was good stuff for media reporting.

I stand by my position that overall there was little or nothing made public about the case that wasn't ultimately part of the truth about what happened to David Milgaard. But the way in which a lot of it came out had a sinister edge and cast people in a light that made them justifiably upset. Some police were made to look like they had hid information or deliberately forced information from witnesses in order to nail Milgaard. Crown attorneys were made to look inept or worse because of non-disclosure.

This is the risk of engaging the media. Media love conflict, and I promoted it. One always has to be mindful that on the other side of the story is a human being who might have done his or her job as best as possible. Just remember that, if you allow others to be demonized, there might come a day when you actually meet them and find out that they are not the devil. Lesson: be careful!

Concurrently, Joyce and her private investigation team set out to speak with the victims of Larry Fisher. I was really worried about this from a human perspective. How would these people react to having the memories of their attacks brought back to them? Amazingly, they all spoke freely about what had happened to them, and on that basis, with dates and details of the attacks, we were able to construct a profile of how Fisher operated.

I still have a copy of that chart because it was David's ticket out of prison. Tragically, most of its information existed before his trial and appeals. If only more people had listened in 1969 to the police officers who had thought that the rapist was the killer. If only we had known our own file better. If only the Department of Justice had done what we legitimately expected of it during its investigation of Fisher.

Armed with this level of detail, we composed a new application and filed it with the Minister of Justice in August 1991. And we continued our public assault on both the Department of Justice and Saskatoon police.

So rowdy had the case become in the media that, when Prime Minister Brian Mulroney visited Winnipeg about a month after we filed the second application, Joyce and some supporters staged a mild protest outside the hotel where he was appearing. I was especially concerned that this would be very public, was a bit worried that Joyce could come into conflict with the PM's security detail, and highly doubted that we could expect another miracle, as had happened with Kim Campbell. But lightning struck twice.

The Prime Minister got out of his car and went straight over to Joyce, in front of all the cameras. He expressed concern over David's health and assured her that all that could be done was being done and that he would speak with his Minister of Justice. In contrast to Campbell, Mulroney looked like a saint. I don't care what motivated him because what he did was the right thing. Mulroney was a lawyer, and perhaps he felt some visceral connection to the justice of David's cause.

One day while testifying at the Milgaard Inquiry, I got a call on my cell phone. After I left law and moved into the world of media business, I got to know Mulroney a bit, and we talked about the case. I guess that he had been following my testimony in the news and decided to call and give me a pep talk. He reminded me that, though we were having a public showdown with the Department of Justice, the Prime Minister's Office (PMO) was extremely concerned about how the *Milgaard* case was being handled and that, by the time we had submitted our second application, the PMO was actively looking into a variety of options for handling the matter.

Finally a Hearing

Two months later, at the end of November 1991, the case was sent by Kim Campbell as a reference to the Supreme Court of Canada. She had to overturn her previous decision, and I both love and hate the fact that she and some of her officials had to eat crow. Why had it come to this?

Chief Justice Lamer wasn't very happy that the case had landed on his lap. In fact, many years later, while enjoying a sunny afternoon together on a patio in Ottawa's Byward Market, he told me so. He also remembered how sick I looked when, after shooting my mouth off to the media during the reference hearing, he hauled me into his chambers for a chat. He reminded me that the politics were over, that the Court was in session, and that I had a different duty now. I had done my job. Now it was time to respect the process and let the evidence lead to a conclusion. That was maybe the most uncomfortable moment that I experienced in the case from start to finish. Trust me, it feels very lonely when you're alone with the Chief Justice of Canada in his office and he's giving you a stern talking to. Chief Justice Lamer ordered complete disclosure and then set a timetable for the hearings, to start soon on January 16, 1992.

Even though Hersh had been very involved with the case from the beginning, he didn't know the granular details of the evidence. As a result, not only did Joyce and I have to get him prepared to examine the witnesses, but also he had to be prepared to digest a mountain of information flowing in under the disclosure order. It was barely manageable, and I was very concerned about how ready we would be when the show started.

Hersh determined that he would examine all of the witnesses. I felt really angry about that. By then, I'd been doing trial work for about six years, had been immersed in the *Milgaard* case, and thought that I should get a chance to participate more actively. And, between the two of us, I thought that I was the better prepared.

But I have to hand it to Hersh. His examination of Larry Fisher was as masterful as it could have been. In preparation, we had consulted a couple of psychiatrists for their advice about how to get into his head. Hersh took Fisher by the hand and walked him down a path frightening in its alignment with how Gail Miller had been killed. At one point, as Hersh was getting him to explain how his method of attack aligned with the Miller murder, Fisher even corrected him in a way that made it even more obvious that he was the killer. It was brilliant, and I don't think that I could have done that.

The reference case formally concluded on April 6, 1992, and the Supreme Court issued its decision on April 14, just eight days later. It quashed the conviction of Milgaard and ordered a new trial, largely on the basis of the Fisher evidence. Two days later, the Government of Saskatchewan said that it would not conduct a new trial and stayed proceedings, and we walked David out of jail. It was a big win, but it wasn't clean because some people still argued that Milgaard was guilty.[24]

At the beginning, I had constructed a vision of what the ending might look like. It had a soundtrack of angelic voices singing as we walked into the sunlit expanse of the prairie outside the prison. But on freedom day, there were still clouds of doubt cast by officialdom. Although we were happy, we were also angry about that. Such doubt was eliminated forever when advanced DNA testing in 1997 showed conclusively that semen on the underwear worn by Miller belonged to Fisher. He was tried and convicted and remains in prison.

As I alluded to at the outset, the crazy part of the story is that, when Milgaard and his friends got to Saskatoon on the morning of January 31, 1969, they were looking for another friend's house, where they eventually arrived. Renting the basement suite of that house was none other than Fisher and his wife, Linda. Several of his attacks, including the murder, had occurred roughly within a zone of comfort around that house. It was true that Milgaard was innocently in the vicinity of the murder on the morning that it happened. When I think of that coincidence and what happened to him, I sometimes think that it's safest in life if you never leave your home.

Lawyering in Retrospect

With that ending, I return to the question posed at the outset of this chapter. Would I have done anything differently if I had known then what we know today?

By the time that I got involved in the case, Milgaard had been given the benefit of a full police investigation, a preliminary inquiry, a trial, and an appeal. Two private lawyers had looked at the case after the conviction but had made no headway in unsettling the verdict against him. Joyce, with precious few resources, had tried her best for decades to right the wrong that had befallen her son. It had destroyed their family and deprived David of the thing that we sometimes take for granted – our freedom.

The lawyer has to walk into that scene with due caution. Cause-based advocacy will undoubtedly bring a personal dimension to how a lawyer looks at a case, and I don't think that I was aware of what drove me at the time. Too often that awareness occurs later, but this shouldn't be surprising. We rarely sit down at the *beginning* of a case and conduct a self-inventory to assess whether something about us could affect how we approach the case. Maybe that's a good lesson for lawyers: to be more aware of what drives us.

Certainly, there were some technical aspects of how I handled myself as a lawyer that I wouldn't do again, such as witnessing statements and handling exhibits. I might have been more cautious about the access and commentary that we gave to the media. Obviously, I would have paid much more attention to the earlier investigative efforts undertaken by the Milgaards.

However, on the main point about the permissible scope of resolute or zealous advocacy, I'm still convinced that we did what we had to do at the time
in order to represent the best interests of our client within the bounds of
the law. I don't like what happened in terms of how Milgaard won the day.
I might have been motivated in part by both noble and selfish reasons,
but anyone who thinks that any of us enjoyed "the gong show" is badly
mistaken.

When we study and learn about the rule of law, it's obvious how much
everything depends on lawyers to make it work effectively. This, in turn,
makes lawyers' codes of conduct extremely important in establishing the
framework within which we should operate. But what happens when the
rule of law has failed? What, then, is the duty of the lawyer? Are the usual
rules thrown out the window? I think that it depends, like all answers to
legal questions, on the circumstances.

I never read Kim Campbell's memoir, which discusses the *Milgaard* case
in passing, but was guided to it by the editors of this book. It was published
after Milgaard was freed and about a year before he was completely exonerated by the DNA evidence in 1997. What she says in it is telling of what we
were up against:

> Fisher is no candidate for the Order of Canada, but he has never been
> linked in any way to the murder of Gail Miller. He has been found guilty
> by the media in the absence of any evidence. Milgaard is in a kind of limbo
> because his innocence hasn't been established in law and probably never
> can be. The attorney general of Saskatchewan at the time of his release,
> Robert Mitchell, said publicly that in his view Milgaard was properly
> convicted.[25]

To be fair, Campbell goes on to acknowledge that there needs to be a
better way for post-conviction review. Yet she reaches the absurd conclusion that the publicity about Fisher was as wrongful a conviction as one in
a court of law. She actually seems to take his side. I think that she might
now regret writing those words, but this attitude is typical of what we faced
in our representation of Milgaard. It makes me go 1990s all over again *sans*
mullet.

The good news is that there hasn't really been a case like that of David
Milgaard since its conclusion. Maybe we all learned something from it. I
know I did. If so, then that's probably the best ending to the story.

Notes

The main title of this chapter, "No One's Interested in Something You Didn't Do," is from "Wheat Kings" by The Tragically Hip. I would like to acknowledge the tremendous assistance of Matthew Armstrong, who was a third-year law student at the University of Manitoba when this chapter was first written.

1 Justice Edward P. MacCallum, *Commission of Inquiry into the Wrongful Conviction of David Milgaard*, vol. 40, April 14, 2005, document no. 214160, exhibit 039103 at 7948, http://www.justice.gov.sk.ca/milgaard/pubdocs/09262005/Linda%20Fisher/214160.pdf; http://www.justice.gov.sk.ca/milgaard/MilgaardTranscripts/V040041405R.PDF.

2 *Ibid.*, exhibit 003734 at 21298, http://www.justice.gov.sk.ca/milgaard/MilgaardTranscripts/V106011606R.PDF.

3 *R. v. Milgaard*, [1971] 2 W.W.R. 266, 1971 CanLII 792 (Sask. C.A.).

4 Justice Edward P. MacCallum, *Report of the Commission of Inquiry into the Wrongful Conviction of David Milgaard* (Regina: Government of Saskatchewan, 2008) at 305, http://www.justice.gov.sk.ca/milgaard/finalPDF/05-Chapter4.pdf.

5 *Ibid.* at 116, http://www.justice.gov.sk.ca/milgaard/finalPDF/04-Chapter3.pdf.

6 *Criminal Code of Canada*, R.S.C. 1985, c. C-46, s. 690, as repealed by *An Act to Amend the Criminal Code and to Amend Other Acts*, S.C. 2002, c. 13, s. 71.

7 *Reference re Milgaard (Can.)*, [1992] 1 S.C.R. 866.

8 Bruce A. MacFarlane, "Wrongful Convictions: The Effect of Tunnel Vision and Predisposing Circumstances in the Criminal Justice System" (2008), prepared for the Inquiry into Pediatric Forensic Pathology in Ontario, Stephen T. Goudge, Commissioner; Keith A. Findley and Michael S. Scott, "The Multiple Dimensions of Tunnel Vision in Criminal Cases" (2006) 2 Wisconsin Law Review 291.

9 MacCallum, *supra* note 1 at 28831, http://www.justice.gov.sk.ca/milgaard/MilgaardTranscripts/V141042806R.PDF. In an odd twist, the cross-examiner, Catherine Knox, a former Crown attorney, had been the subject of the Lamer Inquiry into the wrongful conviction of Gregory Parsons in Newfoundland.

10 MacCallum, *supra* note 4.

11 Jefferson Airplane, "Somebody to Love," *Surrealistic Pillow* (1967).

12 *R. v. Milgaard*, [1971] 2 W.W.R. 266, 1971 CanLII 792 (Sask. C.A.).

13 MacCallum, *supra* note 4 at 491. The evidence presented by John at trial would raise significant questions about how evidence of this type is handled under s. 9(2) of the *Canada Evidence Act*. See http://www.justice.gov.sk.ca/milgaard/finalPDF/11-Chapter9.pdf.

14 By 1986, my father had served as leader of the Liberal Party of Manitoba, was a nationally syndicated columnist, had founded his own law firm, and had built a successful media business that included the Global Television network in Ontario and independent television stations in Winnipeg and Vancouver. He had earned a high profile locally and nationally.

15 *An Act to Amend the Criminal Code and to Amend Other Acts*, S.C. 2002, c. 13, s. 71. Today we operate under the *Criminal Code of Canada*, R.S.C. 1985, c. C-46, s. 696.1.

16 MacCallum, *supra* note 4 at 104, http://www.justice.gov.sk.ca/milgaard/finalPDF/04-Chapter3.pdf.

17 *Ibid.* at 203, http://www.justice.gov.sk.ca/milgaard/finalPDF/04-Chapter3.pdf.

18 *Ibid.* at 128, http://www.justice.gov.sk.ca/milgaard/finalPDF/04-Chapter3.pdf.

19 *R. v. Boucher,* [1955] S.C.R. 16.

20 MacCallum, *supra* note 1, document no. 004601, http://www.justice.gov.sk.ca/milgaard/pubdocs/April6/Ron%20Wilson/004601.pdf.

21 *Ibid.* at 27040, http://www.justice.gov.sk.ca/milgaard/MilgaardTranscripts/V1340 41906R.PDF; document no. 027179, http://www.justice.gov.sk.ca/milgaard/pubdocs/04192006/David%20Asper/027179.pdf.

22 *Ibid.* at 37217, http://www.justice.gov.sk.ca/milgaard/MilgaardTranscripts/V1790 90706R.PDF.

23 Justice Antonio Lamer, *Lamer Inquiry Report on the Administration of Justice* (St. John's: Government of Newfoundland and Labrador, 2006).

24 Kim Campbell, *Time and Chance: The Political Memoirs of Canada's First Woman Prime Minister* (Toronto: Doubleday Canada, 1996) at 202. Campbell is quoted as saying that "perhaps none of us will ever know for certain" whether Milgaard killed Miller. This can be added to comments from former Saskatchewan Attorney General Bob Mitchell, noted in MacCallum, *supra* note 4 at 265, http://www.justice.gov.sk.ca/milgaard/finalPDF/04-Chapter3.pdf.

25 Campbell, *supra* note 24 at 201.

4

"Begun in Faith, Continued in Determination"

Burnley Allan (Rocky) Jones and the Egalitarian Practice of Law

RICHARD F. DEVLIN

> The black people today in North America are the revolutionaries, because they are faced with extermination. We are forced to fight.
>
> – ROCKY JONES (1969)[1]

> You are responsible ... [Y]ou are responsible for learning ... [T]he more you learn, the more you are responsible ... [Y]ou are either part of the solution or you are part of the problem.
>
> – ROCKY JONES (1994)[2]

> But law was never a dream for me. It's more of a way of continuing to do the political things I want to do and have a profession that allows me to make a living without being dependent on government.
>
> – ROCKY JONES (1995)[3]

Lawyers are not well loved in Canadian society. Jokes about lawyers are legion ... and sometimes vicious.[4] Public opinion polls often place lawyers among the lowest ranks of trusted professionals.[5] Even the leaders of the legal profession itself express pointed concerns about its reputation for un-trustworthiness[6] and its ability to ensure access to justice.[7]

Whatever the accuracy or fairness of these criticisms or concerns, there is one segment of the legal community that might merit a kinder, gentler assessment: egalitarian lawyers. They devote their practice to the pursuit of social justice. They recognize the structural forces of inequality – class, race, gender, disability, sexual orientation, and so on – and dedicate their energies to challenging such forces through law.

This chapter provides a snapshot of some of the achievements and chal-lenges of one such egalitarian lawyer: Burnley Allan "Rocky" Jones, one of the first Black lawyers in Nova Scotia. From the 1990s to the early 2000s, Jones established himself as the most high-profile – certainly celebrated, perhaps notorious – Black lawyer in Nova Scotia. An engaging, provocative, and fearless speaker, he took the lead in identifying pervasive racism in Nova Scotia and served as counsel in several of the most significant cases of those two decades. In the first part of this chapter, I discuss three key interven-tions by Jones: his role in helping to establish the Indigenous Black and Mi'kmaq Program at Dalhousie Law School (as it then was); his role as coun-sel in the famous *R.D.S.* case (1997); and his role as co-defendant in a de-famation suit brought by a Halifax police officer in *Campbell v. Derrick and Jones* (2002). The second part of the chapter briefly suggests several the-matic concerns, followed by a conclusion.[8]

Practising Equality

The Nova Scotia Context

Nova Scotia is a storied province. Geographically, it has a stunning coastline and fantastic seascapes. Its lakes, rivers, and valleys are glorious. The island of Cape Breton is a gem. The Fundy tides that ultimately penetrate to the heart of the province, as far as Truro, are a world-class phenomenon. Nova Scotia is also historically rich. The Aboriginal people, the Mi'kmaq, can be traced back more than 11,000 years. Samuel de Champlain landed and built Port Royal (now Annapolis Royal) in 1605. Significant parts of the province were settled by Acadians, who reclaimed large tracts of arable land through the construction of impressive dike systems. The French built Louisburg in 1719. The British built Halifax in 1749. Wars ensued. The Mi'kmaq took sides. The Acadians were expelled. Louisburg fell. Waves of immigrants moved in ... the Scottish, the Irish, the American Loyalists after the Revolution, and the Germans.

Nova Scotian culture reflects this geography and history. Although English is dominant, French and Gaelic are still spoken in parts of the province. The music resonates with the cruel miseries of the sea, the wars, the clearing of the land, and the joy of the dance. Peggy's Cove and Alexander Keith's beer are the province's brands. Nova Scotia is also a community of communities. These subcommunities are often tied closely to their environments – their coastal village, their valley town – and those of their own kind – their religious brethren, their kin, their co-workers.

However, despite – or perhaps because of – this history, Nova Scotia has an uglier side. Racism, in particular anti-Black racism, has been (and unfortunately continues to be) a constitutive dimension of Nova Scotian society.[9] From the enslavement of Mathieu de Costa in Port Royal in 1606; through the forced immigration and emigration of the Black Loyalists, the Maroons, and the Refugees in the eighteenth and nineteenth centuries; to the "racial liberalism" of the twentieth century,[10] African Nova Scotians have experienced a history of violence, murder, oppression, exclusion, false promises, exploitation, segregation, and economic and racial marginalization. After African Nova Scotians received formal equality with the abolition of slavery, they experienced a regime of "liminal citizenship"[11] and the "bondage of dependence."[12] However, in spite of this, drawing on robust family ties and inspirational religious institutions, African Nova Scotians built numerous small but strong cultural communities throughout the province. Usually, these communities were built on the outskirts of town, close, but not too close, for White comfort. One such town is Truro.

Early Engagements

Burnley Jones was born in August 1941 in the town of Truro (population of approximately 10,000). The Mi'kmaq had named the area Wagobagitik, which referred either to "end of the water's flow" or "place of the rushing waters," a reference to the end of the tidal bore of the Bay of Fundy and the Salmon River floodplain. When the Acadians arrived in the early 1770s, they translated the Mi'kmaq name to Cobequid and built a sophisticated system of dikes. After the expulsion of the Acadians in 1755 (which some analogize to ethnic cleansing), the area was resettled in 1761 by Ulster Scots of the Presbyterian persuasion. Truro's motto is "Begun in Faith, Continued in Determination." The settlers built a strong farming community over the next 100 years, and when the industrial revolution arrived it was enthusiastically embraced. Truro became known as the "hub of Nova Scotia" because it emerged as the central point of several railway lines and the most important telephone and communication lines. It also became the hometown of a number of significant manufacturing enterprises, including Stanfields (Truro Knitting Mills), the "unshrinkable" underwear company.

Truro had a small Aboriginal community, though the reserve of Millbrook was close. The Black population was somewhat larger but still small. It is not clear when the first members of the Black community arrived in Truro, but as early as 1788 there was a controversy. The first official Presbyterian minister was the popular Daniel Cock, a Glaswegian, who arrived in the community in 1770, a bare decade after its founding. He was a slave owner. Another Presbyterian minister and fellow Scot, Reverend James MacGregor, had been appointed in 1786 to the Presbyteria of Pictou, just forty-one miles over the Cobequid hills. He was an avowed anti-slavery activist. In his first year in Pictou, MacGregor spent twenty pounds of his annual salary of twenty-seven pounds to purchase the freedom of a young female slave from her Nova Scotian master. Two years later, in 1788, MacGregor published a critique of Cock, admonishing him for the "immorality of a Christian's enslaving of God's children."[13] The letter was unsuccessful in motivating Cock to free the young slave, but it is credited with contributing to "the incipient judicial assault on slavery" and its eventual outlaw.[14]

By 1871, the census reported that there were approximately eighty Black families in Truro, and most of them seemed to be settled in one of three somewhat distinct communities, Young, Ford, or West Prince Street, also known as "the island," "the marsh," and "the hill."[15] Many worked in the railway industry or in the foundries.

The Jones family was well established in the Truro Black community. Family history recounts that Sam Jones – Burnley's great-grandfather – walked from the United States to Nova Scotia in the 1800s.[16] Jeremiah (Jerry) Jones – Burnley's grandfather – was a well-known war hero.[17] During the battle of Vimy Ridge in 1916, his battalion came under heavy fire and could not proceed. Jones single-handedly attacked the gun emplacement and captured it after killing several German soldiers. When the other German soldiers surrendered, he forced them to carry the machine gun back to the Canadian side. It was reported that the commanding officer recommended Jeremiah for the Distinguished Conduct Medal, but it was never awarded.[18] Jeremiah died in 1950, but in 2010 the Government of Canada finally recognized him posthumously with the Canadian Forces Medallion for Distinguished Service.[19]

Burnley's parents, Willena Gabriel (of Springhill) and Elmer Jones, were married in 1935 "at the home of the groom's parents on Ford Street."[20] They had ten children. Prior to getting married, Elmer played hockey for the Africville Brown Bombers. Like his father, Elmer joined the military, and he fought in the Second World War. Willena was a leading community activist, and in due course, at the age of sixty, she received her teaching degree.[21]

Truro of the 1940s and 1950s was a deeply segregated town.[22] In an interview with Stephen Kimber, Jones recalled that

> he couldn't bowl in the local alley, couldn't play pool in the pool hall, couldn't eat in certain restaurants. We were taught at home that we were as good as anyone else ... but we had no experience of Blacks in power. I never even considered the idea that Black people could be lawyers or hold any kind of position of authority.[23]

In another interview, he said, "I knew that town would destroy me ... [It was] so oppressive in such a subtle way ... I had to get out."[24] Jones left school, and Truro, at the age of sixteen, and like his father and grandfather he joined the Canadian military. He served for a couple of years. He moved to Toronto in 1959, where he drove truck.

It was in his early twenties, in Toronto, that Jones appears to have become more politically aware. Two events seem to have triggered this awareness: his relationship with his first wife, Joan, who was politically engaged, and demonstrations by White people outside the American consulate protesting "the denial of voting rights to Blacks in the U.S. South."[25] Jones became a spokesperson at their protests, and the media began to pay attention to him, calling him "Rocky the Revolutionary."[26] He later reflected on his moment: "You do not create history, history creates you."[27]

In 1965, Jones and his wife decided to return to Nova Scotia, which at that point had approximately half of the "African Canadian population" of Canada,[28] to continue the struggle. They and several others were supported by the Student Union for Peace Action to develop a grassroots community development program focused on the needs of Black youth. Jones and his spouse established Kwacha ("Freedom") House, which engaged in educational and activist programs for inner-city Halifax Black youth.[29] Its core philosophy was that "you must free yourself to free others."[30] Kwacha House, always unpopular with Halifax-area politicians, was closed by local authorities in 1968.[31]

Jones also became increasingly active in the Halifax Black community in the mid- to late 1960s. He became disillusioned with the non-confrontational style of the traditional leaders of the Black community, the Nova Scotia Association for the Advancement of Coloured People and the African United Baptist Association. He became interested in the Black Power and Black Panthers movements in the United States. In October 1968, he invited Stokely Carmichael (the "Prime Minister of the Black Panthers") and other Black Panthers to Halifax. This had an electrifying impact on the city.[32] One of the Black Panthers was arrested, as was Jones himself, but only for a brief time.[33] He also helped to establish a new militant group, the Afro-Canadian Liberation movement, which sought "[t]he elimination of all forms of racial oppression, social and economic injustices against Black people – by whatever means necessary ... to this we pledge our lives."[34] It was soon after that the *Globe Magazine* ran a special feature on "Rocky the Revolutionary."[35] This radicalization of the Black community in Nova Scotia ultimately led to the creation of a new "umbrella group" for the community, the Black United Front, though it was not as radical as Jones had hoped.[36] Throughout this period, he was the subject of intense surveillance by the RCMP.[37] At one point, he and his family were the victims of an arson attack on their home.[38]

In the 1970s and early 1980s, Jones consolidated his position of activist leadership in the Black community. He led protests to oppose the appointment of an allegedly racist city manager for Halifax, collaborated with the Black United Front, and challenged police brutality toward the Black community. He became an advocate for prisoners' rights and served as Executive Director of Real Opportunities for Prisoner Employment, and he established the Black Historical and Educational Research Organization, an oral history project gathering information on the Black communities of Nova Scotia. He ran, unsuccessfully, in a by-election as a candidate for the provincial New Democratic Party. He even opened jewellery boutiques with the goal of advancing job opportunities for Black Nova Scotians and to "press the white mall retailers to hire more Blacks ... [E]verything was political."[39] But he also decided to go back to school, first to earn his BA and then to commence an MA in history.

It was during this educational experience that Jones became increasingly concerned about the minuscule number of Black Nova Scotian and Mi'kmaq students attending university and that the universities themselves were part of the problem of racial exclusion and oppression. In collaboration with his friend and graduate student James Walker, Jones conceived (allegedly while on a duck-hunting trip) the idea of a one-year transitional program for Aboriginal and Black youth who had not completed high school in order to prepare them for university education.[40] His aspirations were clear: "It's not just enough to have an education. They had to have an education and then be committed to coming back to the community to use their education to further educate the community."[41] Jones and Walker, with the assistance of others, then began to lobby Dalhousie University to adopt such a program. To their surprise, the university responded positively, and the Transition Year Program (TYP) was established in 1970. Jones and Walker were paid a stipend to design and develop a course on Black history. Jones taught part time in the program for a decade. Since that time, more than 1,000 students have graduated from the program, and it has become a model for other targeted educational support initiatives across Canada, including the Indigenous Black and Mi'kmaq Program at Dalhousie Law School.

The Donald Marshall Jr. Inquiry and the Creation of the Indigenous Black and Mi'kmaq Program

In the mid-1980s, the systemic and pervasive racism of the Nova Scotian criminal justice system was laid bare as a result of the Royal Commission on the Donald Marshall, Jr., Prosecution. In 1971, Donald Marshall Jr., the seventeen-year-old son of the Grand Chief of the Mi'kmaq Nation, was convicted of killing Sandy Seale, a friend, also seventeen years old. Seale was Black. Marshall was sentenced to life imprisonment. Eleven years later, after years of mounting concern that he had been wrongly convicted, the Nova Scotia Court of Appeal acquitted him. However, the egregious failings of the criminal justice system led to calls for a Royal Commission, with a particular focus on the racial dimensions of the prosecution, conviction, and even acquittal. In particular, the final report of the Commission, published in 1989, concluded that the criminal justice system had failed Marshall in making errors that could and should have been prevented had those involved acted professionally and competently. The report made it clear that these failures took place, at least in part, because Marshall was Aboriginal.[42]

The Commission's proceedings actually commenced in 1986. Its mandate made it clear that it would not confine itself to the Marshall situation but focus more generally on racism in the criminal justice system, vis-à-vis not only the Aboriginal community but also the Black community. Given his experience and profile, Jones was selected by the Black United Front to coordinate a research project titled The Black United Front Justice System Review as part of the organization's contribution to the inquiry.[43]

As the hearings unfolded, one of the myriad issues identified was the significant underrepresentation of minorities in the Nova Scotian legal profession. The only law school in the province, Dalhousie Law School, had never graduated a Mi'kmaq person, and only a tiny number of Black Nova Scotians, since it had been established in 1883, almost exactly a century earlier. Perhaps because of his experience with the Transition Year Program, Jones seized a moment of opportunity. On one of the hearing days for the Commission, he found himself seated beside two of the professors from Dalhousie Law School. One he had known from other contexts, and the other was unknown to him.[44] In the course of their conversation, Jones, in his characteristically direct manner, put it to the Dalhousie representatives that the systemic failures of the criminal justice system were partly the fault of the law school. He identified two problems: (1) many of the actors in the criminal justice system were graduates of the law school – lawyers and judges – and their manifest racism stemmed partly from the educational failings of the law school; (2) the law school had failed to graduate students from the Black and Mi'kmaq communities. The Dalhousie representatives did not disagree and suggested that a further meeting take place to develop a strategy.

The receptiveness of the law school representatives had been informed by three other recent developments.[45] First, a few years previously, in 1986, Dalhousie Law School had applied to the American Law School Admissions Council for funding from its Minority Enrollment Challenge Grant Programme for Innovative Projects. The application had been turned down. Second, also in 1986, on the basis of a private grant, Dalhousie University, in conjunction with several Aboriginal organizations, had established the MicMac Professional Careers Project (MCPC) in order to redress the underrepresentation of Aboriginal people in professional programs such as law, health sciences, and administration. Third, in 1988, the university had established The President's Task Force on Access for Black and Native People. Initially, this was conceived of as a review of the Transition Year Program, but as it evolved its ambitions for inclusion and responsiveness became broader.[46]

When the Dalhousie representatives reported to Dean Innis Christie on developments at the Marshall Inquiry in December 1988, he authorized the creation of a committee to enhance minority access to the law school. For the Aboriginal community, an appropriate representative organization already existed, the MicMac Professional Careers Project, under the leadership of Cathy Martin. However, there was no equivalent organization for the Black community. The Dean therefore created an Ad Hoc Committee on the Black Presence at Dalhousie Law School. Jones was an obvious represent-ative, and he was joined by Janis Jones Darrell (co-adviser to the President on minorities and Burnley's sister), Maxine Tynes (poet and member of the Dalhousie Board of Governors), Cynthia Thomas (student), and Donald Oliver (practitioner).

In January and February 1989, Jones and his colleagues had weekly meet-ings with a law school representative to identify sources of the problems and possible solutions to them. Parallel meetings were held with the MPCP representatives. Jones argued forcefully for two separate programs, one for Black students, the other for Mi'kmaq students; a pre-law program; finan-cial support to help defray the expenses of law school for students from disadvantaged communities; and modification of the curriculum to be more responsive to the experiences of Black Canadians. These conversations took place both in formal meetings at the law school and occasionally in the more informal context of the Graduate House. Many of the meetings were opti-mistic, imaginative, and collaborative, but some were conducted in an air of suspicion and confrontation. The most controversial issue was whether it would be a single program for both Black and Mi'kmaq students (with cor-relative questions of proportional participation) or two separate programs. Despite the concerns of Jones and others, the Ad Hoc Committee ultimately concluded that only a unified program would be feasible, both politically and economically. Otherwise, Jones got much of what he wanted. The In-digenous Black and Mi'kmaq Program was unanimously approved in Faculty Council in April 1989, and it commenced operations in July 1989. As a consequence, when the Final Report of the Marshall Inquiry was pub-lished in December 1989, one of the few positive comments in its seven volumes was that

> [t]he Dalhousie Law School's recently announced minority admission pro-gram – which includes special recruitment efforts and a summer program as well as educational and financial support – would appear to include all of the elements we have identified as being necessary to a successful initiative, and we are encouraged by its establishment. But Dalhousie's leadership must be accompanied by the financial support of governments and the bar in order to ensure that the increased participation of visible minorities in the legal profession actually occurs.[47]

Since 1989, the program has graduated more than 150 students, the majority of them indigenous Black Nova Scotians.

But the story of Jones and the IB&M Program does not end there. As James Walker notes, "as the programme began to take shape and Jones was actively recruiting applicants, he came under pressure from the community to 'put his money where his mouth is' and send in his own application."[48] Jones was accepted as one of three Black students in the first cohort. He worked hard, spent an intensive summer term for academic credit at the Dalhousie Legal Aid Clinic, graduated in May 1992, and was chosen as class valedictorian. But this was not the last time that Nova Scotia (and Canada) would hear from him.

The Curious Incident of a Boy on a Bike: The *RDS* Case

After graduation, Jones articled with Jamie Armour in Windsor, Nova Scotia, "working with Mi'kmaq at Shubenacadie; and with the Black Community in Windsor."[49] In 1993, after his call to the bar, now in his early fifties, Jones was hired by the Dalhousie Legal Aid Clinic as a staff lawyer. The clinic was located on Cunard Street, literally just around the corner from what used to be Kwacha House in the 1960s. But the neighbourhood had not changed much: it was still primarily populated by disadvantaged members of the Aboriginal and Black communities. The salary was disappointing (in the low to mid-$30,000 range),[50] but the job put Jones at the centre of the clinic's tripartite mandate: the education of students, the practice of law for the disadvantaged, and community activism/law reform. His appointment as a staff lawyer generated a significant increase in the number of Black people seeking help from the clinic.[51]

After Jones was on the job for just a few months, R.D.S. walked into his life. R.D.S. – the initials of the fifteen-year-old Black youth whose identity was protected under the law – was apparently small and skinny but had been charged, on December 10, 1993, under the *Criminal Code* with several counts of unlawful assault and resisting arrest. The charges stemmed from an incident on October 17, when there was an altercation between R.D.S. and a White constable. Jones was immediately concerned that this was an example of overcharging and agreed to fight the charges. A hearing could not be heard before a Youth Court judge until December 2, 1994, more than a year after the incident. As several commentators have noted,[52] this was a very different Court. Not only were the accused and his lawyer Black, so too were the clerk and judge.[53] This meant that, among the official participants, only the Crown prosecutor, and the only witness other than the accused (the police officer Constable Steinberg), were White.

Even though there were others at the alleged altercation, neither the Crown nor the defence called other witnesses. It would therefore be a "he-said/he-said" determination of credibility. The police officer testified that, in response to a call about a stolen van by "non-white" youth, he chased, caught, questioned, and arrested a suspect, N.R. (another minor referred to by his initials in order to protect his identity). Constable Steinberg claimed that, at that point, R.D.S. rode up on a bike and rammed into him. He stated that, in order to keep the situation under control, he put both N.R. and R.D.S. under restraint until his partner arrived. On cross-examination, Jones pushed Constable Steinberg on two points: use of the description "non-white" and overcharging.

When R.D.S. took the stand, he said that he saw a small crowd, was nosey, saw his cousin handcuffed, and spoke to his cousin. He claimed that he was then put into a chokehold by the police officer and told to shut up or he would also be arrested. He denied ramming his bike into the officer. On cross-examination, the Crown did not contest this version of events.

Judge Corinne Sparks gave an oral decision from the bench. She acknowledged that the case depended entirely on the credibility of the two witnesses. She expressed reservations about the accuracy of Constable Steinberg's testimony, especially the fact that Steinberg had omitted to mention that N.R. had been handcuffed. Judge Sparks then went on to say that R.D.S. seemed to be a "rather honest young boy" and that he had been "struck by the hostility which greeted him by the police officer." Crown counsel had argued that there was "absolutely no reason to attack the credibility of the officer," whose "explanation was straightforward. He was simply doing his lawful duty." Crown counsel asked Judge Sparks to accept the constable's evidence over R.D.S's version of events.[54] She responded:

> I'm not saying that the constable misled the Court, although police officers have been known to do that in the past. And I'm not saying that the officer overreacted, but certainly police officers do overreact, particularly when they're dealing with non-white groups. That, to me, indicates a state of mind right there that is questionable.
>
> I believe that probably the situation in this particular case is the case of a young police officer who overreacted. And I do accept the evidence of Mr S

that he was told to shut up or he would be under arrest. That seems to be in keeping with the prevalent order of the day.

At any rate, based upon my comments and based upon all the evidence before the Court, I have no other choice but to acquit.[55]

Jones and his client were well pleased. The Crown and the police officer were not. Thus began a journey through the courts all the way to the Supreme Court of Canada that would take another three years.[56]

On December 22, 1994, just before the Christmas break, the Crown filed a notice of appeal – it had decided to go after Judge Sparks. Not only did it claim that her oral judgment manifested a reasonable apprehension of bias, but also, almost without precedent, it argued that it manifested actual bias on the basis of race in favour of R.D.S. and against Constable Steinberg.[57]

The appeal was heard on April 18, 1995. The Crown forcefully advanced the actual bias argument. Jones counterargued that Judge Sparks simply made her "findings of fact based on the credibility of the witnesses before her."[58] Chief Justice Constance Glube gave an oral decision from the bench. She held that the remarks of Judge Sparks were not supported by evidence presented in court, and though the comments did not amount to actual bias they did amount to a reasonable apprehension of bias. As a result, the appeal was allowed, and a new trial was ordered before a different judge.

This was a game-changer. The case was no longer just about the credibility of a White police officer and a Black youth getting into an altercation but was now also about the authority, legitimacy, and responsibility of being a Black judge in Nova Scotia.

Jones persuaded the Executive Director of Dalhousie Legal Aid Clinic that the decision of Chief Justice Glube would have to be appealed. But the problem was resources, for the case had morphed from being focused on evidence to involving questions of law: the test for bias and the potential for a *Charter* argument. The solution was to have several members of the Dalhousie Faculty of Law collaborate *pro bono*[59] and to allocate some of the time of some of the students at the clinic. Over the next few months, through multiple evening meetings (and copious amounts of pizza accompanied by the occasional beverage) at the clinic, the team crafted the appeal factum. It was a challenging process requiring not only a technical understanding of the law of bias but also a conceptual capacity to advance both the methodology of contextualism and a substantivist conception of equality.

The appeal took place on October 13, 1995. Jones argued in part that Chief Justice Glube erred in adopting a formal approach to equality in her determination of a reasonable apprehension of bias rather than a substantive approach, as mandated by sections 15, 11(d), and 7 of the *Charter of Rights and Freedoms*. Robert E. Lutes for the Crown argued that the *Charter* argument was not a proper issue for the appeal.[60]

The Court of Appeal issued its reasons for decision surprisingly quickly, just twelve days later. The appeal was denied. The majority (Justices Flinn and Pugsley) excluded the *Charter* argument on the basis that it had not been argued before Chief Justice Glube and that the reasons did generate a reasonable apprehension of bias because they were not based on the evidence. The dissent by Justice Freeman, however, found that there was no reasonable apprehension of bias and that Judge Sparks was entitled to rely on her "wisdom and experience" in making a determination of credibility.[61] Although once again disappointed by the outcome, Jones and his colleagues were encouraged that they had managed to persuade one appellate judge to recognize the validity of at least one of their arguments.

After the debriefing, a consensus was achieved that the Dalhousie Legal Aid Clinic would seek leave to appeal to the Supreme Court of Canada.[62] Some funding was provided by the Court Challenges Program.[63] Again it was decided to advance both the reasonable apprehension of bias argument and *Charter* arguments based on sections 7, 11(d), and 15. Leave was granted in May 1996. The hearing would take place on March 10, 1997.

Much time in the intervening months was spent refining and developing the arguments presented to the Nova Scotia Court of Appeal. Two key strategic issues came to the fore: who should appear on behalf of R.D.S. in the Supreme Court of Canada and what was the best way to pitch the issue of racialization to the Court. For the first, Jones and his collaborators recognized that Supreme Court advocacy required a particular skill set. Obviously, Jones, with only a few years of practice under his belt, did not have that experience. However, he had been the lawyer for R.D.S. from the beginning, and the racialized dimensions of the case made it imperative that he appear. After a discussion during a cigarette break on the street outside the Dalhousie Legal Aid Clinic, it was agreed that Jones would argue the first part of the case – the reasonable apprehension of bias argument – and that Professor Dianne Pothier (a constitutional law scholar and leading equality rights theorist/activist) would advance the *Charter* arguments.

In developing the reasonable apprehension of bias argument, the idea of arguing that Judge Sparks simply took "judicial notice" of racism in Nova Scotia was put on the table. Jones and his collaborators researched the law on judicial notice and eventually determined that, though attractive as a strategy to have the Supreme Court acknowledge systemic racism in Canada, it would be difficult to win because Judge Sparks did not say that this was what she was doing. Instead, it was decided to advance a "contextualist" interpretation of reasonable apprehension of bias as the best way to proceed.

However, one of the interveners in the case – the Women's Legal Education and Action Fund (LEAF) – decided that it wanted to advance the judicial notice argument. In a series of communications, and at least one somewhat testy conference call, Jones and his colleagues argued forcefully against such a move. The concern was that raising the judicial notice argument would allow the Court to ignore or reject the contextualist argument, and if the judicial notice argument failed (which the team thought it would) then the appeal would be lost, Judge Sparks would be rebuked, and R.D.S. would have to face a new trial. Jones and his team were unsuccessful in persuading LEAF to abandon the judicial notice argument.

In the Supreme Court of Canada, Jones was the first to present his argument. He began tentatively and nervously, and his comments were unusually scripted (for him), but as the members of the Court began to ask him questions he found his stride.[64] His most powerful moment came in response to a question from Chief Justice Lamer:

> I want the Court to address the issue if the Court will, that indeed the judge was right to acknowledge the existence of racism, or if not racism of racial overtones in a case, that in fact the same as we would now be aware of the imbalances in our society vis-à-vis women, we should be aware of the imbalances in our society because of race. And it's not asking something far out, it is a reality, and if we don't hide from the reality, if we address the reality, perhaps, and the Appellant submits that it is important for us as Canadians to address these issues and to work on them ...
>
> My Lords and my Ladies, we cannot ignore the fact that for centuries people of colour have made claims about bias in the courts, and the courts have been deaf to those claims, but yet, as soon as one black judge even raises the issue of race, suddenly claims for an apprehension of bias in the judiciary seemed to be well grounded.[65]

Jones spoke to, and for, racial equality – but he never forgot the client. In the closing words of his rebuttal, he reminded the Court of what the case was really about: "That justice must in fact be done for this young person, RDS, and I submit to the Court that his acquittal should be upheld and he should not be faced, years later, as he is now, with going back for a new trial on what was only a summary offence in the first instance."[66]

Jones was followed by his co-counsel, Professor Pothier, who advanced the *Charter* arguments, and then by the interveners and the Crown.

Six months later the Court released its decision. The appeal was granted, Judge Sparks was vindicated, and the acquittal of R.D.S. was reinstated. Jones had won what is still seen to be one of the most significant Supreme Court decisions on race in Canada.[67]

Speaking Truth to Power: The *Campbell v. Derrick and Jones* Defamation Suit

At the same time as the acquittal of R.D.S. was being appealed to Chief Justice Glube in April 1995, Jones took on another controversial file, one that has not garnered the same national attention as the R.D.S. file but is perhaps just as important.

On March 6, 1995, the administration of St. Patrick's–Alexandra Junior High School called the police to report the theft of $300 from the purse of a staff member. The school was "an inner city school in a neighbourhood where many of the students are Black and many are poor."[68] Constable Carol Campbell, who had been with the Halifax Regional Police for two years, was the attending officer. Campbell is White. While she was on the premises, a second theft occurred, this time ten dollars from the backpack of a visiting volunteer university student. Three girls – L.S., J.-L.F., and T.V. (two twelve, the other thirteen, all Black) – were summoned by the Vice-Principal to the Guidance Room. Campbell was left alone in the room with the girls. The evidence was contradictory. The girls claimed that they were told to remove most of their clothing. Campbell claimed that she did not ask them to remove their underwear but only to "pull it away from their bodies so that she could see if the $10.00 was in the underwear."[69] After two of the girls left the room with Campbell, one of them told her that the missing money was between L.S.'s legs. Campbell re-entered the room with a rubber glove and told L.S. that she knew where the money was. At that point, L.S. handed over the ten dollars and was charged with theft and subsequently convicted. She received an absolute discharge.[70]

When the girls' parents found out about the search, they were very upset. Beginning on March 10, several local newspaper articles highlighted girls being "strip-searched." The parents/guardians of T.V. and J.-L.F. retained Jones (still at the Dalhousie Legal Aid Clinic) as their lawyer. The guardian of the third girl, L.S., retained Anne Derrick. She was another high-profile progressive lawyer in Halifax and had served as Donald Marshall Jr.'s lawyer when his conviction was overturned. Derrick is White.

On April 5, Jones and Derrick filed two formal letters of complaint with the Halifax Police Chief. In one part of his letter, Jones claimed that

> [t]here was a complete disregard for the privacy of the girls involved. The girls were instructed to remove their clothes, exposing their private areas ...
>
> The girls were told to remove their clothes in an unsecured area that was totally inappropriate for a strip search ...
>
> ... [I]t is strongly felt that the children would not have been treated in the manner described if they were white and in a school that saw a different social and economic class of society.[71]

Derrick's letter stated in part that

> [L.S.] ... was strip searched by a Halifax Police officer ...
>
> ... [L.S.] was searched by way of patting down at first, including a pat search around her breasts with her shirt pulled partially up. She was then required to take off her pants and other layers including taking down her underwear.
>
> ... [R]ace was a factor in her treatment ... She does not think that white girls in a predominantly white school would have been subjected to the same treatment.[72]

Jones and Derrick also issued the following press release, which stated in part that "B.A. 'Rocky' Jones and Anne Derrick, in their joint capacity as solicitors for the three young women who were strip searched at St. Pat's Alexandra Junior High, will be holding a press conference, on Wednesday, April 5, 1995, 10:30–11:30 a.m. at Club 55 on Gottingen Street."

Two days later Jones and Derrick held the press conference. They made the letters of complaint public, they read letters from the parents and guardians of the three girls, and they responded to media questions. During the press conference, they made explicit connections between what they characterized as the "strip search" and the class and race of the girls. For example, Jones said that

> [w]e have three young women who are prepared to say under oath that they had to remove their clothes because of the directions given to them directly

by a police officer of the City of Halifax and that the vice principal of the school told them that they were to be searched.

... I think that they all presumed powerlessness, and I think that as has been mentioned earlier, because the school is in an area where people are basically poor and because they were black girls, I think both the police officer and the school administrator felt they could do whatever they wanted to these two girls. And so they strip searched them.[73]

Later, in response to a question he said,

I think it's clear that they were all black. All of the children were black. The officer was white. The vice-principal, I do believe, is white. And there's no doubt whatsoever in my mind that this would not have happened to white children.

However, having said that, I do believe that class has a lot to do with this issue also. That because these children are in a community that is basically poor, the school authorities and the police felt that they could trample on their constitutional rights.[74]

Derrick voiced similar concerns. The press conference gained widespread media attention.

In response to the complaint, the Police Chief ordered an internal investigation. The investigation found that Constable Campbell had failed to read the girls their rights and that she had failed to tag the evidence. This was found to constitute discreditable conduct. The complaints that Jones and Derrick had filed according to the *Police Act* were resolved informally, with the Halifax Police Chief acknowledging that the girls' *Charter* rights had been breached during the search for the missing ten dollars.[75]

Several months later, in September 1995, the girls and their parents/guardians sued the Halifax Police Department and the School Board for breach of the girls' constitutional rights. Neither Jones nor Derrick was retained for this action. In due course, both the formal complaint to the Halifax Police Department and the suit were resolved when it was acknowledged that there was a breach of the girls' constitutional rights.

That, however, was not the end of it. Again, as with *R. v. R.D.S.*, the story morphed. On October 4, 1995, Constable Campbell, supported by her union, retained George MacDonald to launch a defamation suit against Jones and Derrick.[76] Campbell claimed that the letters of complaint and the remarks at the press conference defamed her "both in their natural and ordinary meaning and by innuendo."[77] In response, Jones and Derrick claimed that their statements were "either subject to qualified privilege and without malice, or insofar as the words stated matters of fact, they were true, and insofar as they were matters of opinion, they were fair comment on a matter of public interest."[78]

Central to their defence was the argument that lawyers have a particular obligation to speak out in situations in which the administration of justice is being undermined. In particular, they emphasized the following ethical duty as articulated in Nova Scotia's *Legal Ethics and Professional Conduct Handbook:*

> The lawyer has a duty to encourage public respect for justice and to uphold and try to improve the administration of justice.
>
> **Guiding Principles**
> ...
>   The lawyer, by training, opportunity and experience, is in a position to observe the workings and discover the strengths and weaknesses of laws, legal institutions and public authorities. The lawyer, therefore, has a duty to provide leadership in seeking improvements to the legal system. Any criticisms and proposals the lawyer makes in doing so should be *bona fide* and reasoned. In discharging this duty, the lawyer should not be involved in violence or injury to the person.
>
> **Commentary**
> ...
> 21.2 The lawyer's responsibilities are greater than those of a private citizen.
> ...
> 21.4 The lawyer has a duty not to weaken or destroy public confidence in legal institutions or authorities by broad, irresponsible allegations of corruption or partiality. The lawyer in public life must be particularly careful in this regard because the mere fact of being a lawyer lends weight and credibility to any public statements. *For the same reason the lawyer should not hesitate to speak out against an injustice.*[79]

More than five years later the defamation trial finally commenced on April 3, 2001. One of the appeal judges recounted just how gruelling the trial was:

Evidence was presented on behalf of all three parties to this litigation over the course of sixteen days – from April 3–26, 2001. There then followed four days of submissions by counsel to the trial judge on a variety of subjects, including malice, qualified privilege, justification, fair comment, and use of discovery excerpts.

Counsel for the [parties] made their closing submissions to the jury on Thursday, May 3, 2001. The jury was then instructed to return on Monday, May 7, to receive the judge's directions. The trial judge spent all of Monday, May 7, in charging the jury. He brought the jurors back briefly on Tuesday, May 8, for further directions on the defence of justification and to instruct the jury of the requirement for unanimity, but that after deliberating for four hours a majority of five would be sufficient to deliver the jury's verdict.

The jury deliberated for two and a half days before returning a verdict in favour of [Constable Campbell].[80]

In the course of jury deliberations, Justice Moir delivered two brief oral decisions, the first denying the defence of qualified privilege, the second rejecting any evidence of malice. The jury then found Jones and Derrick liable in defamation. It awarded general damages of $240,000 – allegedly the highest defamation amount awarded in the history of Nova Scotia. The trial judge, on August 30, 2001, issued a final written decision, awarded costs against Jones and Derrick for $75,000, plus disbursements. The total was a whopping $315,000!

Jones and Derrick appealed the decision against them on numerous grounds, including the defences of qualified privilege, justification, and fair comment; numerous evidentiary and discretionary rulings; the jury verdict; the damages awarded; and costs.[81] The appeal was heard on June 10 and 11, 2002. After another agonizing four months, the Court of Appeal decision was released on October 24, 2002. It was a split decision of 2:1. The majority decision, written by Justice Elizabeth Roscoe and concurred with by Chief Justice Glube, allowed the appeal. The dissent, by Justice Saunders, affirmed the decision of the trial judge, Justice Moir. Jones and Derrick had been vindicated – but it had been a close one. A careful reading of both decisions is a salutary tale for progressive lawyers who decide to speak to the media about their clients. In this chapter, it is possible to focus only on the outlines of the judges' sharply differing analyses.

Several key points underpinned the majority decision. First, and fatefully for Jones and Derrick, in 2001 the Supreme Court of Canada had issued a decision addressing the powers of the police to conduct strip searches.[82] Justice Roscoe found that the definition of a strip search in that case covered what Constable Campbell had done to the three girls.

Second, Justice Roscoe found that the press conference was an occasion for qualified privilege. Central to her analysis was the argument about the particular responsibilities of lawyers to "speak out against injustice":

> In this case, it was acknowledged by the respondent before trial that the *Charter* rights of three young girls were violated. Though suspected of stealing only $10.00, they were subjected to intrusive personal searches, which were not conducted "incidental to arrest." Their personal dignity and privacy was ignored in the absence of exigent circumstances. Their parents and guardians were not contacted. They were never advised of their rights to counsel. To my mind, such serious violations certainly constituted a patent injustice triggering the duty of the appellants discussed in Chapter 21. In any event, lawyers, by virtue of their role as officers of the court with a specific duty to improve the administration of justice and uphold the law, have a special relationship with and responsibility to the public to speak out when those involved in enforcing our laws violate the fundamental rights of citizens.
>
> ... By analogy, it seems to me that lawyers, who are officers of the court with duties to improve the administration of justice and uphold the law, have a special relationship with and responsibility to the public to speak out when elements of the justice system itself have breached the fundamental rights of citizens and they have reason to believe that complaints pursuant to the *Police Act* will not provide an adequate remedy.[83]

Third, Justice Roscoe invoked a dual-layered contextualist analysis.[84] The constitutional context of overarching constitutional values dovetailed with the social context of the three girls:

> The public interest in the multiple constitutional violations of three young, black girls from a poor neighborhood, was running high at the time of the press conference, as a result of the several press accounts relating the events at the school in which the term "strip search" had figured prominently. The girls were members of a historically doubly-disadvantaged group, whose rights to equal protection of the law were being examined at the press conference. Surely, if equality rights are to be achieved, those who exercise a constitutionally protected right of freedom of expression, on behalf of

disadvantaged persons, in accordance with their duty to ... "encourage public respect for justice and to uphold and try to improve the administration of justice" should be protected by qualified privilege so long as their comments are not motivated by malice, and so far as the comments do not exceed the privilege.

In a case such as this where freedom of expression is exercised not merely for its own sake, or to advance one's own self-interest, but to bring attention to and to seek redress for multiple breaches of such important *Charter* rights as the right to counsel, the right to security of the person, including the right not to be subject to unreasonable search, and the right to equal protection and benefit of the law, one would expect it to be even more difficult to justify its curtailment. In any event, in my view, it was incumbent on the trial judge to at least turn his mind to the myriad of *Charter* rights and values at issue in the case before him. If constitutional rights are to have any meaning, they must surely include the freedom of persons whose *Charter* guarantees have been deliberately violated by officials of state agencies, to cry out loud and long against their transgressors in the public forum, and in the case of children and others less capable of articulation of the issues, to have their advocates cry out on their behalf.[85]

In her summation, Justice Roscoe was clear and unequivocal:

I would conclude that in all the circumstances of this case, observed with "today's eyes," in today's social conditions, that it is in the public interest that the press conference be found to be an occasion of qualified privilege. The appellants, in accordance with the principles of their professional ethics, had a duty to speak about the events at the school, the complaints filed against the respondent and the *Charter* breaches they reasonably understood had taken place. The members of the public in attendance at the meeting had a reciprocal interest in hearing about the exercise of the authority of the police in a neighborhood school.[86]

The dissenting decision of Justice Saunders was an enormous 353 paragraphs compared with Justice Roscoe's 74 paragraphs – and it was equally passionate. Although much of the decision focused either on technical analyses of the complicated law of defamation or on considerations of the more particular grounds of appeal put forward by Jones and Derrick (all of which he rejected), Justice Saunders also reflected on the roles and responsibilities of the vociferous lawyer.

First, he disagreed with Justice Roscoe that Jones and Derrick were within the realm of qualified privilege: "I regret to say that in my opinion, their statements were high handed and careless, void of any semblance of professional restraint or objectivity, were grossly unfair and far exceeded any legitimate purpose the press conference may have served."[87] He characterized the use of the language of "strip searching" as the "repeated endorsement of an attention-grabbing and emotive label."[88] He returned to this theme toward the end of his reasons for decision:

> Mr. Jones and Ms. Derrick are high profile lawyers with a record of service and advocacy in cases of some celebrity. The record reflects that they are used to courting the press. Their convening a press conference could be expected to draw a crowd and lend weight to statements made concerning Cst. Campbell's conduct. The appellants published damaging allegations about the respondent in strong language and consciously and deliberately gave their allegations the maximum possible media exposure. The devastating personal impact of the press conference upon Cst. Campbell was explored at length before the jury ... In my opinion, this constitutes a very grave defamation and the jury had more than enough evidence before it to make a substantial award of damages.[89]

Second, Justice Saunders also emphasized the importance of context but in a manner quite different from that of Justice Roscoe:

> Much has been said, and justifiably so, about the rights of the three complainants. But what of the rights of the respondent, Cst. Campbell? With great respect, it seems to me that the approach taken by my colleagues in the majority places far too much emphasis on the search per se and fails to address the central point of this litigation. The law suit with which we are concerned in this appeal was not a claim by the girls against the police officer, her department or the school board for damages arising from, for example, unlawful detention and search. Rather, we are dealing with a claim by the officer that she was defamed by two lawyers who, so she alleged, said her treatment of these girls was motivated by racism, and discrimination based on their economic status and their youth. That is the central issue, the essence of this case.[90]

Later, in response to the argument that Jones and Derrick were addressing systemic rather than individual racism, he argued that

[i]t was hardly comforting to be thought of as a member of a group that practised "systemic racism" as opposed to being an "overt" or a "direct" racist. The sting is no less sharp. There is arguably no more vile a label in today's parlance than to be described as a "racist." It constitutes one of the most egregious attacks upon character and reputation that one could imagine. It is a human stain and for this generation a scarlet letter.[91]

Third, Justice Saunders took a perspective very different from that of Justice Roscoe on the obligation of lawyers to speak out as a foundation for qualified privilege. For him, the duty of Jones and Derrick "to inform their community and represent the 'disadvantaged' in their dealings with the state was satisfied by their filing the complaint" with the Halifax Police Department.[92] In his eyes, Jones and Derrick were "two highly educated professionals, trained as lawyers and respected members of their community ... [T]heir statements were given in a controlled environment of their own choosing where one assumes their words would be measured and carefully selected. By expressing themselves as they did ... [Jones and Derrick] exceeded whatever privilege attached to their complaints."[93]

In light of this strong difference of opinion between the majority and the dissent in the Nova Scotia Court of Appeal, Constable Campbell decided to seek leave to appeal. Jones and Derrick remained on tenterhooks for another seven months until, surprisingly, leave to appeal was denied by the Supreme Court of Canada.[94] They had been vindicated, but it had been an emotionally and professionally exhausting seven years.

Some Larger Themes

This chapter has provided three glimpses into the career of Burnley "Rocky" Jones to illustrate some of the opportunities and challenges that might be encountered by an egalitarian lawyer. It is impossible, of course, to generalize from a particular case study to any larger claims about egalitarian lawyering. However, the foregoing account does raise several themes that can generate further reflection and consideration.

First, the interventions of Jones help us to reflect on the larger debate in socio-legal theory about the relationship between structure and agency. Clearly, Jones has exercised significant agency in a progressive manner with manifestly positive consequences. However, at the same time, there is little doubt that structures are equally important. The historical and sedimented racism in Truro and Halifax had a major impact on Jones, his family, and his community. He left Nova Scotia, he returned, he battled, and he had victories and defeats. Contexts can be formative but not determinative; individuals can make change happen, but it is complex and can go in unanticipated directions.

Second, egalitarian lawyering can be challenging on multiple levels. Although there might be moments of achievement, even glory, those moments are the consequences of many years of hard graft, drudgery, and stress, usually accompanied by low levels of remuneration. Moreover, the bonds of professional collegiality are frail. Although some members of the Nova Scotian legal profession supported, admired, and collaborated with Jones, others resented and reviled him. Furthermore, the powers of conservatism do not give up without a fight. For many players in society, structural inequality is not just a norm or social condition but also a reality from which they benefit. To preserve that structured privilege, they will not only resist but also go on the offensive.

Third, egalitarian lawyering, to be effective, entails collaboration and support. Although his industry, character, and charisma were vital, Jones was rarely a solo actor. In each of the three instances discussed here, family members, friends, professional colleagues, and even some institutions rallied to his various causes. This did not always mean that there was consensus or that others simply deferred to him. Indeed, as indicated, there were often intense (even testy) arguments at the levels of principle, policy, politics, and strategy. This should come as no surprise, of course, given the issues at stake and the inevitable diversity of normative visions for the good society.

Fourth, and finally, there is the perennial question of the impact of legal education, legal practice, and legal culture on progressive activists. Is the practice of law really an effective mechanism for social reconstruction, or does it result in deradicalization through partial incorporation?[95] Or, more pointedly, did "Rocky the Revolutionary" become "Rocky the Reformer"? How one answers this question, and the correlative question of whether or not such a shift is a good thing, will likely depend more on one's political orientation than on any purportedly objective assessment of the career of Jones.[96]

Conclusion

Many other stories could, and should, be told about Burnley Jones that would provide a richer and deeper understanding of an egalitarian lawyer's ethical identity. Jones retired from the practice of law in the mid-2000s and passed away at the age of seventy-one in July 2013. However, the unfortunate reality is that, despite his best efforts, racism continues in Nova Scotia. As recently as 2012, White lawyers seem not to have learned from the Marshall Inquiry and continue to be incompetent in their representation of members of the Black community.[97] In 2013, the Nova Scotia Human Rights Commission published a report on racialized discrimination in the current marketplace.[98] Nova Scotia needs more lawyers with the "faith and determination" to pursue social equality; it needs more lawyers like Rocky Jones.

Notes

Thanks to John Dickieson, Andrew Nicols, Molly Ross, Philip Girard, Dianne Pothier, Ora Morison, Dick Evans, Faye Woodman, and Vince Kazmierski. Special thanks to Jim Walker for his enthusiastic support of this chapter. Research funding was provided by the Schulich Academic Excellence Fund.

1 Cited in Martin O'Malley, "Rocky the Revolutionary," *Globe Magazine* (15 February 1969) [O'Malley, "Rocky the Revolutionary"].

2 In Almeta Speaks, "Nova Scotia: Against the Tide," part 2, *Hymn to Freedom* (videocassette), dir. Sylvia Hamilton (Mississauga: International Tele-Film, 1994).

3 Cited in Stephen Kimber, "Profile of Rocky Jones" (20 November 1995), online: Stephen Kimber, http://stephenkimber.com/bio/journalism/profile-of-rocky-jones/ [Kimber, "Profile of Rocky Jones"].

4 Kirk Makin, "Tired of Being the Butt of Jokes, Ontario Lawyers Plan Image Overhaul," *Globe and Mail* (6 February 2013), online: Globe and Mail, http://www.theglobe andmail.com/news/national/tired-of-being-the-butt-of-jokes-ontario-lawyers -plan-image-overhaul/article8321520/#dashboard/follows/.

5 Ipsos Reid, News Release, "What Do Pharmacists, Doctors, Soldiers, Pilots and Teachers Have in Common? They're among the Most Trusted Professions in Canada" (4 January 2011); Angela Fernandez, "Polling and Popular Culture (News, Television, and Film): Limitations of the Use of Opinion Polls in Assessing the Public Image of Lawyers" in Lorne Sossin, ed., *In the Public Interest: The Report and Research Papers of the Law Society of Upper Canada's Task Force on the Rule of Law and the Independence of the Bar* (Toronto: Irwin Law in association with the Law Society of Upper Canada, 2007) 209.

6 Justice Ian Binnie, "Sondage après sondage ... A Few Thoughts about Conflicts of Interest," edited version of remarks at a panel discussion at Les Journées Strasbourgeoises in Strasbourg, France, 4 July 2008.

7 Chief Justice Beverley McLachlin, "Remarks of the Right Honourable Beverley McLachlin, P.C.," delivered at the Empire Club of Canada, Toronto, 8 March 2007; Chief Justice Beverley McLachlin, keynote address delivered at the Access to Civil Justice Colloquium, Toronto, 10 February 2011; Chief Justice Robert Bauman, "Remarks of the Honourable Chief Justice Robert J. Bauman," lecture delivered at the Trial Lawyers Association of British Columbia 2013 Bench Bar Awards Luncheon,

5 April 2013; Access to Justice Committeee (CBA), "Reaching Equal Justice Report: An Invitation to Envision and Act" (April 2013), online: CBA, http://www.cba.org/CBA/equaljustice/secure_pdf/EqualJusticeFinalReport-eng.pdf.

8 A preliminary disclosure is essential. I first met Jones in the late 1980s and collaborated with him in establishing the IB&M Program and in helping to develop arguments in the *R.D.S.* case. I would characterize our relationship as one of occasional colleagues. I asked Jones to collaborate on this essay, but for several reasons he was reluctant to do so.

9 Bridglal Pachai, *Beneath the Clouds of the Promised Land: The Survival of Nova Scotia's Blacks, Volumes I and II* (Halifax: Black Educators Association of Nova Scotia, 1990); Robin W. Winks, *The Blacks in Canada: A History* (Montreal: McGill-Queen's University Press, 1971); James Walker, *The Black Loyalists: The Search for a Promised Land in Nova Scotia and Sierra Leone 1783–1870* (Toronto: University of Toronto Press, 1992) [Walker, *The Black Loyalists*]; Barrington Walker, *The African Canadian Legal Odyssey: Historical Essays* (Toronto: University of Toronto Press, 2012) at 3–46; Joseph Mensah, *Black Canadians: History, Experiences, Social Conditions* (Black Point, NS: Fernwood Publishing, 2002); Harvey Amani Whitfield, *From American Slaves to Nova Scotian Subjects: The Case of the Black Refugees, 1813–1840* (Newmarket, ON: Pearson Education Canada, 2005); Joy A. Mannette, "Making Something Happen": Nova Scotia's Black Renaissance, 1968–1986 (Ph.D. diss., Ottawa: Carleton University, 1987); D.G. Bell, J. Barry Cahill, and Harvey Amani Whitfield, "Slavery and Slave Law in the Maritimes" in Barrington Walker, ed., *The African Canadian Legal Odyssey: Historical Essays* (Toronto: University of Toronto Press, 2012) 363; Constance Backhouse, "'Bitterly Disappointed' at the Spread of 'Colour-Bar Tactics': Viola Desmond's Challenge to Racial Segregation, Nova Scotia, 1946" in Barrington Walker, ed., *The African Canadian Legal Odyssey: Historical Essays* (Toronto: University of Toronto Press, 2012) 101.

10 Barrington Walker, *supra* note 9 at 6.

11 *Ibid.* at 20.

12 James Walker, *The Black Loyalists, supra* note 9 at 49.

13 James MacGregor, *Letter to a Clergyman, Urging Him to Set Free a Black Girl He Held in Slavery* (Halifax: Anthony Henry, 1788); Gregory P. Marchildon, "McGregor, James Drummond" in *Dictionary of Canadian Biography*, vol. 14 (Toronto: University of Toronto; Laval: Université Laval, 1998), online: <http://www.biographi.ca/en/bio/mcgregor_james_drummond_14E.html>; Winks, *supra* note 9 at 103.

14 Barry Cahill, "The Antislavery Polemic of the Reverend James MacGregor: Canada's Proto-Abolitionist as 'Radical Evangelical'" in Charles H.H. Scobie and G.A. Rawlyk, eds., *The Contribution of Presbyterianism to the Maritime Provinces of Canada* (Montreal: McGill-Queen's University Press, 1997) 131 at 142.

15 Donna Byard Sealey, *Colored Zion: The History of the Zion United Baptist Church and the Black Community of Truro, Nova Scotia* (Kentville, NS: Gaspereau Press, 2000) at 15–16; Joey Smith, "Golf Is Secondary at Apex," *Truro Daily News* (3 August 2010), online: Truro Daily, http://www.trurodaily.com/Sports/2010-08-03/article-1649919/Golf-is-secondary-at-APEX/1.

16 Speaks, *supra* note 2.

17 Sealey, *supra* note 15 at 203 (Jeremiah's sister, Martha Eleanor Jones, was a cele-brated teacher; see 217–20).

18 Speaks, *supra* note 2; Calvin Ruck, *Canada's Black Battalion: No 2 Construction 1916–1920* (Dartmouth: Society for Protection and Preservation of Black Culture in Nova Scotia, 1986) at 33–35.

19 Veterans Affairs Canada, online: http://www.veterans.gc.ca/eng/remembrance/information-for/students/canada-remembers-times/2011/page3.

20 Sealey, *supra* note 15 at 145.

21 Speaks, *supra* note 2.

22 Sealey, *supra* note 15 at 206, 211–12 (in 1929, there were reports of a "small race riot," and the KKK was active in the 1930s).

23 Kimber, "Profile of Rocky Jones," *supra* note 3.

24 Speaks, *supra* note 2.

25 Kimber, "Profile of Rocky Jones," *supra* note 3.

26 O'Malley, "Rocky the Revolutionary," *supra* note 1.

27 Speaks, *supra* note 2.

28 James Walker, "Black Confrontation in Sixties Halifax" in Lara Campbell *et al.*, eds., *Debating Dissent: Canada and the Sixties* (Toronto: University of Toronto Press, 2012) 173 at 174 [Walker, "Black Confrontation"].

29 Rex Tasker, *Encounter at Kwacha House – Halifax* (short film) (National Film Board, 1967), online: National Film Board, http://www.nfb.ca/film/encounter_at_kwacha_house_halifax/.

30 Speaks, *supra* note 2.

31 Kimber, "Profile of Rocky Jones," *supra* note 3. In 2014, one of Jones's daughters opened a new Kwacha House Café in the Fairview neighbourhood of Halifax.

32 Martin O'Malley, "In the Panthers' Wake," *Globe Magazine* (16 February 1969) 22.

33 *Ibid.*

34 Walker, "Black Confrontation," *supra* note 28 at 14.

35 O'Malley, "Rocky the Revolutionary," *supra* note 1.

36 Walker, "Black Confrontation," *supra* note 28.

37 Kimber, "Profile of Rocky Jones," *supra* note 3.

38 Speaks, *supra* note 2.

39 Kimber, "Profile of Rocky Jones," *supra* note 3.

40 Stephen Kimber, "TYP: It All Began in a Duck Blind" (15 November 2010), online: Stephen Kimber, http://stephenkimber.com/typ-it-all-began-in-a-duck-blind.

41 Patricia Brooks Arenburg, "An Extended Family through Dal's Transition Year Program," Dal News (9 January 2012), online: Dal News, http://www.dal.ca/news/2012/01/09/an-extended-family-through-dals-transition-year-program.html.

42 Nova Scotia, *Royal Commission on the Donald Marshall, Jr., Prosecution* (1989), Digest of Findings and Recommendations at 1.

43 The research project profiled five murder cases in which Blacks had been killed and the community did not believe that justice had prevailed. The project and notes can be found at the Nova Scotia Archives in the Black United Front fonds, vol. 20, re-trieval number 2002-066/020 9.

44 Wayne MacKay had developed a high profile in Nova Scotia as a progressive con-
    stitutional and human rights scholar. I had just arrived in Halifax and was in my first
    year of teaching at Dalhousie.

45 This section draws to some degree on Richard Devlin and Alexander Wayne
    MacKay, "An Essay on Institutional Responsibility: The Indigenous Blacks and
    Micmac Programme at Dalhousie Law School" (1991) 14 Dalhousie Law Journal 296.
    For a critique of this essay, see Carol A. Aylward, "Adding Colour – A Critique of:
    'An Essay on Institutional Responsibility: The Indigenous Blacks and Micmac Pro-
    gramme at Dalhousie Law School'" (1995) 8 Canadian Journal of Women and the
    Law 470.

46 This Task Force was chaired by Professor MacKay, and it issued its final report in
    September 1989.

47 Nova Scotia, *supra* note 42 at 154–55.

48 James Walker, "A Black Day in Court: 'Race' and Judging in *R v RDS*" in Barrington
    Walker, ed., *The African Canadian Legal Odyssey: Historical Essays* (Toronto:
    University of Toronto Press, 2012) 437 at 442 [Walker, "A Black Day in Court"].

49 *Ibid.*

50 Kimber, "Profile of Rocky Jones," *supra* note 3.

51 Speaks, *supra* note 2.

52 Walker, "A Black Day in Court," *supra* note 48 at 442.

53 Judge Sparks was one of two Black judges in Nova Scotia at the time. She is also a
    graduate of Dalhousie Law School (LL.B., 1979) and at the time of the hearing was
    enrolled part time in the LL.M. program (she graduated in 2001). Her thesis was on
    the topic of reparations for Africville. I taught Judge Sparks while she was a graduate
    student.

54 R. Miller (counsel for the prosecution), in the Youth Court for the case of *Her
    Majesty the Queen v. R.D.S.,* December 2, 1994.

55 Judge C. Sparks, in the Youth Court for the case of *Her Majesty the Queen v. R.D.S.,*
    December 2, 1994.

56 The following is an abbreviated version of events, given space constraints. There
    were supplementary reasons given by Judge Sparks and several side actions not
    covered in this account. They are fully discussed elsewhere. See, for example,
    Richard Devlin, "We Can't Go on Together with Suspicious Minds: Judicial Bias
    and Racialized Perspectives in *R v RDS*" (1995) 18 Dalhousie Law Journal 408;
    Walker, "A Black Day in Court," *supra* note 48.

57 Constance Backhouse discusses the accusations of bias against Judge Sparks in her
    contribution to this volume.

58 *R. v. R.D.S.,* [1995] N.S.J. 184, 27 W.C.B. (2d) 147.

59 The three core volunteers were Professor Aylward, Director of the IB&M Program
    and an African Nova Scotian, and Professor Pothier and me, both of whom are
    White.

60 *R. v. R.D.S.,* [1995] N.S.J. 444, 145 N.S.R. (2d) 284.

61 *Ibid.*

62 Three clinic students who played key roles at this stage were Vince Kazmierski,
    Lianne Lagroix, and Bill Watts, all of whom are White.

63 Walker, "A Black Day in Court," *supra* note 48 at 453.

64 See also *ibid.* at 459–62.

65 Cited in *ibid.* at 460.

66 Cited in *ibid.* at 462.

67 The decision has been subjected to a multitude of analyses. See, for example, Carol A. Aylward, "'Take the Long Way Home': RDS v R – The Journey" (1998) 47 U.N.B.L.J. 249; P. Hughes, "S. (R.D.): A New Direction in Judicial Impartiality?" (1998) 9 National Journal of Constitutional Law 251; D.M. Paciocco, "The Promise of RDS: Integrating the Law and Judicial Notice and Apprehension of Bias" (1998) 3 Canadian Criminal Law Review 319; Alan C. Hutchinson and Kathleen Strachan, "What's The Difference? Interpretation, Identity, and R v RDS" (1998) 21 Dalhousie Law Journal 219; Alan W. Mewett, "Secondary Facts, Prejudice, and Stereotyping" (1999) 42 Criminal Law Quarterly 319; Richard Devlin and Dianne Pothier, "Redressing the Imbalances: Rethinking the Judicial Role after *R v RDS*" (2000) 31 Ottawa Law Review 1; April Burey, "No Dichotomies: Reflections on Equality for African Canadians in R v RDS" (1998) 21 Dalhousie Law Journal 199; Jennifer Smith, "R v RDS: A Political Science Perspective" (1998) 21 Dalhousie Law Journal 236; and Christine Boyle *et al.*, "*R v RDS*: An Editor's Forum" 10 Canadian Journal of Women and the Law 159. A careful parsing of the case confirms that it was a victory for R.D.S. and Jones – but it was a close victory.

68 *Jones v. Campbell,* 2002 N.S.C.A. 128 at 2, [2002] N.S.J. 450 [*Jones*].

69 *Ibid.*

70 *Ibid.* at 73.

71 *Ibid.* at 6.

72 *Ibid.* at 6–7.

73 *Ibid.* at 4–5.

74 *Ibid.* at 5–6.

75 *Ibid.* at 4.

76 She also launched a suit against various media outlets. In due course, she reached a settlement with these outlets for a total of $114,500 in damages.

77 *Jones, supra* note 68 at 6.

78 *Ibid.* at 7.

79 Emphasis added. This provision was found in c. 21. A similar provision is found in Federation of Law Societies *Model Code* 5.6–1.

80 *Jones, supra* note 68 at 42.

81 These pleadings included two especially important questions. The first related to the type of expert witness evidence relating to racism that can be admitted. The second focused on the allegedly "inflammatory arguments" to the jury by the lawyer for Campbell, George MacDonald. Space constraints preclude a discussion of these issues.

82 *R. v. Golden,* 2001 S.C.C. 83, [2001] S.C.J. 81.

83 *Jones, supra* note 68 at 31–32.

84 Justice Roscoe had been involved in designing and developing the National Judicial Institute's Social Context Education Program.

85 *Jones, supra* note 68 at 35–37.

86 *Ibid.* at 37.
87 *Ibid.* at 62.
88 *Ibid.* at 66.
89 *Ibid.* at 157–58.
90 *Ibid.* at 71–72.
91 *Ibid.* at 76–77.
92 *Ibid.* at 79.
93 *Ibid.* at 81.
94 *Campbell v. Jones and Derrick,* (2003) 105 C.R.R. (2d) 188, 221 N.S.R. (2d) 400.
95 Karl E. Klare, "Judicial Radicalization of the Wagner Act and the Origins of Modern Legal Consciousness, 1937–1941" (1978) 62 Minnesota Law Review 265.
96 Another response is to argue that this is a false dichotomy and that the preferred position is "radical reformism." See, further, Richard Devlin, "On the Road to Radical Reform: A Critical Review of Unger's Politics" (1990) 28(3) Osgoode Hall Law Journal 641.
97 Richard Devlin and David Layton, "The Cultural Incompetence of Lawyers and the Trial Level Judge: A Legal and Ethical Analysis" (2014) 60 Criminal Law Quarterly 360.
98 Nova Scotia Human Rights Commission, "A Report on Consumer Racial Profiling in Nova Scotia" (2013), online: Nova Scotia Human Rights Commission, http://humanrights.gov.ns.ca/sites/default/files/files/crp-report.pdf.

5

Feminist Lawyering

Insiders and Outsiders

JANINE BENEDET

Three Feminist Lawyers

This legal ethics story begins with some reflections on the career of Carole Curtis, who practised family law in Toronto for three decades before her appointment to the Ontario Court of Justice in 2008. At the time of her appointment to the bench, Curtis had been a bencher of the Law Society of Upper Canada for seventeen years, with a particular focus on supporting sole and small-firm practitioners in providing effective services to their clients.

Although I have never worked with Carole Curtis, or even practised family law, she was one of my role models in the legal profession, a woman who was unafraid to call herself a feminist lawyer and who contributed to feminist law reform and litigation while running a successful practice. Along with women such as Mary Eberts and Marilou McPhedran, she was part of a new generation of women lawyers in the second wave of the women's movement who combined professional success with a commitment to feminist politics. Yet in 1993 Curtis was also the first bencher to face a disciplinary hearing by the Law Society of Upper Canada.[1] She was exonerated and returned to her position as a bencher.

This legal ethics story also reflects on another feminist lawyer, Beth Symes, and her unsuccessful litigation to challenge tax rules that prevented her from deducting child care expenses from her self-employment income as a lawyer. Her case, decided by the Supreme Court of Canada in 1993,[2] attracted considerable attention and debate inside and outside the women's movement. Over time, *Symes* became a case that was less about the disadvantage of women relative to men and more about the divisions between groups of women that tracked along lines of class and race.[3]

In 1993, I was a budding feminist lawyer newly graduated from law school. After graduate school and a few years in private practice, I became a law professor whose work focuses on violence against women, including sexual harassment and sexual assault. So this story is also my story. Two decades later this seems to be an appropriate time to reflect on these events and their impacts on me, then and now.

Carole Curtis: A Feminist Family Lawyer

Carole Curtis was a member of one of the first graduating classes from the University of Windsor Law School.[4] It was the first new law school in Ontario in decades, founded with a particular mission to increase community engagement and access to justice.[5] That does not mean that the law school itself was always a progressive or egalitarian space. As Curtis recalled,

> I went to law school from 1973 to 1976. Less than 10 percent of the students in my graduating class were women. It was a lot like being at a stag party for three years. The women were largely invisible, and were treated as invisible. There was a locker-room atmosphere much of the time, including racist, sexist and homophobic jokes constantly. It was pretty tough. A woman had to want it a lot to stay.[6]

Carole Curtis must have "want[ed] it a lot," because she stayed and graduated. She also took to heart the pressing need to increase access to justice, and after her call to the bar in 1978 she set herself up as a criminal and family lawyer, soon coming to represent mostly women on legal aid certificates in family law cases.

On a number of fronts, these were heady times for the women's movement in Canada. Enactment of the *Charter of Rights and Freedoms* in 1982 explicitly recognized in section 15(1) a constitutional right to sex equality, and the affirmation in section 28 that the rights in the *Charter* were to be guaranteed equally to men and women promised an era of legal and social change. The three-year delay in section 15(1) coming into force was thought to be necessary because of the large number of laws that would need to be amended because they were discriminatory on the ground of sex, especially in the areas of marriage and the family. Organizations such as the National Association of Women and the Law (NAWL) and the National Action Committee on the Status of Women (NAC) had real voices at the legislative table. The Women's Legal Education and Action Fund (LEAF) was formed to use s. 15 of the *Charter* to litigate on behalf of women's rights.

On the other hand, many of the legal protections for women that we now take for granted were not yet achieved. The Supreme Court of Canada would not recognize that sexual harassment in employment was a form of sexual discrimination until 1989.[7] Pay equity legislation had yet to be enacted in any Canadian jurisdiction.[8] Women were moving into the paid labour force in record numbers, but they often faced in the workplace the kind of hostile sexist environment that Curtis recalled from the University of Windsor Law School, especially when they tried to access male-dominated jobs.

In the 1980s and 1990s, feminist law reformers targeted laws governing marriage and the family as one of the key barriers to women's equality. These laws included the marital rape exemption in the *Criminal Code*, the rules governing the division of assets on marital breakdown, and the unequal position of women living in common-law relationships. They pointed out that divorce tended to leave men richer and women poorer than during the marriage. They noted that women's economic inequality made it difficult for women to escape from violent marriages.[9]

In her Toronto practice, Curtis represented many women whose lives were affected by these laws. She also acted as counsel or co-counsel for LEAF in two of its interventions before the Supreme Court of Canada in family law cases,[10] and she appeared before legislative committees on behalf of NAWL.[11] She identified herself as a feminist lawyer committed to legal and social change for women.

Another key issue for feminists that emerged at this time was the widespread but unacknowledged incidence of child sexual abuse. The movement by victims of incest, as they were then usually called, to expose the extent of sexual abuse by male family members gathered momentum in the 1980s and 1990s.[12] Of course, this development intersected with family law on a number of fronts. Some disclosures of sexual abuse led to family breakdowns; in other cases, disclosure by a child was forthcoming only after the marriage had ended and the abuser was no longer living in the home.

In the 1980s and 1990s, mothers most often had primary custody of children after separation and divorce. In most cases, this replicated the division of parental responsibilities during the marriage (mother as primary caregiver), and fathers did not often contest custody applications. However, a fathers' rights movement was growing in strength and influence, and it began to demand presumptive joint custody of children and a more formally equal division of powers and responsibilities after divorce. In addition, men's rights groups began to argue that many claims of sexual and physical abuse were fabricated by vindictive women seeking to keep children away from their fathers.[13]

Accusations and diagnoses of "false memory syndrome" (in which therapists and parents are accused of implanting in children false memories of abuse) and parental alienation syndrome (in which the custodial parent is said to brainwash the child against the non-custodial parent) gained traction in popular discourse and the courts.[14] Criticism soon arose that the system was biased in favour of women. Men's rights groups found a champion in Senator Anne Cools,[15] and in 1999 a controversial report titled "For the Sake of the Children: Report of the Special Joint Committee on Child Custody and Access" endorsed many of these ideas.[16] Feminists did their best to rebut these claims and argued that men were using applications for joint custody to reduce their support obligations or to maintain control over women after spousal relationships ended.

In this highly charged context, family lawyers were left to sort out what to do when the courts ordered contact between a father and a child and the mother believed that the child was at risk of physical or sexual abuse if left alone with the father. This was the situation that Carole Curtis faced in representing one of her clients and that led to her facing a Law Society complaint and disciplinary hearing.

In 1990, Curtis was asked by lawyer Lorna Rudolph to represent Bonnie Scott in an appeal from an order granting custody of Scott's three-year-old daughter Vanessa to her father.[17] Prior to this order, Vanessa had resided with Bonnie. The mother maintained that the child had been sexually abused by the father. The judge did not accept this contention, misreading a doctor's report, which supported the mother, and confirmed that the father was to have primary custody. Before transfer of the child took place, the mother raised new evidence that the child had experienced further abuse while in the father's care on an access visit. An application to vary the trial judge's order, based on the new evidence, was filed. In response to an inquiry about options available to the mother pending the hearing of that application, Curtis and Rudolph had a lengthy phone conversation, which Curtis confirmed in writing:

Further to our telephone conversation this morning, as we indicated to you, we are suggesting the following path with respect to the new disclosure from Vanessa Scott:

1. Contact your client's local Children's Aid Society immediately ...

Also, it is important for you to get a specific answer from them on exactly what they intend to do. This child is disclosing recent evidence of abuse in the context of a custody Order putting her in the custody of this man in approximately 10 days. Why aren't they starting a protection application and apprehending the child (that is, if custody changes on 28 April, 1990). You need a very specific answer to these questions.

2. Advise the lawyer for the child by telephone of what is going on, and ultimately, confirm it in writing ...
3. Your client should seriously consider not allowing this child to be transferred to her father on 28 April, 1990. We appreciate this is a very serious step, and will put her in breach of a Court Order. We strongly urge that she not disappear with the child, but that rather, she keep the father advised at all times that the child is safe. However, if there is any likelihood that he will attend with the police and a certified copy of the Order, then she should not be at her home.

That seems unlikely since, to our knowledge, the Order has not been issued and entered. It is imperative that you issue and enter the Order immediately, whether we proceed with an appeal, a stay motion, or a variation.

4. You should be advising the husband's lawyer, as soon as possible, that you have advised your client not to allow any further contact, including no access and no change of custody. You should also advise him in writing of the reason for that step, and of the proceedings you will be commencing.
5. You should be bringing an immediate motion to vary the terms of the Divorce Judgment ...
6. Also, we suggest that you ask for an interim Order varying the Divorce Judgment prohibiting all contact between the child and her father, whatsoever, at the very least until a further investigation is done.
7. Have you considered contacting the police in this matter? ... In our view, the stay motion can proceed as we had planned.

Rudolph gave the letter to her client, Scott. Ten days later Scott took her child and went into hiding for nearly a year. When she came out of hiding, she had new counsel, who laid the complaint against Curtis with the Law Society. The complaint attracted considerable publicity both because of the seriousness of the allegations against Curtis and because of the alarm that it raised among advocates for abused women and children.[18] The allegations included not only that Curtis had advised her client to disobey a court order and thus violate the law but also that she had communicated with Scott while she was in hiding and had advised her social worker how to get false identification for Scott and her daughter.

By this point, Curtis had been elected a bencher of the Law Society of Upper Canada. She was the first sitting bencher in the Law Society's history to face discipline.[19] She resigned her position as a bencher pending disposition of the complaint, heard in the summer and fall of 1993.

Scott testified before the Law Society disciplinary hearing that she had read and reread the letter from Curtis before going into hiding. She claimed to have told Curtis several times that she wanted to come out of hiding. She testified that she was always looking over her shoulder, subsisting on welfare, and living in a shelter.[20] However, on cross-examination, she acknowledged that she had gone into hiding because she had been worried about further abuse of her daughter and that she had not even mentioned the letter in her affidavit about her actions filed at her new trial.[21]

A social worker who had worked with Scott testified that Curtis had told her to get false identification for Scott and that she might find it by talking to taxicab drivers. On cross-examination, she backtracked, agreeing that she had talked to many people about the case and could not be sure who had given her that advice. Her records of conversations were incomplete or missing.

Curtis testified that she was shocked that her letter, addressed to another lawyer, had been given directly to the client. In her view, a client in that position would be highly emotional and in no shape to review such a letter. She viewed the letter as a roadmap for the trial lawyer and expected that police or children's aid would commence an investigation of the renewed evidence of abuse.[22] That did not happen. Instead, the client was given the letter.

Counsel for the Law Society took a hard line with Curtis in cross-examination, suggesting that her personal views had clouded her professional judgment. Counsel pointed directly to her feminist politics, arguing that Curtis had put feminism above her duty to respect the law.[23] Curtis's lawyer pointed out that the letter stated explicitly that the client should not abscond with the child and instead outlined a number of options that would offer the child protection against the suspected abuse. He also offered doz-ens of letters from judges, lawyers, and members of the public attesting to her high standards, professional ethics, and commitment to serve those who might otherwise go unrepresented.[24]

Convocation unanimously agreed that Curtis had not committed profes-sional misconduct. Her advice to the mother's lawyer was consistent with the ethical rules, which recognize that a court order might not be followed when there is a serious and immediate risk to the safety of another person and when an immediate application is made to appeal or vary the order. The committee also found that Curtis had not made any statement about ob-taining false identification and that she had made it clear to Scott that re-maining in hiding would hurt her application for a stay (which turned out to be true).[25]

This was a complete vindication of Curtis. Unlike in British Columbia, where lawyers found not to have committed professional misconduct are not identified by name in the reports of disciplinary proceedings, her case was covered extensively by national media, and her name is attached to the decision, which has been cited for the appropriate way for a lawyer to respond when faced with a court order that, if executed, could put a child at risk of harm.[26]

Curtis expressed relief at the outcome, noting that she had been treated fairly by the benchers who had heard the case. However, she thought that the Law Society had pursued the case too aggressively.[27] The Law Society went so far as to argue that, where a client is in contempt of a court order, that client ought to be declined further legal representation before the courts until he or she comes forward to purge the contempt, a position rejected by the hearing panel. The Law Society tendered expert evidence on a number of issues, including whether a lawyer is required to counsel a client against breaking the law. There was considerable agreement by the experts on both sides that there is no such rule. Although lawyers cannot counsel clients to break the law, or participate in their illegal actions, the relationship between lawyers and clients would be damaged if lawyers were required to deliver "moral lectures" to clients, lectures that would likely be poorly received.[28]

Curtis testified that she thought it vital not to alienate Scott completely once she had gone into hiding by telling her directly to come out of hiding. Instead, she explained to Scott that hiding made their case much more diffi-cult because Scott was no longer wearing "the white hat." Curtis resumed her duties as a bencher and was repeatedly re-elected to that position by her peers until her elevation to the bench.[29]

Beth Symes: A Feminist Litigator and Test Case Plaintiff

I arrived at the Supreme Court to begin a judicial clerkship while Curtis's hearing was ongoing and just as the Court was releasing its decision in *Symes v. Canada*.[30] Beth Symes was another prominent Toronto lawyer who had achieved success as a litigator while advocating for sex equality in the legal profession and in Canadian society. A founding member of LEAF, she acted as counsel in a number of high-profile cases dealing with the rights of pregnant women, social and economic rights, and other social justice causes. In the mid-1980s, she decided to bring a *Charter* challenge to the *Income Tax Act*, which disallowed her from claiming child care costs as a business expense against her self-employment income. Symes argued that the rules discriminated against women, primarily responsible for child care, in violation of section 15(1) of the *Charter*. She noted that other kinds of expenses, such as golf course memberships, could be deducted, and she argued that the current rules favoured deductions claimed primarily by men. Existing deductions for child care expenses were much less advantageous than treating such costs as business expenses.

What made this case so interesting is that gendered assumptions about valid expenses required to earn business incomes threatened to become overshadowed by arguments that the case privileged wealthier, mostly white, women over economically disadvantaged, often racialized, women who performed that child care. Hiring a nanny itself was seen as an assertion of dominance and privilege, one that ought to disentitle Symes from assuming the position of a victim of discrimination. Counsel for the government explicitly picked up on these themes, asking Symes if her employee was legally in the country and criticizing Symes for paying her no more than the minimum wage.[31]

Ultimately, the Supreme Court, in a 7:2 decision, dismissed the case. Writing for the majority, Justice Iacobucci, with the six other male justices concurring, held that child care expenses were not business expenses within the meaning of the *Income Tax Act* and that existing deductions in section 63 of the *Act* comprised a complete code of allowable expenses. He went on to find that this interpretation did not violate section 15(1) of the *Charter* because, though women bear the social burden of child care, the evidence was far from clear that they also bore the financial burden of child care. In dissent, Justice L'Heureux-Dubé, writing for herself and Justice McLachlin, held that child care expenses are not precluded as business expenses and that an interpretation of the *Income Tax Act* that denies such a claim would violate section 15(1). She disagreed with the majority's analysis that allowing the claim would fail to take into account the larger context that would leave Symes privileged compared with other mothers and parents who might be worse off, noting that the question for the Court was simply whether or not the law disadvantages self-employed businesswomen compared with self-employed businessmen.

In a recent Canadian Bar Association newsletter article on the twentieth anniversary of the decision, Symes was interviewed about her reflections on the case.[32] She noted that the Supreme Court's split along gendered lines demonstrated that this "is clearly gendered, and without child care I couldn't practice law." She added that "I was struggling with how to juggle the responsibilities of family and the practice of law ... And if I was having such difficulty, I thought, 'What about most other women in Canada who didn't have as good a support system as I did and didn't have as much money as I did?'" As this quotation indicates, Symes saw herself as sticking up for self-employed women who were not, relatively speaking, as advantaged as she was and for whom the cost of unsubsidized child care might make it impossible for them to run businesses. The article went on to note that the flight of women from the private practice of law continued to be a serious problem, with the inability of the profession to reshape itself to permit family care responsibilities the most important explanation for this result.

A few years earlier Mary Eberts, who acted as counsel for Beth Symes in the case, said the following in response to a question about how she decided which cases to adopt and the role of her political beliefs in her practice:

> Well, I think that there are several stages in my development as a person and lawyer that come into play on this. Specifically, with respect to the Symes case, I think that both Beth Symes and I made a strategic calculation at the beginning of that case that either was not well understood or accepted or turned out to be mistaken in the end. Our strategic thought when going into that case was really predicated on what happens when you win constitutional challenges. We thought that if you could at least take out the provision of the law the way it stood then there would have to be legislative and policy processes that followed the take-out of that provision. Our thinking was that after having opened the door, then we would be followed through it by a whole range of women and women's groups that would participate in a policy process to change the child-care deduction. I think that in the heat of things that this strategy was not understood or maybe people just thought that it was a bad strategy. Either way, that strategy never really got legs. And yes, people did criticize Beth and myself for doing that case ...

[Another] thing about that case – and this has to do with the way that it was written up by the Court – was that we actually had before the Court quite a lot of evidence about women entrepreneurs and that evidence showed that the vast majority of women entrepreneurs are quite poor. These women run part-time businesses often in their homes – they are hairdressers; they make dried flower arrangements; they run daycares in their homes. In this way, they are often marginally attached to the economy. But, for its own reasons, the Court really stressed the privilege of Beth Symes, and it totally ignored that evidence. The Court wanted to portray her as a highly privileged woman looking for her own advancement. We did, however, have demographic and economic evidence before them about the profile of women entrepreneurs.

... I think my approach now would actually rule out the kind of strategic thinking Beth and I had with respect to the Symes case. If I am not right there in the moment, I don't do the case anymore.[33]

These comments prompt a few observations. First, clearly Symes and Eberts understood that the challenge was only one piece of the complex web of legal and public policy decisions that contributed to women's economic inequality. But all that a *Charter* claim, even at its most innovative, can really hope to do is knock out one piece or a few pieces of the affirmative steps taken by government decision makers that hold women back. The hope is that such a result attracts sufficient media coverage and public interest that it can serve as a rallying point for more systemic change. The comments above suggest that Eberts had come to doubt the wisdom of that strategy. We need further study of the real results of high-profile *Charter* cases, successful and unsuccessful, before we can conclude whether this is true.

Second, the wealth of evidence on the precarious nature of self-employment for many women was overshadowed by the personal details of the case. Would the result have been different if the challenge had enlisted the support of a coalition of women who ran small businesses and picked a more diverse range of representative plaintiffs?[34] We cannot know the answer to this question. Yet, at the end of the day, Symes, despite her relative privilege, was on the receiving end of sex discrimination, and the *Charter* was designed to allow her to challenge that discrimination. It seems odd to suggest that it was wrong for her to try to do anything about it, any more than it was wrong for the white, male, Scottish lawyer in *Andrews* to challenge the citizenship requirements for entry into the BC legal profession.[35]

Symes continued to practise law and has had an illustrious career as a lawyer. Like Curtis, she was elected a bencher of the Law Society of Upper Canada and has made plain her commitment to promoting equality in the legal profession. Symes has been a fierce supporter of the program in Ontario designed to provide financial support for self-employed lawyers who take parental leave.[36] In 2011, she was named a Member of the Order of Canada for her demonstrated commitment to women's equality.

Conclusion

Twenty years ago it seemed to me that Carole Curtis and Beth Symes were outsiders in the legal profession and were punished in different ways for being feminists. Not surprisingly, twenty years later the ways in which their stories resonate for me have been reshaped by my own experiences over that time.

Looking back on the legal ethics story of Curtis today, as a feminist law professor and occasional *pro bono* lawyer, I am struck by how important it was to me then. In September 1993, when the disciplinary citation was being heard and decided, I had just graduated from law school and started a judicial clerkship at the Supreme Court of Canada. I had not had much exposure to feminist politics before entering law school. At most, I was a "liberal" feminist who believed that women should be able to do anything and prove their worth against any man. My law school education expanded my thinking. I realized that the playing field was still far from level and that questions of class, race, and other factors contributed to the understanding of "merit" and the creation of legal and professional norms. I graduated with the conviction that I would be a lawyer who would contribute in some way to the fight for women's rights.

The disciplinary citation against Curtis scared and angered me. How could the first bencher to be disciplined in Ontario happen to be a feminist? I saw the case as a kind of attempt at collective revenge by the establishment against an outsider who had dared to become an insider. It was part of the backlash against the inroads that feminism had made in countering male privilege. It reminded me that being outspoken came at a cost. I welcomed her exoneration but wondered why, if the applicable ethical rules were either non-existent or in her favour, the case had been prosecuted at all.

Today, as a teacher of legal ethics, I have a better understanding of how disciplinary citations find their way into law society hearings. I still believe that anti-feminism influenced some of the decisions made in the case, but I also recognize that the complaint was brought by lawyers representing the mother, not the father. Most of those attacking Curtis were other women. I also see that, as a bencher and later a judge, Curtis is also an insider of sorts and that being an outsider on the inside is a difficult position to maintain, since you risk both criticisms for feminist bias and accusations of selling out.

When I first heard about the *Symes* case, as a childless young woman entering the legal profession, I thought that the claim was self-evidently just. Of course child care expenses were necessary for women to earn income, whether from their jobs or from self-employment. Surely such expenses were more socially useful than the business entertaining done by men judged to be an allowable deduction. I dismissed as regressive and absurd the reasoning of conservative commentators that having children was a woman's choice, such that the woman should be expected to bear the costs of caring for them if she chose to enter the labour force. No one expected men to choose between career and family in the same way. But I was also chastened by claims that the *Symes* case represented the essentializing of the experiences of women and the privileging of the claims of white, middle-class, professional women above those who were much worse off economically. In the end, I felt embarrassed for hoping that Symes would win.

Looking back at this case, two children and a professional career of my own later, I see it as a lost opportunity of sorts. The goal of accessible and quality child care for all women could not have been achieved by the *Symes* case. Nor could it have addressed the inequalities endured by the mostly racialized women who provide that care. But the Supreme Court could at least have recognized a case of sex discrimination against women under section 15(1) of the *Charter*, something that it has yet to do in any case over a quarter century after this provision came into force. Moreover, there could have been clear recognition not only of the social value of reproduction but also of women's labour force participation as tied directly to women's equality.[37]

The *Symes* case is not a "legal ethics story" in the strict sense of raising issues of professional misconduct or unethical behaviour. Yet the choices of cases that one pursues are profoundly ethical questions for lawyers, even (or especially) when acting as litigants. Symes argued that female lawyers were outsiders in the private practice of law, a claim amply supported by the many reports on the flight of women from this kind of practice. She met resistance from those who viewed her as too much of an insider compared with working mothers more generally. Like Carole Curtis, like me, and like most women in the legal profession, Beth Symes was probably some of both, insider and outsider. These dual vantage points sometimes seem hard to reconcile. Yet they should be understood as positions that carry the possibility of informing one another, and bettering both the lives of women and the legal profession.

Notes

1 *Re Curtis,* 1993 CanLII 1183 (O.N. L.S.D.C.).
2 *Symes v. Canada,* [1993] 4 S.C.R. 695.
3 See, for example, Susan B. Boyd and Claire F.L.Young, "Feminism, Law, and Public Policy: Family Feuds and Taxing Times" (2004) 42 Osgoode Hall Law Journal 545, and the accompanying commentary by Sonia Lawrence, "Feminism, Consequences, Accountability" (2004) 42 Osgoode Hall Law Journal 583.
4 The University of Windsor Law School opened in 1968, with the first students graduating in 1971. Annette Demers, "A History of the University of Windsor Faculty of Law" (2010), online: University of Windsor Faculty of Law, http://www1.uwindsor.ca/law/system/files/law40thBook.pdf.
5 *Ibid.* at 9–10.
6 Carole Curtis, "Carole Curtis: Q & A," with Mark Tamminga, (2007) 33 Law Practice 20, online: American Bar Association, http://www.americanbar.org/publications/law_practice_home/law_practice_archive/lpm_magazine_articles_v33_is5_an15.html.
7 *Janzen v. Platy Enterprises,* [1989] 1 S.C.R. 1252.
8 Most Canadian jurisdictions today still lack separate pay equity legislation, and only two (Ontario and Quebec) extend it to the private sector. See Ontario Pay Equity Commission, "An Overview of Pay Equity in Various Canadian Jurisdictions" (2011), online: Ontario Pay Equity Commission, http://www.payequity.gov.on.ca/en/about/pubs/genderwage/pe_survey.php.
9 Mary Jane Mossman was one of the trailblazers in this field. See, for example, Mary Jane Mossman and Morag MacLean, "Family Law and Social Welfare: Toward a New Equality" (1986) 5 Canadian Journal of Family Law 79; and Mary Jane Mossman, "Running Hard to Stand Still: The Paradox of Family Law Reform" (1994) 17 Dalhousie Law Journal 5. Other early feminist family law scholars in Canada included Carol Rogerson and Anne McGillivray.
10 *Goertz v. Gordon,* [1996] 2 S.C.R. 27; *New Brunswick v. G.(J.),* [1999] 3 S.C.R. 46.
11 For example, testimony before the Special Joint Committee on Custody and Access, March 16, 1998, online: Parliament of Canada, http://www.parl.gc.ca/HousePublications/Publication.aspx?DocId=1038476&Mode=1&Language=E.
12 June Callwood, "Openness about Childhood Sexual Abuse Brings Flood of Pleas for Help" *Globe and Mail* (June 14, 1989) A2.
13 Susan B. Boyd, "Demonizing Mothers: Fathers' Rights Discourses in Child Custody Law Reform Processes" (2004) 6 Journal of the Association of Research on Mothering 52.
14 In Canada, criminal defence lawyer Alan Gold was one of the most vocal proponents of "false memory syndrome" as a way to attack historical sexual abuse claims. See

Campbell Perry and Alan D. Gold, "Hypnosis and the Elicitation of True and False Memories of Sexual Abuse" (1995) 2 Psychiatry, Psychology, and Law 127. For a rebuttal, see Michele Landsberg, "False Memory Label Invented by Lobby Group" *Toronto Star* (November 13, 1993). For a more nuanced assessment of the possibility of forgetting and recalling past abuse, see Linda M. Williams, "Recovered Memories of Abuse in Women with Documented Child Sexual Victimization Histories" (1995) 8 Journal of Traumatic Stress 649.

15 Cools made it clear that it was the "feminist analysis" that had relegated fathers to the role of mere observers in their children's lives. She believed that false reports of sexual abuse by mothers were commonplace: "I have studied this issue, its injustice, and its consequences for the children of divorce and their families. I have studied the legal documents of hundreds of fathers falsely accused during divorce and custody proceedings by mothers of sexually abusing their children. This phenomenon is a heart of darkness. Such false accusations are soul-destroying to those afflicted fathers and families." *Debates of the Senate,* 36th Parl., 1st Sess., June 8, 1999 (Senator Anne Cools), Senate of Canada, http://senatorcools.sencanada.ca/Speech-in -Senate-Chamber-Senator-Cools-urges-the-Senate-to-affirm-its-support-for-the -entitlements-of-children-of-divorce-to-the-financial-support-of-both-parents -according-to-respective-abilities/.

16 Special Joint Committee on Child Custody and Access, "For the Sake of the Children: Report of the Special Joint Committee on Child Custody and Access," Landon Pearson and Roger Galloway, Chairs (December 1998), online: Parliament of Canada, http://www.parl.gc.ca/HousePublications/Publication.aspx?DocId=1031529 &Language=E&Mode=1&Parl=36&Ses=1. Cools was a Senate member of the committee.

17 The account of the facts and the arguments of the parties in the following paragraphs are taken from the Discipline Committee decision, *supra* note 1.

18 Stephen Bindman, "Prominent Lawyer Goes on Trial for Misconduct" *Calgary Herald* (August 16, 1993) A3.

19 "Lawyer's Letter Prompted Year in Hiding, Woman Says" *Windsor Star* (August 17, 1993) A2.

20 Margot Gibb-Clark, "Mother Tells Hearing of Hiding with Child: Lawyer Accused of Advising Woman Not to Turn Child over to Father" *Globe and Mail* (August 17, 1993) A10.

21 *Ibid.*

22 Margot Gibb-Clark, "Lawyer Says Letter Mis-Directed: Advice Given in Custody Case" *Globe and Mail* (August 20, 1993) A12.

23 "Lawyer Too Loyal to Feminism" *Montreal Gazette* (September 13, 1993) C1.

24 Margot Gibb-Clark, "Lawyer Celebrates Vindication: Law Society Clears Curtis of Professional-Misconduct Charge" *Globe and Mail* (October 1, 1993) A18.

25 Margot Gibb-Clark, "Lawyer Says Legal Route Failed: Law Body Probes Member's Advice in Custody Case," *Globe and Mail* (August 21, 1993) A13.

26 See, for example, *Re Sussman,* 1995 CanLII 537 (O.N. L.S.D.C.).

27 Tracey Tyler, "Cleared Family Lawyer Getting over 'Worst Thing that Ever Happened to Me'" *Ottawa Citizen* (October 4, 1993) A6.

28 *Re Curtis, supra* note 1.

29 About three dozen of her judicial decisions are available on Quicklaw. They demonstrate the value of having specialists in family law on the bench deciding such cases, which often involve fundamental decisions such as applications for Crown wardship of children for the purpose of adoption. If any pattern can be gleaned from her decisions, it is that Justice Curtis has a keen commitment to the safety and welfare of children and is willing to criticize both litigants and their counsel for failing to use court resources wisely or for attempting to manipulate the process. She has held a mother in contempt for failing to respect an order denying her any access to her son; see *Peers v. Poupore*, [2012] O.J. No. 2259.

30 *Symes v. Canada, supra* note 2.

31 For an excellent and detailed treatment of *Symes*, see Rebecca Johnson, *Taxing Choices: The Intersection of Class, Gender, Parenthood, and the Law* (Vancouver: UBC Press, 2002). The cross-examination of Symes is described at 69–71.

32 Rachel Gardner, "Twenty Years after the Symes Trial, Child-Care Still an Obstacle for Many Businesswomen" (August 2013), online: Touchstones, http://www.cba.org/CBA/equity/newsletters2013/symes.aspx. The CBA intervened in support of Symes at the Supreme Court of Canada.

33 "Interview: Mary Eberts," with Amy Salyzyn (2004) 3 Journal of Law and Equality 97 at 104–5.

34 For a discussion of the strategies that led to the choice of claimant in this case, see Johnson, *supra* note 31 at 49–50.

35 *Andrews v. Law Society of British Columbia*, [1989] 1 S.C.R 143.

36 As of 2014, the program is restricted to those who are not receiving special Employment Insurance benefits and have a net income of less than $50,000. The maximum benefits are $9,000.

37 The Supreme Court recognized the social value of reproduction in the context of pregnancy discrimination under human rights legislation in *Brooks v. Canada Safeway*, [1989] 1 S.C.R. 1219, and recognized that sexual discrimination in employment is a barrier to women's equality in *Janzen v. Platy Enterprises, supra* note 7, in the context of sexual harassment in the workplace.

6

Gender and Race in the Construction of "Legal Professionalism"

Historical Perspectives

CONSTANCE BACKHOUSE

It was twelve years ago, in the moot courtroom at the University of Western Ontario Law School, when I first delivered a summary of the chapter that follows. I was distinctly nervous, not only because I recall feeling that I was the least qualified of the presenters on the panel but also because three distinguished Chief Justices and a former Premier spoke alongside me that day. Collectively, my fellow panelists sought to elevate the debate regarding "professionalism," which they understood to represent the best aspirations of the legal community. It was the start of a multifaceted project to raise issues about civility in the courtroom, the responsibilities of self-regulation, community service, *pro bono* representation, and such. Although I had some sympathy for aspects of these matters, my concerns about the need for change within the profession were somewhat different. My cynicism about the profession to which I belonged left me impatient with efforts that I saw as less than fundamentally transformative.

Much has happened in the intervening years, as many of the chapters in this volume illustrate. And I have come to know much more about the legal profession than I did in 2003, largely because of my subsequent experience as an elected bencher of the Law Society of Upper Canada, charged with supervising admissions, disciplining lawyers, promulgating codes of conduct, compensating victims of lawyer dishonesty, overseeing legal insurance, and more. I have come to have a somewhat deeper regard for lawyers and judges who seek to elevate the conduct and behaviour of lawyers and to recognize more fully the complexities of the task.

However, I have not changed my views about the history of a profession undeniably riddled with discrimination and inequality. The roots of our profession remain profoundly troubling, and though our membership has begun to show somewhat greater diversity there has been little evidence that we are successfully grappling with the gendered, class-based, ethno-racist, heterosexist, or ablist presumptions welded onto the concept of professionalism at the outset. Tinkering at the edges of the profession will not dismantle discriminatory privileges. Many predict that the future will herald draconian changes for the practice of law. Whether these changes will serve to cement or reduce imbalances of power is the question that we need to probe.

This chapter is based on a paper solicited for a colloquium canvassing issues of legal professionalism. When first asked to participate, I was advised that the colloquium had been designed by the Chief Justice of Ontario's Advisory Committee on Professionalism to "promote professionalism, civility, and a spirit of community and collegiality in the legal profession."[1] The concept of professionalism has always caused me a certain degree of hesitation. I think back to the Osgoode Hall classroom in which I sat as a third-year law student, decades ago in the mid-1970s, listening to Dean Harry Arthurs lecture on "The Legal Profession." Try as I might, I could never quite get over my bewilderment that the hallmarks of "professions" apparently included self-regulating codes of conduct and an ethic of public service. I remember leaning back in my chair, surprise twinned with skepticism, and wondering, as I have more than once in subsequent years, "just whom do they think they are kidding?"

So I wondered whether I was the right person to contribute to the colloquium. While mulling over this question, I was out walking with a professor of history who teaches at Carleton University. I told her about the colloquium on professionalism and mentioned my hesitation. She retorted, "Professionalism? Professionalism is all about power and exclusion." I returned home slowly from that walk, pondering the connections among professionalism, power, and exclusion. My expertise is within the field of history. And what I have learned about the history of the Canadian legal profession resonates far more with words such as *power, exclusion,* and *dominance* than it does with concepts such as civility or the extension of community and collegiality.

In the end, I resolved to prepare a paper for the colloquium that attempted to chronicle what we know about how lawyers have resorted to ideas of professionalism to exercise power and exclusion based on gender, race, class, and religion. It describes some of the barriers placed before working-class, Black, Jewish, Aboriginal, and female individuals who sought admission to the legal profession.[2] It examines some of the discriminatory practices used by lawyers and judges against those who managed to obtain admission to the profession despite the barriers. And it considers the wider impacts that such discrimination has had on disadvantaged communities and society more generally.

But a word of caution at the outset. Historical records are frequently produced at the behest of the powerful, and it is their achievements and victories that grace the pages of most written sources. Disadvantaged communities rarely maintain full accounts of their experiences of discrimination, and the fragmentary records that they do create are often lost over time.[3] What I have been able to uncover so far is, without a doubt, the tip of the iceberg.

The Notion of "Professionalism"

The very concept of professionalism has been inextricably linked historically to masculinity, whiteness, class privilege, and Protestantism. In its formative years, when the Law Society of Upper Canada first established entrance examinations, the objective was to winnow out candidates who did not possess the "gentlemanly" accoutrements of fluency in the classics. In 1820, describing the first admissions tests as important to "secure to the Province a learned and honorable Body to assist their fellow subjects," the Law Society passed Rule 18, requiring candidates "to give a written translation in the presence of the Society of a portion of one of Cicero's Orations or perform such other exercise as may satisfy the Society of his acquaintance with Latin and English composition, and that no person who cannot give these proofs of a liberal education shall hereafter be admitted upon their Books."[4]

In 1825, the Law Society determined that its efforts to weed out the "ungentlemanly" had not gone far enough. "No small injury" had been done, it noted, "to that portion of the youth of this country intended for the profession of law" by "confining their examination to Cicero's Orations." An additional resolution was promulgated:

> It is unanimously resolved that in future the Student on his examination will be expected to exhibit a general knowledge of English, Grecian and Roman History, a becoming acquaintance with one of the ancient Latin

Poets, as Virgil, Horace or Juvenal, and the like acquaintance with some of the celebrated prose works of the ancients such as Sallust or Cicero's Offices, as well as his Orations or any author of equal celebrity which may be adopted ... and it will also be expected that the student will show some reasonable portion of mathematical instruction.[5]

The notion of "becoming acquaintance" conveys so much all on its own. The second resolution was not subsequently approved by the judges and was not therefore enforced, but the classical foundation that the benchers of the Law Society wished to see carried unmistakable connotations of class, gender, and race. Training in the classics was largely restricted to Anglo-Canadian families of means, who reserved such education primarily for promising young boys.

Some sense of this imbues the account of Patrick MacGregor, a white, male, Scottish immigrant who set himself the task of preparing for the entrance examination in 1834. Building upon the classical education that he had already received at school, he devoted the months of February through April to studying "with great earnestness and application." His diary recounts the ordeal:

> Went over six books of Euclid. Read Paley's Moral Philosophy twice-over, and read the revised Algebra, Tyler's Elements of General History, Goldsmith's Greece and Rome (abridged), Revised Geography and Astronomy, Cicero's Select Orations, and some of Virgil ... On the 19th of April 1834, in the morning, after being furnished with money and a new suit of clothes by my uncle, I set out for the City of Toronto, Capital of Upper Canada (formerly Little York) to be examined by the Benchers of the Law Society ... Presented my Petition and fee of £10 to the Secretary ... After delaying some time, till there was a quorum, we were examined. I was called in, and Baldwin gave me the 7th chapter of Cicero's speech on the Manilian Law to translate ... We were afterwards called in to read our translations. Knowing their prejudices, I imitated the English style, as well as I could and succeeded.[6]

A formidable task successfully completed. And how clearly the relieved young Scot seems to have been the beneficiary of his ethnicity, class, and gender. Each had given him a foundation upon which to build and the time and resources with which to prepare. Equally important, he was also the recipient of a fresh suit of clothes in which to make the sort of impression that would help to convince the crusty old benchers that he had, indeed, the proper "proofs of a liberal education."[7]

The lawyers who became members of the Law Society of Upper Canada in the nineteenth century were quite homogeneous, mostly drawn from the ranks of the privileged, and closely linked through firm partnerships, intermarriages, and social connections. Family names that lawyers still recognize today stretch back generations, in some cases far back into the nineteenth century: McCarthy, Osler, Blake, Cartwright, Fasken, Beatty, Smith, Robinette. The very notion of professionalism embodied the image of a tightly knit community, with shared culture, traditions, and expectations. Established lawyers hired family members and friends, and the dynastic legacies lengthened.[8]

By way of comparison to medicine, recent research into the admissions process of the University of Toronto medical school has revealed that the rules were dramatically bent to accommodate the sons of physician parents, at the same time as quotas were installed to reduce the numbers of female and Jewish students at various points during the 1940s, 1950s, and 1960s.[9] It is still only a matter of speculation, but one wonders what a similar historical scrutiny of the admissions practices at Canadian law schools and hiring decisions within Canadian law firms would reveal. That Bora Laskin, who would later become the first Jewish Chief Justice of the Supreme Court of Canada, was forced to take unpaid articling positions, and after graduation from Harvard Law School to write headnotes for a law publisher because he could not secure a permanent paid position with a law firm, is instructive.[10]

Differential Treatment Accorded to Path Breakers

In spite of the homogeneous image of the legal profession, there have always been individuals from outside the circle who sought elevation to the rank of lawyer. Delos Rogest Davis claimed publicly in the late nineteenth century that he wished to become the first Black lawyer in Canada.[11] His reception by the legal profession was anything but civil. Davis was unable to find a lawyer who would agree to serve as his principal, so he was not allowed to obtain the requisite years of articling experience. Instead, he had to petition the Ontario legislature for admission. Pointing out that he had already been appointed a commissioner of affidavits and public notary, and had studied law for eleven years, Davis successfully convinced the legislators to admit him by special statute. On May 19, 1885, at the age of thirty-nine, he was finally admitted to the bar as a solicitor, and in 1886 he became a barrister. Both admissions were over the protests of the Law Society.[12]

Black law students who followed Davis throughout the first half of the twentieth century often had trouble finding articling positions and typically worked only for other Blacks or with Jewish lawyers.[13] Neither Blacks nor Jews, it seems, fit the "professional" mould according to those who set the dictates of the white, Protestant, wealthy men who had founded the Law Society and fashioned it in their own image.

The ordeal that Davis went through was soon equalled by that of Clara Brett Martin, the first woman lawyer admitted to the Law Society of Upper Canada. A well-to-do, white Torontonian of Anglican Irish heritage, with a degree from Trinity College, Martin fit the contemporary image of the legal professional in every respect but gender. In 1891, at the age of seventeen, she formally petitioned the Law Society for registration as a student member. A committee of benchers, chaired by Samuel Hume Blake, ruled her ineligible because of her gender.[14] The decision was cheered by legal commentators, one of whom wrote that there must be "a more suitable place in life" for women than that of counsel: "A woman does not, as a rule, arrive at a conclusion by logical reasoning, but rather by a species of instinct, which, no matter how unerring, cannot assist others to arrive at the same conclusion."[15] Some who contemplated women becoming lawyers labelled the mere idea "hilarious," asserting that the prospect of women exercising a profession would "banish all maiden mawkishness," something that was "so novel, so contrary to all notion of feminine sweetness, modesty, and delicacy," that it deserved nothing but mockery.[16] The *Canada Law Journal* editors had previously counselled that refusing to allow women "to embark upon the rough and troubled sea of actual legal practice" was "being cruel only to be kind."[17]

Martin then followed the same route as Davis. She petitioned the Ontario legislature to require the lawyers to admit women. The debates that ensued on the floor of the legislature inspired another bencher of the Law Society, William Ralph Meredith, also the leader of the opposition, to rant against the admission of women. He claimed that the dictates of female fashion would never allow women to wear "the same official robes" as men, and he was backed up by the *Canada Law Journal*, which insisted that "a new and becoming headgear would have to be devised in place of the hideous horse-hair wig; some bewitching structure of dainty curls, of the particular shade of gold fashionable at the moment."[18] Meredith argued that the presence of women would wreak havoc on jury trials because male jurors would find their chivalrous instincts running out of control as they tried to compare the positions of male and female lawyers. "It would upset the whole equanimity of the twelve good men and true," he warned, closing with these words: "Women were not intended for the position of advocate. Nature intended women should occupy [a] different position to men in the community. If the House were carried away by gush and sentiment, it would be disastrous to the best interests of women."[19] Another legislator, Nicholas Awry, insisted that the very "homes and womanhood of Ontario" were at stake.[20] Catastrophic disruption was predicted: nurseries attached to courtrooms, shrill demands to change laws perceived as discriminatory, abandoned families in unkempt homes as mothers who should have been attending to domestic duties lingered in law offices.[21] The entrenched masculinity of the legal profession was transparently arrayed in the types of arguments put forward. The feminization of law was viewed with consternation and dismay as heralding an end to the very foundation of the profession.

It took Clara Brett Martin two separate statutes of the Ontario legislature, a series of contentious votes within the Law Society, and six full years to obtain admission, on February 2, 1897, as the first female barrister and solicitor in Canada.[22] She sat through taunting, hissing, and vicious classroom harassment during the student lectures by the benchers. Her race and class privilege enabled her to secure articles, unlike Delos Rogest Davis, but she found articling to be a miserable experience, for the other articled clerks avoided her and made things "as unpleasant as they possibly could."[23] When Martin was called to the bar, no one would hire her initially, and she was forced to place a self-deprecating advertisement in a Toronto newspaper: "Miss Clara Brett Martin, Barrister &c., desires position in a law firm, where experience can be had in practical work, that being the object rather than salary."[24] The barriers erected by the all-male legal profession were so high that Martin almost abandoned her goal, stating at one point that, "[i]f it were not that I set out to open the way to the bar for others of my sex, I would have given up the effort long ago."[25] In one of the ironies of history, documentation has recently surfaced showing that Martin was anti-Semitic, illustrating how experience of discrimination in one format does not always teach people to prize principles of egalitarianism more generally.[26] Her anti-Semitism also indicates just how well Martin fit into the dominant mould of the legal profession in every aspect but gender.

The barriers facing early Aboriginal applicants were, if anything, even more impenetrable. One of the best examples is the case of Andrew Paull, an Aboriginal man from British Columbia, who obtained a position with the law offices of Hugh St. Quentin Cayley in 1917. After a four-year stint there, Paull sought admission as a student-at-law. Vancouver lawyer D.W.F. McDonald wrote to the British Columbia Law Society on Paull's behalf in 1922:

> Mr. Paul [sic] has had a thorough education at the Mission and High Schools ... and is looked upon as one of authority by the Indians. He is desirous of taking up the study of law; he is about twenty-eight years of age, and speaks and writes English fluently. He has not had much instruction in Latin, though he speaks and writes French.

The Law Society denied his application, indicating that "no concessions will be made as to the subject of Latin." The secretary of the Law Society also noted that Paull was barred by another criterion for admission: all applicants had to be entitled to vote in the province. Aboriginal individuals were barred by statute from voting in BC elections until 1949.[27] Paull went on to a very distinguished career as an advocate for First Nations land claims in British Columbia, but he never became a lawyer.[28]

Indeed, the historical understanding of Aboriginality and professionalism was such that the federal government had enacted a provision, in effect for more than seventy years from 1876 to 1951, providing that, if Aboriginal individuals became a lawyer (or doctor or minister) or held a university degree, they were no longer capable of holding the status of "Indian."[29] To be a lawyer meant, in legal terms, not to be Aboriginal.

It is unclear how this affected the first Aboriginal lawyer to be called to the bar in Ontario (and the first in Canada), Norman Lickers. Born in Tuscarora Township on the Six Nations Territory, and orphaned by the time that he reached school age, Lickers was raised at the Mohawk Institute in Brantford. He graduated from Brantford Collegiate Institute and then obtained a BA from the University of Western Ontario in 1934. In the fall of that year, he was admitted as a student-at-law to Osgoode Hall Law School, and he articled with J.O. Trepanier in Brantford. Lickers was called to the bar in 1938 and set up practice in Brantford, where he specialized in criminal law. Disbarred in 1950, Lickers moved on to a successful career as an ironworker and a leader in Aboriginal politics.[30]

The theme of disbarment, which plagued a number of early racialized lawyers, including some early Black lawyers, sends up a discordant note that suggests the need for further research on the difficulties that beset such path breakers and the discriminatory types of disciplinary supervision that they might have been accorded by provincial law societies.[31]

Further Harassment of Path Breakers

It was not just admission to law that created consternation. Those who broke down barriers, and many who came after them, were often additionally burdened by gendered, racist, or classist treatment by white, male lawyers. The experience of some of the first judges to break the traditional mould is filled with examples. Both Emily Murphy and Alice Jamieson, the first two women appointed as police magistrates in Canada in the early twentieth century, faced complaints from male counsel who objected that as "non-persons" women had no legal entitlement to preside over courtrooms. Supreme Court of Alberta Judge David Lynch Scott, who ultimately upheld women's right to sit, could not resist adding that he personally "entertain[ed] serious doubts" whether a woman was "qualified to be appointed," but the government of the day apparently thought otherwise, and he could not find any legal impediment.[32]

Justice Bertha Wilson became the first woman appointed to the Ontario Court of Appeal in 1976 and to the Supreme Court of Canada in 1982.[33] She found her entry into both courts marred by incidents of exclusion and hostility from some of the other judges. Her biographer described the treatment that Justice Wilson received from Justice Arthur Jessup at the Court of Appeal; he made it clear that he disliked sitting on panels with her, asked that she be replaced on "complex" cases, and ignored her completely whenever possible.[34] The biography also recounts the awkwardness exhibited by Chief Justice Bora Laskin when he spoke at Justice Wilson's swearing-in at the Supreme Court and Justice Antonio Lamer's pointed refusal to rise from his chair along with the rest of his colleagues when Justice Wilson entered the conference room for her first judicial conference. Even more troubling was the fact that she was routinely isolated from the informal decision-making discussions of male judges at the Supreme Court, a phenomenon that deeply disturbed her and impeded her ability to influence the Court.[35] Professional norms of civility and collegiality were used to demarcate, bolster, and protect the masculine judicial circle. These ethical norms, so touted in professional rhetoric, were used not to extend collegial community to the first woman as an equal but to isolate and exclude her. Her treatment underscored that the judiciary was, first and foremost, masculine and that the introduction of a female judge on the bench was viewed as highly intrusive and inappropriate.

Justice Claire L'Heureux-Dubé became the first woman appointed to the Quebec Court of Appeal in 1979 and the second female Supreme Court of Canada appointee in 1987.[36] She described her shock when one of the judges at the Supreme Court initially refused to speak with her. "He wouldn't talk to me for three months. After that, he sent me a note saying: 'You've passed your probation.'"[37] She characterized her early years at the Supreme Court as akin to an "old boys' club" in which she and Justice Wilson were "isolated" and "felt the sting of exclusion." She even considered resigning from the bench during that early period because of "ideological battles among the judges over the Charter, loneliness, and the reluctance of [some of the male judges] to accept a second woman judge."[38]

Justice L'Heureux-Dubé was also subjected to a barrage of remarkably disrespectful and uncivil comments by other judges and lawyers. In 1999, she released the *Ewanchuk* decision, in which she articulated the egalitarian principles that applied to the assessment of consent in sexual assault law. Her decision was signed by one of her colleagues, and concurred in by another, who wrote a shorter and more general judgment.[39] The decision was later characterized by academic commentators as strongly worded but by no means aberrant.[40] Yet, in what has been described as an "unprecedented and unparalleled personal attack," Justice John Wesley McClung, whose decision she overturned, published an open letter in the *National Post* in which he disparaged Justice L'Heureux-Dubé for "feminist bias" and a "graceless slide into personal invective." In a surprising assertion, he also wagered that her "personal convictions ... delivered again from her judicial chair" could be responsible for the "disparate (and growing) number of male suicides being reported in the Province of Quebec."[41] Alan Gold, a prominent Toronto defence lawyer, was quoted in the *Toronto Star* as describing Justice L'Heureux-Dubé's "radical feminist judgment" as "ridiculous" and in the *Calgary Herald* as "totalitarian."[42] The *National Post* reported that lawyer Gwen Landolt, founder of REAL Women, had "branded Judge L'Heureux-Dubé as a feminist out of step with ordinary Canadians," quoting her as stating that "[w]e shouldn't have to pay the salary of a radical feminist who sits on the bench and uses her position to promote her own personal agenda."[43]

Perhaps the strongest invective came from Edward L. Greenspan, a Toronto defence lawyer. His letter to the editor, published in the *National Post,* began with this remarkable image: "When the Supreme Court judges swore their oath ... [t]hey were not given the right to pull a lower court judge's pants down in public and paddle him." The letter continued:

> She was intemperate, showed a lack of balance, and a terrible lack of judgment ... It is clear that the feminist influence has amounted to intimidation, posing a potential danger to the independence of the judiciary ... Feminists

have entrenched their ideology in the Supreme Court of Canada and have put all contrary views beyond the pale ... The feminist perspective has hijacked the Supreme Court of Canada and now feminists want to throw off the bench anyone who disagrees with them. Judge L'Heureux-Dubé was hell-bent on reeducating Judge McClung, bullying and coercing him into looking at everything from her point of view. She raked him over the coals for making remarks that may, in fact, be accurate in the given case. I don't know. But just as he had no empirical evidence to support his view (if you discount all of human history), she has no empirical evidence to say what she says (if you discount Catharine MacKinnon's collected works) ... Madam Justice L'Heureux-Dubé has shown an astounding insensitivity and an inability to conceive of any concepts outside her own terms of reference and has thereby disgraced the Supreme Court.[44]

Justice McClung was ultimately the recipient of a mild reprimand from the Canadian Judicial Council, but none of the lawyers was faced with a complaint of unprofessional behaviour or conduct unbecoming a barrister and solicitor. Critiques of a female judge because she expressed feminist views seem to border on hysteria. Harsh comments about male judges from other judges and lawyers are rarely if ever publicly circulated and suggest the fragility of acceptance of women on the bench. Widespread tolerance of such commentary within professional circles underscores the fact that concepts such as professionalism, civility, community, and collegiality do not extend to female judges perceived as feminist.

Some of the first Black judges also experienced attacks. Justice Corinne Sparks was subjected to a serious challenge when she acquitted a Black male teenager of assaulting and resisting a white police officer in 1994, stating that the young officer had "probably overreacted," which police officers were known to do when "dealing with non-white groups."[45] Justice Sparks was the only Black person then sitting on the bench in Nova Scotia and Canada's first African Canadian woman judge.[46] Complaints from the white Crown attorney resulted in an appeal and a finding by the white judges of the Nova Scotia Court of Appeal that the remarks had created a reasonable apprehension of racial bias, a ruling later narrowly overturned by a divided Supreme Court of Canada, in which the majority censured Sparks for her "worrisome" comments.[47]

Numerous official reports have documented racial inequities within the Canadian legal system, and many commentators have suggested that the decision of Judge Sparks actually reflected her sensitivity to racism within the community rather than "racial bias" against the police.[48] Perhaps the most astonishing feature of the entire episode was that it appears to have been the first Canadian case in which there was a finding of apprehension of racial bias among the judiciary.[49] Scores of white judges, many of whom have made far more inflammatory racial statements, have escaped critique,[50] but the first Black female judge in Nova Scotia incited censure in highly debatable circumstances. Elsewhere I have argued that the position of Judge Sparks as a Black judge made her more vulnerable to such challenges and that this case, among others, reflects the pervasiveness of racial inequality within our legal system.[51] It is also an indication that the traditional deference extended to members of the judiciary by lawyers and other judges is not accorded to those perceived as different from the norm. In fact, during jury selection in the 1993 case of *R. v. Parks,* white male Ontario Court of Appeal Judge David Doherty foreshadowed Judge Sparks, articulating the existence of racism as part of the Canadian "community's psyche" in words substantially stronger than she used. There was no appeal, and there was no complaint of racial bias against the white male judge.[52]

Lawyers receive their training at law schools, and here, too, differential treatment of those who represent diversification has interfered with the rhetorical objectives of professionalism. Many female law professors in the 1970s, 1980s, and 1990s reported experiencing a "chilly climate" within Canadian law schools, which impeded their ability to teach, participate in administration, and write. They described serious devaluation, trivialization, and harassment from some male professors, administrators, and students. They reported abusive attacks in the classroom and during faculty meetings, discrediting rumour campaigns, a failure to acknowledge gender bias, and rationalization of male abuse.[53] The attacks were clearly motivated by gender. They constituted deliberate and protracted efforts to diminish the scope of authority of female law professors and to maintain law schools as bastions of masculinity. Some of the first Aboriginal female law professors reported abuse specific to their racialization: tokenism, disrespectful challenges to their authority, teaching evaluations complaining that they wore "too many beads and feathers to class," and a general unwillingness to open up space for Aboriginality within legal education.[54] Even at the front end of professional development, at the root and foundation of legal training, white male dominance has been evident.

Consequences of a Masculine, White, Privileged Legal Profession

Why does it matter that the norms of the legal profession historically have

been framed around deeply entrenched notions of masculinity, white su-
premacy, and class privilege? Obviously, the costs to those excluded from
the profession because of their gender, race, and class have been enormous
in terms of career opportunities, economic benefits, and social status. But
the consequences run much deeper. The homogeneous nature of the profession and its resistance to diversification in the name of preserving professionalism have serious implications for the services that lawyers offer to the
public, the arguments that lawyers make in courtrooms, and the decisions
that judges hand down.

Our understandings of the most beneficent theories of professionalism
suggest that legal services should be available to all and that lawyers should
provide well-honed advocacy skills that properly represent the interests of
their clients. Yet communities that have gone underrepresented in the profession have substantially less access to information about legal rights and
to the lawyers who could represent them. If and when they do identify the
legal aspects of their problems and retain legal services, the lawyers are
often unable to represent them properly.

Nowhere is this more evident than in Aboriginal communities. The
historical record is replete with examples of completely inept lawyering
on cases of critical importance to Aboriginal clients. When Euro-Canadian
legal authorities first attempted to assert jurisdiction over Aboriginal communities – in terms of criminal, civil, and property law – many arguments
should have been made contesting the validity of this assertion. There had
been no conquest of and no surrender of sovereignty by Aboriginal nations,
and where there were treaties they were woefully vague on issues of legal
jurisdiction. Yet Euro-Canadians blithely arrested Aboriginal individuals,
imposed their own understandings of substantive law, and conducted trials
under Euro-Canadian procedural rules, presided over by Euro-Canadian
judges. Aboriginal peoples frequently contested the right of European new-
comers to assert such jurisdiction, but their voices were ignored. When
Aboriginal clients were represented by white lawyers, almost every effort to
put the question of jurisdiction on the record was misconstrued by counsel,
unheard, or mangled.[55] White lawyers seem to have been incapable of com-
prehending the complex Aboriginal political and justice systems that had
been operating for centuries before contact or of imagining that the Euro-
Canadian system was not the only option. The basic questions of sovereignty, then, were never truly considered or adjudicated. Not only did this
result in the failure to accord Aboriginal communities basic legal rights, but

also it left these questions outstanding, continuing to plague Aboriginal Canadian relations into the present and future.

Court archives are also full of examples of white male lawyers making blatantly racist and sexist arguments. Hamilton barrister C.W. Reid Bowlby represented a group of Ku Klux Klansmen from southwestern Ontario after they used mob intimidation in 1930 to prevent a marriage in Oakville between a white woman and an African Canadian man. During the criminal trial, Bowlby proclaimed that his clients had done "a humane, decent thing in taking her away from that man." He begged the court for a dismissal of all charges, adding that "I am sure that there are hundreds of parents throughout the Dominion of Canada who would be eternally thankful that such a step had been taken."[56]

Regina lawyer Douglas J. Thom appeared before Regina City Council in 1924 to argue that Chinese Canadian restaurateur Yee Clun ought not to be granted a licence that would enable him to hire white female employees. In an unabashedly racist argument, Thom asserted that "Chinatowns have an unsavory moral reputation" and that "white girls lose caste when they are employed by Chinese."[57] Nineteenth-century and early-twentieth-century sexual assault and seduction trials are filled with misogynistic arguments. Generally without any evidentiary basis, male lawyers asserted that victims of sexual abuse lied and were sexually promiscuous, rabble rousing, foul tongued, ill mannered, and intemperate with alcohol. They accused women and children of fabricating sexual complaints out of delusional fantasies, desires for revenge, and conspiracies to blackmail. These character assassinations, pursued in zealous efforts to protect accused men, frequently convinced all-male juries to acquit in trials in which evidence of the crime was strong and convincing.[58]

The fact that so many lawyers were drawn from the ranks of privileged white men also affected their understandings of the world when they later became judges. Indeed, the feminist decisions of Justices Wilson and L'Heureux-Dubé, and the anti-racist decision of Judge Sparks, which provoked such critique, form an intriguing comparative backdrop to some of the comments and decisions issued by white male judges, whose decisions inspired few complaints and no discipline. George T. Denison, a white judge who became Toronto's most famous magistrate from 1877 to 1921, openly referred to Jews as "neurotic," southern Europeans as "hot-blooded," Chinese as "degenerate," Aboriginal people as "primitive," and Blacks as "child-like savages."[59] William Renwick Riddell, a white Court of Appeal judge in early-twentieth-century Ontario, described the Inuit and First Nations of western and northern Canada as people with "savage appetites," who "seldom considered themselves to be bound by anything but their own desires," in contrast to whites, whom he designated as a "higher race." Riddell publicly portrayed Blacks as incompetent and uncivilized.[60] The historical record reveals countless statements made by male Canadian judges exhibiting explicit suspicion of, and hostility toward, women.[61] William Campbell, who served as Chief Justice of Ontario in the early nineteenth century, heard a family law dispute in which a husband had brandished a whip over his wife in front of multiple witnesses after beating her repeatedly for some time. Justice Campbell declared that "a man had a right to chastise his wife *moderately*" and ruled that the wife had had no justification in leaving the marital home.[62] This legitimation of wife battering stood for years as the prevailing Canadian judicial edict on a husband's rights. More recently, Judge R.M. Bourassa, a white male Territorial Court judge in the Northwest Territories, made a series of statements that attracted widespread criticism as being both racist and sexist. The judicial inquiry into his conduct found no reasonable apprehension of bias.[63]

The shocking revelation of the wrongful criminal conviction of Donald Marshall Jr., an Aboriginal man from Nova Scotia, resulted in an inquiry into the behaviour of the five white appellate judges who upheld his conviction. The white judges of the Canadian Judicial Council concluded that there was nothing to impugn the impartiality of the court.[64]

The Future of Legal Professionalism

The examples that I have produced in this chapter cannot capture the fullness of the historical record, in part because this research is so new, and in part because the recipients of such behaviour did not commit thorough accounts to writing in forms that have survived in archival collections. Yet what I have presented allows us to get some sense of the climate that fostered a deep and long-standing intolerance of lawyers and judges who were not male, white, economically privileged Gentiles. The history of the legal profession illustrates that concepts such as professionalism, civility, community, and collegiality have been imbued with discriminatory intent and practice. These are ideas, indeed, that have been pressed into service to allow the most privileged of lawyers and judges to exercise power and promulgate exclusion based on gender, race, class, and religion.

What does this mean for the future? Are such concepts so tainted by their historical foundations that they are impossible to rehabilitate? Are efforts to promote an ethic of professionalism doomed to failure? Certainly, I would argue, some of these concepts are irretrievably misconceived. *Collegiality* is a word that has long been used within the academy to justify the need to hire and retain faculty members who "fit the mould," who blend well into existing structures and ways of doing things. It almost never represents a desire to extend camaraderie to individuals and groups who have long been outside the fold. When previously excluded groups articulate the problems that they perceive, they are accused of "lack of collegiality," of "lack of civility," of failure to behave "professionally." The concepts are turned on their heads, and those who have exercised power for the purpose of exclusion claim that they are the ones who have been aggrieved.

Perhaps it is better to turn away from words so laden with historical baggage. I think that we can move forward from our history of exclusion more quickly if we focus on different ideals, such as anti-racism, gender equality, respect for Aboriginality, religious tolerance, reduction in wealth disparity, and social justice. The legacy left by our profession's historical practices continues to have impacts. Major structural changes are required to set things right. These, far more than professionalism and civility, are the principles that require urgent attention if we are to achieve a profession worthy of the name.

Notes

I am indebted to Ella Forbes-Chilibeck for her research assistance. Financial assistance from the University of Ottawa, the Social Sciences and Humanities Research Council of Canada, the Bora Laskin Human Rights Fellowship, and the Law Foundation of Ontario is gratefully acknowledged.

1 The objectives of the colloquium, including these, are set out in the promotional flyer announcing the October 20, 2003, event.
2 This list is not, of course, exhaustive. I have not dealt with discrimination against other ethnic and religious minorities, persons with disabilities, gays, and lesbians. These areas all require more historical research and examination of the continuing impacts that discrimination has on such communities within law.
3 See, for example, Jacalyn Duffin, "The Quota: 'An Equally Serious Problem' for Us All" (2002) 19(2) Canadian Bulletin of Medical History at 327–49, which discusses the search for historical proof of the quotas on women in medicine at the University of Toronto. Duffin describes how difficult it was to "prove historically" what she "knew to be true existentially." After a difficult search, she managed to locate several written records as well as a living witness who could offer evidence regarding the existence of quotas. "What happens to the history of entrenched practices that leave no tracks?" she asks. "We are confronted with the poverty of a historical method that privileges the written word. Had those two archival documents not been kept, or had

[the witness] not been found, the quota would have existed anyway, encased in a paper silence, characterized as strident rumour mongering, suppressed by retrospective shame, and potentially lost to our contemplation forever ... Historiographically, then, we know that some histories are not and cannot be told through the usual channels."

4 William Renwick Riddell, *The Legal Profession in Upper Canada in Its Early Periods* (Toronto: Law Society of Upper Canada, 1916) at 39.

5 *Ibid.* at 40–41.

6 These extracts of MacGregor's diary are taken from D.G. Kilgour, "A Note on Legal Education in Ontario 125 Years Ago" (1959–60) 13 University of Toronto Law Journal at 270–72.

7 Other accounts of young lawyers during this era suggest that studies at Upper Canada College often provided a thorough background in classics with which to impress the benchers during admission examinations. Larratt William Violett Smith, who immigrated to Canada from England as a child, described the course of study that he had pursued at Upper Canada College: "The pupils began Latin in the first form and by the time they reached the sixth form they could construe Horace, Cicero, and Virgil, and were proficient in Greek as well." He successfully passed his admission examinations at the age of nineteen in 1839. See Mary Larratt Smith, *Young Mr. Smith in Upper Canada* (Toronto: University of Toronto Press, 1980) at 7–9, 14.

8 For details on the intergenerational nature of some of these legal families, see Christopher Moore, *The Law Society of Upper Canada and Ontario's Lawyers, 1797–1997* (Toronto: University of Toronto Press, 1997).

9 Duffin, *supra* note 3. For more general discussion on Jewish quotas, see Charles Levi, "The Jewish Quota in the Faculty of Medicine, University of Toronto: Generational Memory Sustained by Documentation" (2003) 15(1) Historical Studies in Education 130; and W.P.J. Millar, "'We Wanted Our Children Should Have It Better': Jewish Medical Students at the University of Toronto 1910–51" (2000) 11(1) Journal of the Canadian Historical Association 109.

10 On Bora Laskin's experience as an articling student, see Philip Girard, *Bora Laskin: Bringing Law to Life* (Toronto: University of Toronto Press, 2005). On the headnote writing experience, see Irving Abella, "The Making of a Chief Justice: Bora Laskin, the Early Years" (1990) 24(3) Law Society of Upper Canada Gazette 187. Gretta Wong Grant, who would become the first Chinese Canadian female lawyer when she was called to the Ontario bar in 1946, recalled that anti-Semitism was rife among the Osgoode Hall student body and that Jewish students who wished to find articling positions outside Jewish firms had an almost impossible task. See "Oral History Interview with Gretta Grant," conducted by Constance Backhouse and Anna Feltracco, July 11 and September 17, 1991, typescript on file with the author at 16–17; and Constance Backhouse, "Gretta Wong Grant: Canada's First Chinese-Canadian Female Lawyer" (1996) 15 Windsor Yearbook of Access to Justice 3 at 33.

11 Although Davis was the first to lay public claim to this achievement, there were others of mixed race who preceded him. Robert Sutherland, now acknowledged to be the first Black person called to the bar in Ontario, was called in 1855. His parents were a Scottish father from Jamaica and an African Jamaican mother. He was

identified as "coloured" when he attended Queen's University in Kingston from 1849 to 1852, graduating with honours in classics and mathematics, subjects that would have stood him in good stead on admission criteria. Sutherland set up practice in Walkerton after his call. Whether because he did not seek it or for other reasons, he does not appear to have received public recognition as the first "coloured" lawyer until recently. See Ian Malcolm, "Robert Sutherland: The First Black Lawyer in Canada?" (1992) 26(2) Law Society of Upper Canada Gazette 183.

12 Subsequent to his admission, Davis set up practice in Amherstberg, Ontario, near the county of his birth. His son, Frederick Homer Alphonso Davis, eventually joined him in practice in 1900. Davis became the first Black King's Counsel in 1910. See *An Act to Authorize the Supreme Court of Judicature for Ontario to admit Delos Rogest Davis to practice as a solicitor,* S.O. 1884, c. 94; *An Act to authorize the Law Society of Upper Canada to admit Delos Rogest Davis as a Barrister-at-Law,* S.O. 1886, c. 94; Lance C. Talbot, "History of Blacks in the Law Society of Upper Canada" (1990) 24(1) Law Society of Upper Canada Gazette 65; and Robin W. Winks, *The Blacks in Canada: A History,* 2d ed. (Montreal: McGill-Queen's University Press, 1997) at 328.

13 See Talbot, *supra* note 12. Ethelbert Lionel Cross, who appears to have been the fourth Black admitted to the Law Society of Upper Canada, and the only one between 1900 and 1923, was called in 1924, after articling with E.F. Singer. Bertrand Joseph Spencer Pitt, the fifth, articled with Cross and was called in 1928. Blacks who articled with Pitt included James Watson, Myrtle Blackwood Smith, and George Carter. Many of the early Black lawyers in Nova Scotia articled with Joseph Eaglan Griffith, a Black immigrant from the British West Indies, who was called to the bar in 1917 and practised in Halifax until his death in 1944. For details, see Constance Backhouse, *Colour-Coded: A Legal History of Racism in Canada, 1900-1950* (Toronto: The Osgoode Society and University of Toronto Press, 1999), Chapters 4 and 5 [*Colour-Coded*].

14 Constance Backhouse, *Petticoats and Prejudice: Women and Law in Nineteenth-Century Canada* (Toronto: Women's Press, 1991) at 293–326 [*Petticoats and Prejudice*].

15 A.H. O'B. [Arthur H. O'Brien], "Legal Scrap Book" (1892) 28(7) Canada Law Journal 202 at 205.

16 "Woman's Rights" *Canadian Illustrated News* (Montreal) (November 21, 1874) at 323–24.

17 See (1879) 15 Canada Law Journal 146, and (1880) 16 Canada Law Journal 161.

18 "Female Students-at-Law" *Daily Mail* (Toronto) (April 6, 1892); "Women as Lawyers" *Daily Mail* (Toronto) (April 7, 1892); (1896) 32 Canada Law Journal 784.

19 "Female Students-at-Law" *Daily Mail* (Toronto) (April 6, 1892); "Women as Lawyers" *Daily Mail* (Toronto) (April 7, 1892).

20 *Globe* (Toronto) (April 5, 1895).

21 Backhouse, *Petticoats and Prejudice, supra* note 14 at 334.

22 *Ibid.* at 293–321; *An Act to Provide for the Admission of Women to the Study and Practice of Law,* S.O. 1892, c. 32; *An Act to amend the Act to provide for the admission of Women to the Study and Practice of Law,* S.O. 1895, c. 27.

23 The articling period at this time was three years, and Martin secured a position with the prominent Toronto firm of Mulock, Miller, Crowther, and Montgomery, in part

because of her long-standing friendship with Sir William Mulock's daughter. She switched articles partway through to another well-known Toronto firm, Blake, Lash, Cassels. In an interview with the Buffalo *Express*, Martin described feeling like "an interloper, if not a curiosity," at these firms and confessed that she found the articling experience an "obstacle" that nearly "doomed [her] to failure." See Backhouse, *Petticoats and Prejudice, supra* note 14 at 309–14; *Express* (Buffalo) (undated clipping *ca.* 1896), Archives, Women's Law Association of Ontario.

24 *Telegram* (Toronto) (February 3, 1897). She eventually secured a position with a two-man law firm operated by John Shilton and William H. Wallbridge and practised with them until 1906, when she established her own firm. She went to court several times in the early years, but the fuss that always greeted her presence ultimately discouraged her, and she began to retain male barristers to act for her clients when they needed courtroom representation. Her practice centred on wills, real estate, and family law. See Backhouse, *Petticoats and Prejudice, supra* note 14 at 321–23.

25 *Express* (Buffalo) (undated clipping *ca.* 1896), Archives, Women's Law Association of Ontario.

26 For detailed discussions of Martin's anti-Semitism, see Backhouse, *Petticoats and Prejudice, supra* note 14 at 323–24; Constance Backhouse, "Clara Brett Martin: Canadian Heroine or Not?" (1992) 5(2) Canadian Journal of Women and the Law 263; Lita-Rose Betcherman, "Clara Brett Martin's Anti-Semitism" (1992) 5(2) Canadian Journal of Women and the Law 280; Brenda Cossman and Marlee Kline, "'And if Not Now, When?' Feminism and Anti-Semitism beyond Clara Brett Martin" (1992) 5(2) Canadian Journal of Women and the Law 298; Lynne Pearlman, "Through Jewish Lesbian Eyes: Rethinking Clara Brett Martin" (1992) 5(2) Canadian Journal of Women and the Law 317; Constance Backhouse, "Response to Cossman, Kline, and Pearlman" (1992) 5(2) Canadian Journal of Women and the Law 351; and Lita-Rose Betcherman, "Response to Cossman, Kline, and Pearlman" (1992) 5(2) Canadian Journal of Women and the Law 355.

27 For details of the exclusion of Aboriginals from the legal profession in British Columbia, see Joan Brockman, "Exclusionary Tactics: The History of Women and Visible Minorities in the Legal Profession in British Columbia" in Hamar Foster and John McLaren, eds., *Essays in the History of Canadian Law: British Columbia and the Yukon,* vol. 6 (Toronto: Osgoode Society, 1995) 508 at 519–25 and 549; E. Palmer Patterson, "Andrew Paull and Canadian Indian Resurgence" (Ph.D. diss., University of Washington, 1962). The requirement that applicants have the right to vote, Law Society of British Columbia Rule 39, had been passed in response to the efforts of several Japanese and Chinese men to be admitted as students-at-law in 1918–19 and stated that "[n]o person shall be admitted or enrolled who is not the full age of sixteen, is a British subject, and who would, if of the age of twenty-one years, be entitled to be placed on the Voter's List under the Provincial Elections Act." Asians were prohibited from exercising the provincial suffrage until 1949. For details regarding the prohibitions on voting for Aboriginals and Asian Canadians, see Backhouse, *Colour-Coded, supra* note 13 at Chapters 4 and 5.

28 In the mid-1920s, Andrew Paull, Peter Kelly, and their lawyer, A.E. O'Meara, brought a successful claim on behalf of the Allied Tribes of British Columbia before a Joint Committee of the Senate and House of Commons. Almost immediately after, in

1927, Parliament made it a crime to raise money from Aboriginal communities for the prosecution of Aboriginal claims, unless the Department of Indian Affairs had given prior written consent. See *An Act to Amend the Indian Act,* S.C. 1926–27, c. 32, s. 6. The prohibition on fundraising was not removed until enactment of the *Indian Act,* S.C. 1951, c. 29. George Manuel and Michael Posluns attributed enactment of the prohibition to a backlash in response to Paull, Kelly, and O'Meara's success; see their *The Fourth World: An Indian Reality* (Don Mills: Collier-Macmillan Canada, 1974) at 86–87.

29 The *Indian Act, 1876,* S.C. 1876, c. 18, s. 86(1), provided that "[a]ny Indian who may be admitted to the degree of Doctor of Medicine, or to any other degree by any University of Learning, or who may be admitted in any Province of the Dominion to practice law either as an Advocate or as a Barrister or Counsellor or Solicitor or Attorney or to be a Notary Public, or who may enter Holy Orders or who may be licensed by any denomination of Christians as a Minister of the Gospel, shall *ipso facto* become and be enfranchised under this Act." Section 88 provided that the effect of enfranchisement was that such individuals "shall no longer be deemed Indians within the meaning of the laws relating to Indians, except in so far as their right to participate in the annuities and interest moneys, and rents and councils of the band of Indians to which they belonged."

30 Lickers was born on 10 June 1913. His father, a farmer, was Henry Lickers. His degree from Western was an Honours BA in political science and economics. His call to the bar took place on 17 November 1938, and his disbarment occurred on 28 September 1950. Although details of the disbarment are not publicly accessible, the press referred to misappropriation or failing to account for a client's funds. His iron-working career involved work at Hamilton Bridge and Tank, service in the ironworkers' union, and establishing courses to teach Aboriginal youths the trade. In 1951, Lickers acted as a consultant to the federal government on amendments to the *Indian Act.* He was one of the most vocal protesters against the white paper issued by Indian Affairs in 1969, served as a founding president of the Association of Iroquois and Allied Indians, and was active on his band council from 1958 to 1974. Lickers was also an accomplished athlete. For details, see Law Society of Upper Canada Archives, Past Member Files, "Canada's First Native Lawyer Dies on Six Nations Reserve" *Expositor* (Brantford) (March 16, 1987). I am indebted to Susan Lewthwaite of the Law Society of Upper Canada Archives for this information.

31 E. Lionel Cross was disbarred in 1937. Of the five Black lawyers practising in Ontario in the 1940s and 1950s, two were disbarred, one in 1948 and another in 1953. See Talbot, *supra* note 12 at 66–68. On the disciplinary vigilance that the Law Society showed toward Black lawyers, accused of "touting" and "conduct unbecoming," see the Oral History Transcript of Charles Roach, Osgoode Society, November-December 1989.

32 Although neither woman was a lawyer, as was the case for many non-legally trained police magistrates of the time, their experiences in judicial posts set a precedent that is important to examine. Emily Murphy became the first woman police magistrate in the British Empire in 1916 when she was appointed to the Women's Court in Edmonton. She was joined the same year by Alice Jamieson, named a police magistrate in Calgary. During her first year on the bench, Magistrate Murphy was

advised by one of the male lawyers who appeared before her that she was not "legally a 'person' under the British North America Act and had no right to be holding court." The argument was temporarily resolved until Magistrate Jamieson was similarly challenged in 1917. Defence counsel attempted to quash Jamieson's conviction of Lizzie Cyr for vagrancy because a woman was "incompetent and incapable of holding the position of police magistrate." In *Rex v. Cyr* (1917), 12 Alta. L.R. 321, Judge David Lynch Scott of the Supreme Court of Alberta concluded that, "[w]hile I entertain serious doubts whether a woman is qualified to be appointed to that office, I am of opinion that the legality of such appointment cannot be questioned or inquired into on this application." The accused appealed, and the Alberta Court of Appeal declared that "in this province and at this time in our presently existing conditions there is at common law no legal disqualification for holding public office in the government of the country arising from any distinction of sex" and that "Mrs. Jamieson is not disqualified from holding the office of police magistrate." Discomfort with these attacks led Murphy to launch a campaign, which took more than a decade to complete, to have women judicially declared "persons." The "Persons Case" resolved the matter permanently when the Privy Council overturned the Supreme Court of Canada decision that had held that women were not qualified to sit as "persons" in the Senate. *Henrietta Muir Edwards et al. v. Attorney-General for Canada*, [1930] A.C. 124 (P.C.), reversing [1928] S.C.R. 276; Catherine L. Cleverdon, *The Woman Suffrage Movement in Canada* (Toronto: University of Toronto Press, 1950) at 73–74, 102, 142. For another example, see the description of the "petty tyrannies" that plagued Helen Gregory MacGill, appointed assistant judge in the Vancouver Juvenile Court in 1917, in Elsie Gregory MacGill, *My Mother the Judge* (Toronto: Peter Martin Associates, 1981).

33 Ellen Anderson, *Judging Bertha Wilson: Law as Large as Life* (Toronto: University of Toronto Press, 2001) at 85, 128.

34 *Ibid.* at 94.

35 *Ibid.* at 128, 150, 153–54, 164. After his retirement, former Chief Justice Antonio Lamer took issue with Justice Wilson's biographer's assertion that Wilson had felt excluded at the Court. "There was no little clique," he told *Lawyers Weekly*, "no little gang. Like-minded people tend to congregate ... I guess some of us just figured, 'well, there's no point in going and trying to convince Bertha that it's going to be this, and not that,' because she is not going to change her mind ... and maybe she felt isolated about that, but we never isolated her." Cited in Cristin Schmitz, "Former Chief Justice Lamer Reflects on His Brightest, Darkest Moments as Canada's Top Jurist" *Lawyers Weekly* (March 29, 2002) 1 at 7. University of Toronto law professor Jim Phillips, a former clerk for Justice Wilson, wrote back that Justice Lamer had failed "to take into consideration that, had she been invited to participate in more of the informal discussions among the judges forming majority opinions without the benefit of her input, she might have been able to change their minds." Jim Phillips, "Says Lamer's Reaction Confirms Wilson's Version," Letters to the Editor, *Lawyers Weekly* (April 18, 2002) 5.

36 Teresa Scassa, "Claire L'Heureux-Dubé (1927–)" in Rebecca Mae Salokar and Mary L. Volcansek, eds., *Women in Law: A Bio-Bibliographical Sourcebook* (Westport, CT: Greenwood Press, 1996) at 136–43.

37 "Gatecrashing the Old Boys Club" *Globe and Mail* (May 2, 2002) A8. The judge was not named in the article.

38 "Top Court 'Can Always Be Improved'" *Ottawa Citizen* (May 5, 2002) A4.

39 *R. v. Ewanchuk*, [1999] 1 S.C.R. 330. The Alberta Court of Appeal judgment under appeal had characterized the accused's coercive advances as "clumsy passes" more "hormonal" than "criminal." It dismissed the complainant's repeated "no's" as irrelevant and implied that a woman who had had a child out of wedlock, living common law with a male partner, was not capable of refusing consent. The decision had also rebuked the complainant for being dressed in shorts, commenting that she "did not present herself to Ewanchuk or enter his trailer in a bonnet and crinolines." The portion of Justice L'Heureux-Dubé's judgment that came under scrutiny, concurred in by Justice Charles Doherty Gonthier, read (at 369, 372, 376) as follows: "Complainants should be able to rely on a system free from myths and stereotypes, and on a judiciary whose impartiality is not compromised by these biased assumptions ... It is part of the role of this Court to denounce this kind of language, unfortunately still used today, which not only perpetuates archaic myths and stereotypes about the nature of sexual assaults but also ignores the law." Chief Justice Beverley McLachlin issued a shorter concurring opinion.

40 Academic researchers who have examined the substance and tone of appellate decisions have concluded that the type of "censure" contained in Justice L'Heureux-Dubé's decision in *Ewanchuk* was by no means unique. Barbara Billingsley and Bruce P. Elman characterized the opinion as "an example of the Supreme Court accusing the Court of Appeal of a serious or flagrant misunderstanding of the law" that was "relatively rare but certainly not aberrant." Barbara Billingsley and Bruce P. Elman, "The Supreme Court of Canada and the Alberta Court of Appeal: Do the Top Courts Have a Fundamental Philosophical Difference of Opinion on Public Law Issues?" (2001) 39(3) Alberta Law Review 703 at 728. The *Ethical Principles for Judges* promulgated by the Canadian Judicial Council used language very similar to that adopted by Justice L'Heureux-Dubé: "Judges should not be influenced by attitudes based on stereotype, myth or prejudice. They should, therefore, make every effort to recognize, demonstrate sensitivity to and correct such attitudes. Judges should avoid comments, expressions, gestures or behaviour which reasonably may be interpreted as showing insensitivity to or disrespect for anyone. Examples include irrelevant comments based on racial, cultural, sexual or other stereotypes and other conduct implying that persons before the court will not be afforded equal consideration and respect." Canadian Judicial Council, *Ethical Principles for Judges* (Ottawa: Canadian Judicial Council, 1998) at 23–24. For a fuller analysis of the decision and the response to it, see Constance Backhouse, "The Chilly Climate for Women Judges: Reflections on the Backlash from the Ewanchuk Case" (2003) 15(1) Canadian Journal of Women and the Law 167 ["Chilly Climate"].

41 Mr. Justice J.W. McClung, Court of Appeal of Alberta, Edmonton, "Right of Reply," Letters to the Editor, *National Post* (February 26, 1999) A19. On the unprecedented and unparalleled nature of the attack, see Alanna Mitchell, Jill Mahoney, and Sean Fine, "Legal Experts Outraged by Personal Attack on Supreme Court Judge" *Globe and Mail* (February 27, 1999) A1.

42 "Defence Lawyer Criticizes 'Radical Feminist' Ruling" *Toronto Star* (February 26, 1999) A7; "L'Heureux-Dubé Attacked as Support for McClung Builds" *Calgary Herald* (March 4, 1999) A12.

43 "Top Judge 'Tore Him to Pieces'" *National Post* (March 4, 1999) A05.

44 Edward L. Greenspan, "Judges Have No Right to Be Bullies" *National Post* (March 2, 1999) A18.

45 The case, ultimately decided by the Supreme Court of Canada, was *R. v. S. (R.D.)* (1997), 10 C.R. (5th) 1 (S.C.C.).

46 Constance Backhouse, "Bias in Canadian Law: A Lopsided Precipice" (1998) 10(1) Canadian Journal of Women and the Law 170 at 176 ["Bias in Canadian Law"].

47 *R. v. S. (R.D.)* (1997), 10 C.R. (5th) 1 (S.C.C.).

48 See, for example, *Royal Commission on the Donald Marshall, Jr., Prosecution* (Halifax: Royal Commission, 1989); *Report of the Aboriginal Justice Inquiry of Manitoba* (Winnipeg: Queen's Printer, 1991); *Report of the Royal Commission on Aboriginal Peoples* (Ottawa: Minister of Supply and Services, 1996); *Justice on Trial: Report of the Task Force on the Criminal Justice System and Its Impact on the Indian and Métis People of Alberta* (Edmonton: Task Force, 1991); *Report of the Royal Commission on Systemic Racism in the Ontario Criminal Justice System* (Toronto: Royal Commission, 1995). On the analysis of the decision of Justice Sparks, see Christine Boyle, "Case Comments, *R. v. R.D.S.:* An Editor's Forum" (1998) 10(1) Canadian Journal of Women and the Law 159.

49 Richard Devlin, "We Can't Go on Together with Suspicious Minds: Judicial Bias and Racialized Perspective in *R. v. R.D.S.*" (1995) 18 Dalhousie Law Journal 408 at 423.

50 See below for examples.

51 Backhouse, "Bias in Canadian Law," *supra* note 46; Backhouse, "Chilly Climate," *supra* note 48.

52 *R. v. Parks* (1993), 84 C.C.C. (3d) 353 at 369 (Ont. C.A.), leave to appeal denied [1994] 1 S.C.R. x.

53 See, for example, Sheila McIntyre, "Gender Bias within the Law School: 'The Memo' and Its Impact" in The Chilly Collective, eds., *Breaking Anonymity: The Chilly Climate for Women Faculty* (Waterloo: Wilfrid Laurier University Press, 1995) 211; and Bruce Feldthusen, "The Gender Wars: 'Where the Boys Are'" in The Chilly Collective, eds., *Breaking Anonymity: The Chilly Climate for Women Faculty* (Waterloo: Wilfrid Laurier University Press, 1995) 279. For a wider appraisal of these patterns, which beset women and racialized professors both inside and outside law faculties, see Constance Backhouse *et al.,* "The Chilly Climate for Faculty Women at Western: Postscript to the *Backhouse Report*" in The Chilly Collective, eds., *Breaking Anonymity: The Chilly Climate for Women Faculty* (Waterloo: Wilfrid Laurier University Press, 1995) 97; and The York Stories Collective, *York Stories: Women in Higher Education* (Toronto: TSAR, 2000).

54 See, for example, Patricia A. Monture-O Kanee, "Introduction: Surviving the Contradictions: Personal Notes on Academia" in The Chilly Collective, eds., *Breaking Anonymity: The Chilly Climate for Women Faculty* (Waterloo: Wilfrid Laurier University Press, 1995) 11; and Patricia Monture-Angus Thunder, *My Soul: A Mohawk Woman Speaks* (Halifax: Fernwood, 1995).

55 See, for example, Cornelia Schuh, "Justice on the Northern Frontier: Early Murder Trials of Native Accused" (1979) 22 Criminal Law Quarterly 74; Backhouse, *Colour-Coded, supra* note 13 at Chapters 3 and 4.

56 For a discussion of the activity of the KKK in Canada, the trial, and the appeal, which resulted in a short jail term for one of the Klansmen, see Backhouse, *Colour-Coded, supra* note 13 at Chapter 6.

57 Saskatchewan had been one of four Canadian provinces to pass a law limiting the right of Asian Canadian men to hire white women in the early twentieth century. For a discussion of the legislation and its enforcement, including the Yee Clun case, see *ibid.* at Chapter 5.

58 Backhouse, *Petticoats and Prejudice, supra* note 14 at Chapters 2 and 3; Constance Backhouse, "Attentat à la dignité du Parlement: Viol dans l'enceinte de la Chambre des communes, Ottawa 1929" (2001–2) 33(1) Ottawa Law Review 95; Constance Backhouse, "The Doctrine of Corroboration in Sexual Assault Trials in Early Twentieth Century Canada and Australia" (2001) 26(2) Queen's Law Journal 297; Constance Backhouse, "'Don't You Bully Me ... Justice I Want if There Is Justice to Be Had': The Rape of Mary Ann Burden, London, Ontario, 1907" in Constance Backhouse and Jon Swainger, eds., *People and Place: Historical Influences on Legal Culture* (Vancouver: UBC Press, 2003) 60.

59 T. Denison, *Recollections of a Magistrate* (Toronto: Musson Book Company, 1920), as cited in Carolyn Strange, *Toronto's Girl Problems: The Perils and Pleasures of the City, 1880–1930* (Toronto: University of Toronto Press, 1995) at 16, 153, 250; Winks, *supra* note 12 at 298; Backhouse, *Petticoats and Prejudice, supra* note 14 at 404; Gene Howard Homel, "Denison's Law: Criminal Justice and the Police Court in Toronto, 1877–1921" (1981) 73(3) Ontario History 171; Library and Archives Canada, MG29, E29, Denison Papers (Diaries 1850–1923 and Scrapbooks 1859–1925).

60 Strange, *supra* note 59 at 250; Winks, *supra* note 12 at 298; William Renwick Riddell, "Administration of Criminal Law in the Far North of Canada" (1929) 20 Journal of Criminal Law, Criminology, and Police Science 294.

61 Backhouse, *Petticoats and Prejudice, supra* note 14.

62 *Hawley v. Ham,* Midland District Assizes in Upper Canada, September 1826, unreported, as discussed in *ibid.* at Chapter 6.

63 *Re Inquiry Pursuant to Section 13(2) of Territorial Court Act: Re Inquiry into Conduct of Judge Bourassa,* [1990] N.W.T.R. 337.

64 "Report to the Canadian Judicial Council of the Inquiry Committee Established Pursuant to Subsection 63(1) of the Judges Act at the Request of the Attorney General of Nova Scotia" (August 1990).

7

The Helping Profession

Can *Pro Bono* Lawyers Make Sick
Children Well?

LORNE SOSSIN

Can *pro bono* lawyers make sick children well? Surprisingly, the answer might be yes. Or at least *pro bono* lawyers can improve patients' experiences and health outcomes for families caught up in the hospital system. There is an oft-repeated (perhaps apocryphal) story told of a child in Boston taken to the hospital for a respiratory disorder. After checking the chart, the doctor realized that he had treated the same child for the same illness twice before. After interviewing the child's distraught mother, the doctor realized that the heat in their apartment was routinely shut off by the landlord for non-payment of rent. "I can treat his lungs," the doctor said, "but this child needs a good lawyer to make him well."

Such stories led to a pioneering initiative in Boston to locate legal clinics in hospitals.[1] Word of this experiment reached Pro Bono Law Ontario (PBLO), an organization active in referring hospital cases to lawyers willing to take on *pro bono* cases. The benefits of coordinating such cases through a hospital-based *pro bono* clinic were clear, and the Family Legal Health Program, renamed PBLO at SickKids, was born. The press release accompanying the launch of the program in 2009 featured this perspective from the Director of Social Work at the hospital:

> Every day at SickKids, we see children who are affected by the social determinants of health, which are defined as the conditions in which people live and work that impact their health and well-being ... Being able to offer

onsite legal guidance to families who might not otherwise have access to lawyers will play a significant role in improving the health and well-being of these children and their families.[2]

Are lawyers working with PBLO at SickKids any different from lawyers working with paying clients with health-care or hospital administration disputes? Again, surprisingly, the answer might be yes. Below I explore this claim and its implications for legal ethics and professionalism.

What Is *Pro Bono,* and Why Is It Different?

Pro bono publico literally means "for the public good." The Canadian Bar Association, in adopting its 1998 resolution Promoting a *Pro Bono* Culture in the Legal Profession, defined lawyers as engaging in *pro bono* practice when they

> voluntarily contribute part of their time without charge or at substantially reduced rates, to establish or preserve the rights of disadvantaged individuals; and to provide legal services to assist organizations who represent the interests of, or who work on behalf of, members of the community of limited means or other public interest organizations, or for the improvement of laws or the legal system.[3]

For my analysis, I use the term simply to refer to legal services provided without expectation of compensation or personal gain. This should not suggest, however, that all *pro bono* practice serves the public interest or is focused on social justice.[4] As Deborah Rhode began her memorable inquiry into the principles and practice of *pro bono,*

> The American bar's commitment to provide legal service "pro bono publico" expresses what is most and least admirable in our profession. Over the course of their careers, many members of the bar contribute hundreds of unpaid hours to causes that would otherwise be priced out of the justice system. Some lawyers also give significant financial support to legal assistance for the poor. Yet the majority do not. Most lawyers make no contributions, and the average for the bar as a whole is less than half an hour a week and fifty cents a day. Moreover, much of what passes for "pro bono" is not aid to the indigent or public interest causes, but favors for friends, family, or clients, or cases where fees turn out to be uncollectible. The bar's pro bono commitments are, in short, a reflection of both the profession's highest ideals and its most grating hypocrisies.[5]

Although we are not always sure what *pro bono* practice is, nonetheless there has been a robust debate over whether it should be seen as an ethical requirement of legal professionalism. The rationale for this link between *pro bono* practice and legal professionalism has a clear point of departure. Since lawyers typically enjoy a monopoly on the delivery of many legal services, and since this creates an artificially high market value for these services, which in turn precludes large swaths of the public from accessing those services, do lawyers have a moral duty to address this gap? In other words, *pro bono* is the *quid pro quo* for lawyers' wealth and privilege.[6]

More recently, the debate has shifted to whether *pro bono* service should be a mandatory requirement for law students and/or lawyers.[7] *Pro bono* in this context lies at the intersection of two unsettled questions: the scope of legal ethics and professionalism, on the one hand, and the solution for improving access to otherwise unaffordable legal services, on the other. In other words, though few believe that the provision of *pro bono* services is a bad thing, the jury is still out on whether it should be a requirement for every lawyer and even more so on whether it is a solution to the dilemma of access to justice.

In May 2012, New York became the first state in the United States to require those wishing to become lawyers to engage in *pro bono* practice. As one observer noted,

> The legal profession faces a number of unprecedented challenges. They include an awful employment market, students graduating with sky high debt, competition from overseas, and lawsuits against law schools for fraudulently reporting employment data. Everybody who cares about the legal profession needs to be rethinking legal education and the delivery of legal services in light of these challenges. Given this state of affairs, I was somewhat surprised that Chief Judge Jonathan Lippman's May announcement that New York would become the first state to require bar applicants to perform pro bono service in order to gain admission received so much attention.[8]

While the debate over *pro bono* as a policy matter rages on, rarely do we hear about the realities of *pro bono* practice.[9] What are the unique challenges to legal professionalism to which *pro bono* practice gives rise? This chapter seeks to fill this lacuna. My focus is on the particular and compelling ethical issues that arise distinctly, if not uniquely, in the context of *pro bono* practice. Although one could examine ethical issues in *pro bono* practice across an array of settings (housing, immigration, etc.), I focus on the health setting, in which client problems are particularly compelling and access to legal services, for the most part, is out of reach to those who need it most. The insights from one *pro bono* setting might not all be applicable to others, but I believe that most will be and as a whole are sufficiently distinct from legal practice that is not *pro bono* so as to raise different but important ethical challenges.

PBLO at SickKids

One of the most innovative *pro bono* initiatives in Canada is PBLO at SickKids, launched at the Hospital for Sick Children (SickKids) in Toronto in 2009. Its mission is to provide legal services free of charge for patients and families referred by clinical staff (particularly social workers) in addition to engaging in other forms of informal dispute resolution and systemic advocacy in collaboration with doctors, lawyers, and other health professionals. This program has expanded to the Children's Hospital of Eastern Ontario, London Children's Hospital, and Holland Bloorview Kids Rehab Hospital, and it is poised to expand to several other hospitals in Ontario (and elsewhere in Canada).[10]

The program focuses on legal assistance that can have impacts on a child's health or a family's capacity to care for a sick child. The program involves training doctors, nurses, and social workers to identify cases that might require legal intervention; referring families to a lawyer whose office is at the hospital; offering legal information to families who need it; and providing access to legal services (sometimes through the lawyer at SickKids, sometimes through referral to a network of participating *pro bono* lawyers, in addition to a range of other legal services in the community). The lawyer at SickKids is also available to meet with families in the office or, if necessary, at the child's bedside, enabling parents to focus on their child. Cases dealt with to date have included housing, immigration, employment, special education, social benefits, and taxation, just to scratch the surface.

The Desbiens family has been featured in a number of discussions about the merits of the program and represents the kind of compelling legal need to which the program responds.[11] Charolette, the daughter of Cindy and Jeff Desbiens, was born with a rare form of congenital heart disease. She spent the first four and a half months of her life at SickKids with her parents by her side. When Cindy and Jeff tried to claim a tax credit for the more than

$12,000 in expenses incurred while travelling to and from their home in Waterloo during their daughter's stay at SickKids, the Canada Revenue Agency (CRA) denied their claim. They were told that the claim would be accepted only if Cindy or Jeff were travelling to receive treatment themselves. Since this was not the case, they were simply considered "visitors" and thus ineligible for the credit. "We needed to be by our daughter's side," Cindy told the CRA. "She was a newborn. She needed her parents' help to recover. How could they say we were just visiting?"[12]

The Desbiens family attempted to appeal the CRA's decision. A referral from their SickKids social worker to Pro Bono Law Ontario connected them with *pro bono* tax lawyers from McMillan LLP, one of the partner law firms of the program. With the assistance of counsel Michael Friedman, Ryan Morris, and Michael Templeton, who filed a Notice of Appeal in the Tax Court of Canada, they were able to resolve the issue and get reimbursed for their expenses. They continue to work with the lawyers to effect change in the current tax laws to help prevent other families from having to face the same challenges. "You never expect your children to be sick and when that happens, it has a huge impact on your family. This program reduced a lot of stress for our family. It means a lot to us," Cindy stated in an endorsement of the program.[13]

Although some of the *pro bono* work is meant to solve problems faced by families of sick children, other legal issues have impacts on children directly, such as the young boy told that he could not attend school because he was on oxygen or the young girl excluded from school because of recurring seizures.[14] In both cases, lawyers negotiated with the schools to ensure that both young people could continue to be educated with their peers rather than being isolated at home. Other clients present PBLO at SickKids with more complex and therefore time-consuming problems. For example, a *pro bono* lawyer successfully appealed the denial of health insurance coverage for a child referred to a hospital in the United States for life-saving treatment.[15] Particularly challenging are cases in which sick children belong to families that have been or are in the process of spousal disputes.[16]

What kinds of lawyers seek out *pro bono* services in this type of setting? Torkin Manes LLP lawyers Duncan Embury and Lisa Corrente are good examples. Both have taken on a range of Family Legal Health Program matters. The lawyer at SickKids can call on outside law firms for matters beyond quick advice or filling out forms. Torkin Manes indicates that more than a dozen of its lawyers have been involved with PBLO at SickKids, tackling the following range of cases:

- Obtaining continuation of long-term disability benefits for the mother of a severely ill child, allowing the mother to remain at her daughter's bedside
- Persuading an employer to change its workplace practices by which a child's illness was being exacerbated through airborne pollutants brought home on her father's clothing
- Assisting a mother in obtaining death benefits following the tragic death of her daughter
- Advising a disabled employee (who continues to receive treatment as an adult patient) on improvements to be made in her workplace so that she may continue to perform her job
- Representing a family dealing with living conditions that are adversely affecting their ill child.[17]

Typical of lawyers engaged in *pro bono* practice, the program partner lawyers at McMillan, Torkin Manes, and Bellissimo Law Group also manage busy practices of paying clients. In other words, they are not *pro bono* lawyers, but lawyers who happen to take on the occasional *pro bono* case.

The *pro bono* files, however, take on special significance for many of these lawyers. This might be because there is a particular quality and "payback" to volunteer work or because such files can enable a lawyer to mix the delivery of legal services with systemic change and law reform. Lisa Corrente, a partner in the Torkin Manes Labour Relations and Employment Group, for example, reported that her work on the program's Systemic Issues Working Group is particularly rewarding: "Helping health practitioners identify legal problems and advocate for legal change in fields that affect family health – where else would you be able to do that?"[18]

Systemic advocacy is the third part of the program, in addition to education of staff to spot legal issues and direct legal representation of families. The on-site lawyer is in a unique position to identify broader legal issues that can have impacts on the patient population. As part of the program, lawyers working with social workers, doctors, and nurses can identify and provide expertise on issues that affect children's health. This has resulted in advocacy with governments at all levels, test cases challenging the constitutionality of laws, and submissions on proposed legislation that will have impacts on the health and welfare of children. As evidence of the unique collaboration, a social worker and a lawyer made joint oral submissions to the Ontario legislature on the gaps in protection of and services for the most vulnerable, young people with complex medical issues, who lack the capacity to speak in their own best interests.[19]

Pro Bono Legal Ethics

Pro bono representation raises a host of distinct issues for legal ethics and professionalism. Using PBLO at SickKids as a case in point, I discuss three of these issues below.

Gatekeeping Ethics

When a lawyer charges for services or earns a salary to perform a set range of roles, gatekeeping is a relatively straightforward affair. When you pay for a lawyer's services, there is a legal ethics infrastructure that governs when and in what circumstances the lawyer will or will not act on your instructions. When a lawyer offers services without an expectation of being paid, however, the ethical canons governing when and in what circumstances a lawyer can or should take a case are less clear.

Under the "cab rank rule,"[20] a lawyer is supposed to take the next client in line regardless of how notorious the alleged wrongdoing or how odious the client. The rule underscores the difference between the role of counsel to advocate zealously on behalf of a client and other players in the legal system (*e.g.*, judges and juries) who pass judgment. There is an important exception to the cab rank rule, however, for clients who cannot pay. It is not unethical for a lawyer to refuse to represent a client who is unwilling or unable to pay for his or her services (though it becomes more complicated if the lawyer signed on when the client could pay and wants to abandon the case when the client no longer can pay).

In *pro bono* cases, the systemic logic of the cab rank rule is no longer available. Rather than asserting the right not to be turned away by a lawyer, a potential client must have a matter deemed by the lawyer worth taking on. Whereas a lawyer might be reconciled to representing people or institutions whether or not they seem to be worthwhile because she is getting paid (recognizing that, without such cases, the rent would go unpaid and payroll could not be met), the lawyer engaged in *pro bono* work makes a different calculus: is this matter worth the effort? This kind of gatekeeping creates new ethical dilemmas for *pro bono* counsel. Lee Ann Chapman, the PBLO lead at SickKids, describes the hardest moments for her when she has to say no to a family in need because there is no reasonable chance of a successful legal outcome.[21] Particularly challenging are immigration cases in which families face deportation. Although the program now has the expert assistance of Bellissimo Law Group, an immigration law firm, such cases lay bare the limitations both of law itself and of a way of meeting legal needs premised on finding the right lawyer to take on a case without charge.

Even in potentially promising cases, it is important to "manage the expectations" of clients. Referrals from PBLO at SickKids tend to be for consultations only. The firms then determine their own retainers and often impose limits on them. So, while in paid work clients might assume that as long as they pay the fees the lawyer will keep going and exhaust all possible legal avenues, the same is rarely the case in the context of *pro bono* work. Each step in a case is subject to the *pro bono* lawyer (and of course the client) being willing to take it to the next level.

Advocacy within and outside Boundaries

We tend to think of legal problems in a bubble. To most lawyers, legal problems are self-contained. They have a beginning, a middle, and an end. In reality, however, people do not tend to have "legal" problems. Rather, they just have problems. A relationship breaks down. A child is in trouble. A person loses his or her house or job, or a debt goes unpaid. It is the law itself that turns these personal problems into legal problems. Family law regulates how income is divided and children's needs are addressed when a relationship breaks down, provides recourse for people who have lost their homes or jobs, and dictates what happens after a debt goes unpaid. Just as laws define the scope of legal problems, so too can legal professionalism demarcate the scope of problem solving in which lawyers can engage.

Pro bono legal services can free lawyers to go beyond the silo of legal solutions to legal problems. At PBLO at SickKids, for example, lawyers work with doctors, social workers, hospital administrators, and a range of government officials to solve problems. Lee Ann Chapman, the staff lawyer for the program at SickKids when it was launched, viewed this "relationship building" among hospital staff as critical to the success of the program.[22] This relationship can also, in turn, change a lawyer's understanding of the scope of a "legal" problem. For example, because of family status issues, some children at SickKids have faced barriers in attempting to access the Make-A-Wish program, which grants seriously ill children the chance to fulfill a wished-for experience (e.g., going to Disneyworld or meeting a sports idol). Outside the SickKids context, it is unlikely that this would be seen as a legal problem to which a lawyer's advocacy is the solution. Through the PBLO at SickKids lens, however, it falls within the spectrum of dilemmas that can improve health outcomes, for which doctors, social workers, and other health professionals lack the skills to resolve on their own.

Similarly, in the context of the Desbiens family, the legal solution was not simply to ensure that the family had its tax credit but also to ensure that the

CRA changed its policy with respect to "visitors" when the family of a sick child is involved. In such cases, *pro bono* lawyers can more easily pursue systemic solutions.

The ethics of a lawyer's actions in the context of PBLO at SickKids might relate as much to particular health outcomes as to particular legal outcomes. *Pro bono* practice, in other words, often involves pushing past the boundaries of a lawyer's role and in this sense adds a fluidity and variability to legal professionalism that is often missing from the realm of paid work.

Pro Bono Work and the "Good Lawyer"

Just as PBLO at SickKids can expand the scope of advocacy, so too can it have a similar effect on legal professionalism. The act of volunteering or "donating" one's time is arguably an ethical act in the way that exchanging one's time for pay is not. *Pro bono* lawyering is encouraged by every branch of the legal community, from the judiciary to the Canadian Bar Association, from the law societies to the law schools. There is also a plausible argument that *pro bono* lawyers cannot act unethically. That is, even if a *pro bono* lawyer violates a well-accepted ethical rule – acting in a conflict of interest,[23] for example – there is the sense that what would otherwise be viewed as unethical is not when the lawyer is pursuing an altruistic goal. For example, a lawyer who contravenes a rule of professional conduct to increase fees might well be viewed differently than a lawyer who contravenes the same rule in a *pro bono* context in order to help a vulnerable client. This ambivalence toward legal ethics in the context of *pro bono* work stems from the fact that we associate unethical conduct with self-dealing or gaining an improper advantage. In addition, many ethical rules arise only in the context of paid work (e.g., rules related to financial disputes between lawyers and clients over billing practices). Put simply, does *pro bono* practice give lawyers a "get out of jail free" card that might make an otherwise unethical act acceptable (or at least mitigate any consequences for the lawyer)?

In several jurisdictions, the *Rules of Professional Conduct* themselves have been adjusted to reflect the fact that *pro bono* practice is "different." In Ontario, for example, conflict of interest rules for "unbundled" legal services are less strict where the limited retainer is part of a *pro bono* initiative. The "commentary" to this rule provides that

> Short term limited legal service programs are usually offered in circum-
> stances in which it may be difficult to systematically screen for conflicts of

interest in a timely way, despite the best efforts and existing practices and procedures of Pro Bono Law Ontario (PBLO) and the lawyers and law firms who provide these services. Performing a full conflicts screening in circumstances in which the pro bono services described in subrule (15) are being offered can be very challenging given the timelines, volume and logistics of the setting in which the services are provided. The time required to screen for conflicts may mean that qualifying individuals for whom these brief legal services are available are denied access to legal assistance.

Subrules (15) to (19) apply in circumstances in which the limited nature of the legal services being provided by a lawyer significantly reduces the risk of conflicts of interest with other matters being handled by the lawyer's firm. Accordingly, the lawyer is disqualified from acting for a client receiving short-term limited legal services only if the lawyer has actual knowledge of a conflict of interest between the pro bono client and an existing or former client of the lawyer, the lawyer's firm or PBLO. For example, a conflict of interest of which the lawyer has no actual knowledge but which is imputed to the lawyer because of the lawyer's membership in or association or employment with a firm would not preclude the lawyer from representing the client seeking short-term limited legal services. The lawyer's knowledge would be based on the lawyer's reasonable recollection and information provided by the client in the ordinary course of the consultation and in the client's application to PBLO for legal assistance.[24]

This approach to the *Rules of Professional Conduct* alleviates lawyers from taking on clients for *pro bono* work with PBLO at SickKids, where, for example, a client's dispute is with a large health insurance company that the lawyer's firm, in separate retainers, might represent. That said, conflicts of interest continue to be barriers to *pro bono* representation, particularly in settings (as is often the case with PBLO at SickKids) in which the lawyer must provide more than just summary advice.

Although a *pro bono* lawyer will be subject to somewhat different rules than other lawyers, the basis for this differentiation merits closer scrutiny. A number of behavioural theories reject the notion of pure altruism as a motivating factor in voluntary activities such as *pro bono* lawyering. A range of self-interested motivations might enter the calculations of a lawyer who agrees to provide services without charge – from feeling good about oneself to stature in the community to gaining valuable experience and profile to more situational benefits (e.g., helping out a friend or colleague). The very premise of *pro bono* practice, as noted above, contemplates that personal gain should not enter into the equation. As PBLO at SickKids demonstrates, however, the dividing lines are not always so clear.

The law firm of Torkin Manes, for example, derives no revenue or personal gain for its lawyers when they take on *pro bono* cases from the program. The firm as a whole, however, can enjoy a range of tangible benefits from its involvement in the program. Its website markets the program as a way to enhance the goodwill of the firm to clients to generate new business and enhance existing business and to recruit students. The firm goes on to highlight that two of its lawyers have received a Lexpert Zenith Pro Bono Award for their work at SickKids.[25]

Pro bono representation can generate value for a lawyer or firm in more concrete ways than just goodwill and positive profile. *Pro bono* representation can be used by lawyers or law firms, for example, to enhance the training of lawyers (based on the problematic belief that "less" might be at stake when a client is not paying). Typically (though the practice varies), lawyers who engage in *pro bono* practice can "count" the hours spent toward their billable hour totals. Paul Schabas (the lead partner for *pro bono* activities at the law firm of Blake, Cassels and Graydon LLP) has described this practice as "a way of putting your money where your mouth is."[26] Although this signals to the lawyer that the work matters, at some point it ceases to represent work undertaken without expectation of compensation.

An interesting question has also arisen with respect to *pro bono* representation and costs. If a case is taken on *pro bono*, but with the expectation that a victory might bring a costs award, is it truly *pro bono* (i.e., work done for the public good without compensation)? If so, how does this differ from contingency fee arrangements (i.e., a lawyer who expects to be compensated if successful but willing to bear the financial risk of an unsuccessful outcome)? One key difference is the *expectation* of compensation. The *pro bono* lawyer does not expect to be paid a fee but might receive costs if successful and if the court awards costs. The lawyer who undertakes representation on a contingency basis, in contrast, does expect to receive compensation at the conclusion of a case if the client is successful and enters into a formal agreement with the client setting out this contingent entitlement to compensation.

The Ontario Court of Appeal addressed this issue in the 2006 *Cavalieri* case,[27] a corporate matter involving a default judgment that the successful party's lawyer had taken on *pro bono*. Neither the Ontario *Rules of Civil Procedure* nor the *Courts of Justice Act*, two authorities governing the awarding of costs in civil matters in Ontario, address the *pro bono* issue. In its decision, the Court of Appeal accepted that costs should be available at least in some circumstances for parties represented by *pro bono* counsel and adopted "access to justice" as a newly recognized cost criterion in Ontario. To do otherwise, it was argued, would be to place significant disincentives for lawyers who take on cases on this basis (particularly lawyers who practise on their own or in small firms).

Although the Court concluded that it was appropriate for lawyers to have incentives to undertake *pro bono* cases, should they forfeit the benefits of taking on a *pro bono* matter as an ethical matter, where they might stand to profit at the end of the day after all? Perhaps the ethical lens of *pro bono* work should not be that of the virtue of the lawyer but the needs of the client. To the child and her or his family at SickKids, does it matter whether the lawyer at Torkin Manes includes the hours spent on their legal matter as part of his or her billable hours? Either way the needs of clients are being met at no cost to them. From this lens, however, the distinction between *pro bono* and contingency fee representation (or, for that matter, representing a party that qualifies for a legal aid certificate) appears to be less clear.[28] In other words, how and why a lawyer takes on a case at no charge to the client matters (at least to the model of legal professionalism being pursued). The ethics of *pro bono* practice, in this sense, must be attentive both to the lawyer's perspective and to the client's perspective.

Conclusion

Although lawyers are encouraged to undertake *pro bono* work for mostly good reasons, the implications for legal ethics and professionalism are less clear. Deborah Rhode once referred to a "trickle up" effect of *pro bono* work.[29] PBLO at SickKids certainly has witnessed some trickling up. The program, as noted above, is expanding to additional hospitals in Toronto, Ottawa, and London, with more lawyers and firms signing on. Although *pro bono* legal service might not be the answer (or the *only* answer) to access to justice, its success leads to important questions for legal ethics and professionalism. When fees and charges are removed from the equation, how is serving a client's needs (or solving a client's problem) viewed differently? As PBLO at SickKids vividly demonstrates, many lawyers have a deeply rooted desire to help others that their "day job" might not satisfy.

As former Chief Justice Roy McMurtry said at the founding of Pro Bono Law Ontario (and on many other occasions), law is a "helping profession."[30] *Pro bono* representation of the kind featured in PBLO at SickKids allows this aspect of legal professionalism to be given fuller expression. This does not mean that *pro bono* practice does not have its share of ethical challenges and dilemmas. And many of them remain to be fully worked out. Even with its complications, however, the *pro bono* story might well be the one that most captivates the imagination of the public. If lawyers can help to heal sick children, and act in the interests of vulnerable groups without expectation of personal benefit, then there might be hope yet for the legal profession.

Notes

I am grateful to Lee Ann Chapman for sharing some of her experiences with PBLO at SickKids that inform and enrich this chapter. All errors and omissions are my own.

1 Erik Eckholm, "When Doctor's Visit Leads to Legal Help," *New York Times* (March 23, 2010), referring to Barry Zuckerman, Chief of Pediatrics at Boston Medical Center, as pioneering this model in the early 1990s, online: New York Times, http://www.nytimes.com/glogin?URI=http%3A%2F%2Fwww.nytimes.com%2F2010%2F03%2F24%2Fus%2F24legal.html%3F_r%3D1.

2 "SickKids and Pro Bono Law Ontario Launch Canada's First Program to Prescribe Legal Remedies in a Hospital Setting" (November 10, 2009), online: SickKids, http://www.sickkids.ca/AboutSickKids/Newsroom/Past-News/2009/Family_Legal_Health_Program%20.html.

3 CBA Resolution 98-01-A. See Standing Committee on Pro Bono, online: CBA, http://www.cba.org/CBA/groups/probono/.

4 I have explored this question in earlier work, including, for example, L. Sossin, "Professionalism and Pro Bono" in K. Tranter, ed., *Re-Affirming Legal Ethics* (London: Routledge-Cavendish, 2009); and L. Sossin, "The Public Interest, Professionalism, and Pro Bono Publico" (2008) 46 Osgoode Hall Law Journal 131. See also Rob Atkinson, "A Social-Democratic Critique of Pro Bono Publico Representation of the Poor: The Good as the Enemy of the Best" (2001) 9 Journal of Gender, Social Policy, and the Law 129, online: http://digitalcommons.wcl.american.edu/cgi/viewcontent.cgi?article=1386&context=jgspl; and Justice J.C. Major, "Lawyers' Obligation to Provide Legal Services" (1995) 33 Alberta Law Review 719.

5 Deborah Rhode, "Pro Bono in Principle and Practice" (2003) Stanford Public Law and Legal Theory Research Series, Research Paper No. 66 at 1.

6 See the discussion in Alice Woolley, "Access to Justice" in Alice Woolley *et al.*, eds., *Lawyers' Ethics and Professional Regulation*, 2d ed. (Toronto: LexisNexis, 2012) at Chapter 12.

7 See Robert Granfield and Lynn Mather, eds., *Private Lawyers and the Public Interest: The Evolving Role of Pro Bono in the Legal Profession* (New York: Oxford University Press, 2009).

8 B. Cooper, "Mandatory Pro Bono for New York Bar Applicants: Why Not?" (2012), online: American Bar Association, http://www.americanbar.org/content/dam/aba/administrative/professional_responsibility/tpl_21_3_20121105.authcheckdam.pdf.

9 See Granfield and Mather, *supra* note 7.

10 Christopher Guly, "A Legal Prescription for Families with Sick Kids: Pro Bono Law Ontario Program Expands to Ottawa Region" *Lawyers Weekly* (March 28, 2014) 22; P. Small, "Lawyers Donate Expertise to Sick Kids Families" *Toronto Star* (January 8, 2012), online: Toronto Star, http://www.thestar.com/news/gta/2012/01/08/lawyers_donate_expertise_to_sick_kids_families.html.

11 *Supra* note 2.

12 *Ibid.*

13 *Ibid.*

14 Interview with Lee Ann Chapman, December 2013.

15 *Ibid.*

16 *Ibid.*

17 Torkin Manes listed these aspects of its work with PBLO as it shared in a Zenith Leadership Award in 2010 for its participation in the Family Legal Health Program See http://www.newswire.ca/fr/story/630399/innovative-family-legal-health-program-wins-award.

18 *Ibid.*

19 *Supra* note 14.

20 See Gavin MacKenzie, *Lawyers and Ethics: Professional Responsibility and Discipline* (Toronto: Carswell, 1998) at 4-4.

21 Interview with Lee Ann Chapman, December 2013.

22 *Ibid.*

23 See 3.4-1 of the Law Society of Upper Canada *Rules of Professional Conduct.*

24 Law Society of Upper Canada, *Rules of Professional Conduct,* Rules 2.04(15)–(19).

25 See online: Torkin Manes, http://www.torkinmanes.com/about-us/community-involvement.

26 Law Society of British Columbia, "The Future of Pro Bono in Canadian Law Firms" (2004) Bencher Bulletin No. 3, online: Law Society of British Columbia, http://www.lawsociety.bc.ca/page.cfm?cid=1450.

27 *1465778 Ontario Inc. v. 1122077 Ontario Ltd.* (2006), 82 O.R. (3d) 757 (C.A.).

28 Law Society of Upper Canada, "Contingency Fees," online: Law Society of Upper Canada, http://www.lsuc.on.ca/ContingencyFees/.

29 Deborah L. Rhode, "Legal Education: Professional Interests and Public Values" (2000) 34 Indiana Law Review 23 at 43.

30 R. Roy McMurtry, "The Legal Profession and Public Service" (2004) (remarks to the Third Colloquium of the Chief Justice Advisory Committee on Professionalism), online: Law Society of Upper Canada, http://www.lsuc.on.ca/media/third_colloquium_mcmurtry.pdf at 3.

8
A New Wave of Access to Justice Reform in Canada

TREVOR C.W. FARROW

There is a tide in the affairs of men
Which, taken at the flood, leads on to fortune;
Omitted, all the voyage of their life
Is bound in shallows and in miseries.
On such a full sea are we now afloat,
And we must take the current when it serves
Or lose our ventures.

– WILLIAM SHAKESPEARE, *JULIUS CAESAR*,
ACT IV, SCENE III, LL. 218–24[1]

This chapter is about access to justice. In particular, it is about a new wave of access to justice reform starting to wash over Canada's legal community. At first blush, this might seem like an odd choice of topic for a collection of Canadian legal ethics stories – particularly one focused primarily on individual lawyers, their cases, and their clients. However, though this is admittedly not a chapter about an individual lawyer, case, or client, it involves stories relevant to all lawyers, cases, and clients. Put differently, it is a discussion about an issue – access to justice reform – becoming one of the defining challenges, as well as one of the most promising developments, for the Canadian legal profession. How lawyers regulate themselves and how they practise law are central questions of legal ethics and professionalism.

As the new wave, or tide, of access to justice research, thinking, and reform demonstrates, current approaches to practice and regulation fail to address the everyday legal needs of Canadians as well as the barriers that they face in trying to address those needs. New approaches to professionalism are needed.

In the spirit of the storytelling approach of this collection, I develop this chapter largely by weaving together two stories. The first is a story about justice, access to justice, and in particular what everyday Canadians think about those issues. Over the past number of years, I have been involved in numerous academic conferences and policy debates – with members of all sectors of the legal community – discussing what to do about access to justice. There is no lack of promising ideas from those who work within the system about what we should do for those who use the system. In the context of those discussions, I heard myself saying more and more often that, if we asked people on the street what they think about justice and access to it, we might get a very different view. Rather than continue to guess what people might say, I decided to ask them.[2] When first approached about their views on justice, people who participated in this survey provided some candid and amusing responses, including "Shit ... this is like a test!" and "Oh my God this is terrible!"[3] However, what people ultimately said, some of which I will share in this chapter, is enlightening in terms of how to think about and potentially reform the justice system.

The second story in this chapter, really my main focus, is about a particular organization that represents, and in many ways defines, a new reform agenda. That organization is the Action Committee on Access to Justice in Civil and Family Matters.[4] It is a national initiative, created in 2008 at the invitation of the Chief Justice of Canada, designed to address the growing inaccessibility of civil and family justice in this country. Although the story of the Action Committee is not linked formally in any way to the story of the justice survey, told together they form a dialectic designed to animate our understanding of the challenges, and some potential solutions, facing Canada's legal system today.

Access to Justice

What Does It Mean?
An increasing amount of thinking is being devoted to the topic of access to justice and access to justice reform.[5] I will be relatively brief here.[6] There are essentially two ways to think about access to justice. One view, the

traditional view, largely sees access to justice in terms of access to legal services – primarily including lawyers, courts, and judges.[7] The other view, more recent, sees access to justice more in terms of what those processes can and should provide for those who use the system: namely, the public.

The traditional approach to access to justice primarily brings a systems perspective to the issue, meaning that it approaches the discussion largely from the perspective of the legal system (the provider) as opposed to the user (the public). According to this systems view, to the extent that we increase people's access to courts and tribunals by lowering wait times, making trials more efficient, and to the extent that we increase the availability of lawyers, perhaps by increasing the number of lawyers who can practise law in a given jurisdiction or decreasing what they charge, we increase access to justice. Put simply, people will have an easier time accessing lawyers and getting their matters to and through the courts more efficiently and cost effectively if we improve the systems of law. These systems-based procedural considerations and improvements are important, particularly in the context of issues and conflicts that require these kinds of legal interventions. There is no doubt that, if a matter needs to go to court, and if a client needs to pay for a lawyer in order to get advice on that matter, access to the system will have been improved if the system and the people providing those services are available more efficiently and cost effectively, allowing more people access to those services.

However, as a preliminary concern, this traditional view of access to justice – which starts primarily from the perspective of the system as opposed to the user – often downplays or disregards the nuances and complexities of everyday social problems that people face and that either do not always need or never reach the formal justice system. It assumes that all problems are legal problems, it assumes that they all need lawyers and courts, and it assumes that most people can access and afford legal assistance. Although many social issues benefit greatly from legal assistance, many problems dressed up as legal problems also involve numerous other challenges and issues. For example, a young person struggling with behavioural problems at school might have a learning challenge or disability. Such issues often lead to anti-social and other problematic behaviours that bring young people into contact with the law. If the issue is seen as a social issue, early on, and not (only) as a legal issue, then appropriate support can be provided.

The point here, as many have commented, is that to a hammer everything looks like a nail. If we always come from a legal perspective, we see problems largely as legal problems. Alternatively, in this example, the young person might be struggling at school because, as a result of a parent's termination of employment the previous year, home life has become chaotic (or even violent and traumatic). The learning issue might still be a learning issue, but in fact it might be a derivative behavioural issue. If the parent's employment issue had been identified and addressed earlier – perhaps both with legal assistance and with job retraining and support – the other domestic problems could have been mitigated, and the child's school issues might never have come up. To the extent that we try to solve all social issues with legal tools, or to the extent that we do not see social issues as having legal components, much is missed. When thinking about access to justice, we need to recognize at least the complex, multidimensional realities of everyday social and legal problems.

Of course, this is not merely an abstract, theoretical discussion. As several respondents to the justice survey indicated, access to justice is about much more than courts and lawyers. For example, according to one respondent, "[t]here are people ... working 16 hours a day ... who have to choose between food and shelter. That's not just. And why ... we're not ... able to take care of our own population in a way that meets anybody's basic ... standards ... is beyond me."[8] According to another, "[t]he biggest thing is taking care of the disenfranchised ... because what's enfranchisement other than accessibility ... ?"[9] These are real people with real concerns about everyday challenges. To the extent that the system is unable to engage with those challenges, there are real questions about its utility and accessibility.

To the degree that we improve how we address everyday social issues (including legal issues) in order to provide those things that people need and want, then – in line with a more modern view of justice – we succeed in increasing access to justice. And to do so, we need to start from the premise of what the public needs, not – at least as a starting point – what the legal system currently can offer. We need to start seeing our role as providers of justice in terms of the real stuff of life: help with addictions, food, housing, empowerment, and dignity. Ultimately, these are the types of help that people want. Starting with the end in mind, a focus on the public is a defining feature of a more modern and expansive approach to justice and access to it. It starts with both the simplicity and the complexity of everyday legal problems and tries to build an approach to justice from the perspective of those who experience those problems.

What Is the Problem?
Although in Canada we enjoy one of the strongest legal systems in the world, there is currently a major problem of access to justice. Many members of

various sectors of our system have recognized the problem. For example, according to the Chief Justice of Canada, "we do not have adequate access to justice in Canada."[10] Bluntly put, as the former Chief Justice of Ontario commented, the system is in "crisis."[11] More recently, Justice D.M. Brown described the civil justice system as "sinking" and having "a life of its own" that "grinds relentlessly on and downward."[12] These are not flattering descriptions.

And our judiciary is not alone in its concern. For example, according to responses from a recent survey of Canadian court workers, the "general public has no idea about court procedures, requirements, the language, who or where to go for help," and as a result the "civil system [is] ... very much open to abuse by those with more money at their disposal."[13] Similar concerns were also raised by members of the public through the justice survey. For example, according to one respondent, "[p]eople with money have access to more justice than people without."[14] According to other respondents, "I think it comes down to class. The higher class have more access to justice"; similarly, "[a]ccess to justice looks really different depending on who you are and where you come from ... because so much of justice and so much of anything related to justice ... intersects [with] ... class, gender, race."[15] Furthermore, according to a recent report from the Law Society of Upper Canada, the problem is not going away and seems to be getting worse, so the need for reform is even greater.[16]

On what basis are these various comments from the judiciary, court workers, the public, regulators, and others being made? Unfortunately, there is a growing body of research – a "mountain of evidence"[17] – to support this view. As a starting point, it is important to acknowledge that justice, and access to it, do not comprise a niche issue. Quite the opposite: almost half of Canadians will encounter a legal problem over a three-year period; put differently, essentially all Canadians will encounter one over their lifetimes.[18] Furthermore, not all Canadians will experience legal issues in the same way. Vulnerable and equity-seeking groups are more likely to face legal problems.[19] As we have seen from important work on various equity-seeking groups in our communities, the justice system is often particularly inaccessible and alienates those who need it most.[20] Similar views were expressed by respondents to the justice survey, many of whom identified the following factors as hampering access to justice: "language," "education," "culture," "age," "sexual orientation," "poverty," "homeless[ness]," "immig[ration]," and "mental illness."[21] Research also indicates that legal problems tend to cluster and can lead to other legal, social, and health-related problems,[22] making life more difficult[23] and leading to the use of other sources of public assistance and services.[24]

Overall, there is a gap in justice: a divide between which legal services people need and what they can afford and access. The result, of course, is that a significant number of legal needs go unmet and result in social, economic, and health costs individually and societally. The following anecdote from one of the justice survey respondents makes this point clearly:

> I paid down on an apartment ... I didn't get it ... so I wanted my money back. I couldn't get my money back because the guy ... didn't give me back my cash and I didn't know how to go about it, I was new to the country ... I just checked at the tenant board ... But it just looked like it was gonna be a lot stressful for me just to take that upon myself to try to figure that out. So I was just like, whatever, leave that.[25]

Not only did this person not get the apartment, and not only did he not get his deposit back, but also he suffered the stress and lost opportunity and related costs that go with these challenges and systemic failings. And he is far from alone. According to other justice survey respondents, "I have a family law situation that I can't afford to address – I have to just let it go"; "[a]s far as I know, it's going to cost you ... [S]o ... when I have issues, I just leave it – whatever"; "I work three jobs – am I gonna take off ... my full day to go pursue this? Probably not, so I'm just gonna let this slide"; and "[m]ost people ... if it's not criminal ... won't pursue it – like if it's a racial thing ... employ[ment] ... discrimination, I don't think they would pursue it."[26] These stories represent, in real-life terms, the concrete, everyday failings – and resulting costs – of our increasingly inaccessible justice system. Something significant needs to be done.

Action Committee on Access to Justice in Civil and Family Matters

Background
It was with this problematic access to the justice landscape in mind that the Action Committee was created in 2008 at the invitation of the Chief Justice of Canada, the Action Committee's Honorary Chair. She was motivated by her opinion that, at the turn of the millennium, we were "increasingly failing in our responsibility to provide a justice system that was accessible, responsive and citizen-focused."[27] Several specific aspects of her opinion animated the creation and work of the Action Committee, including its focus on

broad national collaboration ("*our* responsibility") and its primary emphasis on accessibility for those who use the system ("accessible, responsive and *citizen*-focused").

The Action Committee's focus on collaboration is a unique and distinguishing feature of this initiative. According to the Chief Justice of Canada, the "broad consensus among the stakeholders on the Action Committee ... is unprecedented and gives us an important foundation for change."[28] Unlike many other important reform efforts, which typically have been pursued by individual organizations,[29] the Action Committee's approach was to bring together a collaborative, wide-ranging, and nationally diverse group that represents as many aspects of and voices in the civil and family justice system as possible. Specifically included in the Action Committee's membership are governments, the judiciary, the bar (including regulators and lawyers' organizations), legal aid, legal education, *pro bono* and other non-governmental organizations, court administrators, the academy, and – perhaps most importantly – the public.[30] The work of this large group was primarily directed by a smaller Steering Committee.[31] The entire process was chaired by the Honourable Thomas Cromwell of the Supreme Court of Canada.

In terms of the interest of the Action Committee in being "accessible, responsive and citizen-focused,"[32] it started by clarifying which definition of access to justice would guide its work. Not surprisingly, of the two approaches discussed earlier in this chapter, the Action Committee was guided by a more expansive, public-centred approach. Specifically, according to the Action Committee,

> [w]hen thinking about access to justice, the starting point and consistent focus of the Action Committee is on the broad range of legal problems experienced by the public – not just those that are adjudicated by courts. Key to this understanding of the justice system is that it looks at everyday legal problems from the point of view of the people experiencing them.[33]

Taking an expansive, public-centred approach to access to justice is significant – in fact it is revolutionary – in terms of civil and family justice reform in Canada. Reaching a broad national consensus and involving all major justice stakeholders had not happened before in this country. Without it, no meaningful, transformative reform could follow. If this was the only thing that the Action Committee had accomplished, then its work would have been significant in terms of signalling the importance – to all justice stakeholders – of adopting a public-focused, legal needs approach to access to justice.

Working Groups and Final Report

Of course, that was just the start. From there, the Action Committee looked at the needs of the users of, and the problems facing, the civil and family justice system, and it decided on four key areas of reform most needed: court process simplification; access to legal services; prevention, triage, and referral; and family law – again all with the public as the primary focus of attention. Working groups were formed for each topic and included members of the Action Committee as well as other members of the Canadian legal community. Over the next several years, research and surveys were conducted, and ultimately four working group reports were produced.[34] These reports were essentially designed to identify key issues, fundamental needs, current problems, promising initiatives, and future areas for action-oriented reform. Again, if these reports were the end of the Action Committee's work, then much would have been accomplished: specific, issue-focused reports with broad consultation, broad consensus, and significant practical potential.

Following this working group process and with the working group reports in hand, the Steering Committee, in consultation with the full Action Committee, began the process of producing a final report. In the spirit of the Action Committee's earlier work, this process was also very collaborative, leading to publication of the final report in October 2013.[35] Having been directly involved, I can say that I have never been part of such an active and engaged writing project. All stakeholders were consulted and engaged, which resulted in a rich and diverse approach as well as broad support and buy-in.

There are several defining aspects of the report, which I briefly mention here, not only because of their significance for the Action Committee's work, but also because I think that they could be very useful for future reports and reform processes of a similar nature. In terms of its format, the report needed to be accessible to a number of audiences, including policy makers, researchers, service providers, the media, and the public. It therefore needed to be relatively short, written in accessible language, and replete with enough research and detail to be practically useful for all readers.

In terms of its content, the final report was also not meant simply to summarize the four working group reports, which had already been published. Rather, it was designed to provide something new – not just different from

the working group reports but also different from any prior report on justice reform. It also needed to be acceptable to all of the Action Committee
members. Again, several key elements emerged. The first part of the report
was designed to do two things.[36] First, the report provides an expansive view
of access to justice, pursuant to expanding the accepted scope of national
access to justice thinking. Second, the Action Committee wanted plainly to
acknowledge the access to justice problem, in unvarnished terms, together
with the justice gap that currently exists between what people need and
what they can access and afford. Various voices are heard, including those of
respondents to the justice survey. A clear acknowledgment of the significance of the problem is important in terms of understanding the scope of
the issue and getting the attention of those who need to be involved in the
process of reform.

The second part of the report, in my view, is its most innovative and
important contribution.[37] In a nutshell, it provides a basis for change in the
way that we approach justice reform in Canada. In order to make significant
changes, a necessary first step is to lay the groundwork for a culture shift.
Specifically, unless we change how we approach reform, we will continue
along well-trodden paths that, though important, have not been successful
in seriously addressing the challenges of access to justice in this country. Six
key elements were identified as necessary parts of that culture shift.

First, we need to put the public first. All reform thinking needs to start
from the perspective of those who use the system to deal with various everyday problems that they face. Responsiveness to actual needs is critical;
otherwise, the system will continue to recreate itself in its own image.

Second, we must collaborate and coordinate. In a country that largely
administers justice provincially (particularly civil and family justice),[38] it has
become all too common for projects to be pursued in isolation, without any
coordination in terms of lessons learned, best practices, and funding strategies. Furthermore, to address everyday problems that often share both
legal and non-legal dimensions, coordination among legal and other social
and health-care providers is necessary if we want to provide the services
that people actually need.

Third, the system must prevent and educate. We are better off preventing
legal problems at the outset, largely by equipping people to recognize,
understand, and try to avoid legal issues as far as possible before they become major problems.

Fourth, in terms of the justice system, we need to simplify it and make it
more coherent, proportional, and sustainable, particularly if we are to draw

the public into the process of justice care. At the moment, as we know from many reports,[39] the public finds the system foreign and inaccessible. Respondents to the justice survey had the same view. For example, according to several respondents, "[t]he language of justice tends to be ... foreign to most people," and "I never really know anything about justice."[40]

Fifth, we need to take action. Although research and thinking are important, we are at the stage now at which action needs to occur. According to one of the working group reports, we need to "move beyond wise words"[41] if we are going to make any kind of meaningful change on the ground.

Sixth, we need to focus on outcomes. In line with the public-focused approach to access to justice discussed earlier, and as expressed by many of the respondents to the justice survey, people typically want not more process but better results.[42] Our approach to justice reform must recognize that reality.

The Action Committee believes that this six-point culture shift, though not a sufficient precondition, is a necessary precondition for any meaningful transformation of justice to occur.[43]

The third part of the report provides a concrete plan for action – a nine-point "roadmap" to help bridge the current access to justice gap.[44] The idea was not to provide generalities and principles but to provide specific and measurable suggestions for concrete action. Several aspects are worthy of note.

First, because of the local nature of how civil and family justice is largely administered in Canada,[45] the Action Committee did not take a top-heavy approach. Rather, it saw its role as collaborative, facilitative, and suggestive, one ultimately of a leadership as opposed to an authoritative nature – because, in the end, mostly local stakeholders will implement significant and "on the ground" reforms. For that reason, animated by the specific concerns and principles set out in the first two parts of the report, this roadmap suggests avenues for reform that provide ideas and examples of promising practices and options.

Second, animated by an expansive understanding of access to justice, the roadmap is designed to speak to all members and aspects of the civil and family justice system, including not only judges and lawyers but also – primarily – the public. It understands the system in terms of the public's everyday problems, and it provides suggestions and solutions directed at those problems.

Third, it speaks at several different levels of reform. It provides suggestions for specific, on-the-ground action items for innovation (expanding

the "front end" of the justice system, including triage and public legal education, redeveloping courts as multi-service centres for dispute resolution,
reimagining family services, *etc.*). Some of these front-end, prevention-
oriented goals resonate with the views of some of the respondents to the
justice survey. For example, according to one respondent, "[p]erhaps a little
more of an effort can be spent in education campaigns [in] ... public school
... to prevent maybe heading off to jail or heading off to court or heading off
to probation ... Prevent it before it starts."[46] Similarly, according to another
respondent, "[j]ustice incorporates our life ... [P]erhaps it can be taught in
school as a life skill so that kids are more aware of what it means to make a
choice and do the right thing for themselves and each other."[47]

Fourth, the roadmap provides suggestions for new structural thinking
(creation of access to justice implementation mechanisms, suggestions for
legal education reform, *etc.*). Furthermore, it provides research and funding
goals (an access to justice research agenda and sustained and coherent funding strategies).

Fifth, the roadmap does all of this with an eye on progress and concrete
measurement, through the use of specific goals and timelines. The motivation behind this aspect of the third part of the report came from the Millennium Development Goals of the United Nations.[48] Important for this
approach was that the suggestions be specific, both practical and aspira-
tional, achievable by a specific date, and measurable in terms of development and success.

With the final report in hand, there were two options in terms of what
to do next. One option was simply to publish the report and then sit back
and hope that people would notice it and do something. The other option,
which the Action Committee adopted, was to be more active and engaged.
Following an initial press release,[49] the Action Committee, largely through
the efforts of Justice Cromwell and several members of the Steering Committee, took the final report on a "road show." Over the late fall of 2013,
stopping in most major centres, they delivered, discussed, and often "work-
shopped" the report. Events were typically hosted by local bar or other
justice stakeholder groups, attended by many members of various legal
groups and stakeholders, and very successful in terms of raising the profile
not only of the final report but also, more importantly, of the challenges to
and opportunities for improving access to justice that the report is designed
to address. This active, whistle-stop approach to justice reform was another
unique and significant feature of the Action Committee's work.

Finally, in January 2014, the Action Committee held a two-day colloquium in Toronto.[50] There were several purposes behind this initiative. The Action Committee wanted to bring together leaders of the various national and provincial justice communities – those who will be the change makers – to discuss the report, the results of the road show, and most importantly the next steps. The idea was to develop a shared vision of action items that could be taken back to local and regional organizations for discussion and, hopefully, piloting and implementation. The Action Committee also wanted to stimulate the development of local and national coalition groups – access to justice commissions – to help with implementing, monitoring, and measuring access to justice initiatives on the ground. Finally, the Action Committee wanted to discuss the next steps for its work, the first phase of which came to an end with the colloquium.[51] Those discussions are ongoing.

What will come of all this is still to be seen. Based on the early uptake of many of the Action Committee's recommendations, there is good reason to be hopeful, but there is also reason to be cautious. Many reports and reform efforts, predating the work of the Action Committee, came and went with relatively little major improvement to the justice system. Skeptics cannot be faulted for wondering whether this report, and these efforts, will be any different. The Action Committee itself recognizes that it is not the body that will ultimately create change. Rather, it can simply provide leadership by laying out a plan that, if implemented, should lead to significant improvements. Furthermore, much more engagement with the public is necessary if we are going to see major gains in making the system more accessible to and reflective of the communities that it is meant to serve. Although the Action Committee went out of its way to include a representative of the public in all of its work, much more should be done going forward to increase the number and diversity of members of the public actively engaged in these reform efforts.

However, having said all that, and notwithstanding potential reasons for skepticism, the creation of the Action Committee, the process by which it conducted its work, and the fruits of its labour have been significant successes. Largely through the vision of its leadership, but also because of the collaborative hard work of an extremely dedicated group of access to justice champions across the country, a major event has happened in Canada's justice sector – one the nature of which we have not seen before. According to the Chair of the Association of Legal Aid Plans Canada, the "Action Committee's report provides a much-needed roadmap for reform of the

Canadian justice system."[52] More pointedly, Richard Zorza described the report as a "model for the world" and a "force for the future."[53] With the Action Committee's work in hand, the question now facing us is "what next?" or, put differently, "what can I do next?" That question, to which I now turn, is of fundamental importance to the legal profession.

Access to Justice and the Legal Profession

The work of the Action Committee contemplates a major role for the legal profession. For example, one of the nine elements of its access to justice roadmap focuses on legal services and the relationship between lawyers and legal services and the access to justice agenda. Put simply, access to justice must become a central element of legal professionalism. According to the Action Committee,

> Access to justice must become more than a vague and aspirational princi-
> ple. Law societies and lawyers must see it as part of a modern – "sustainable"
> – notion of legal professionalism. Access to justice should feature promin-
> ently in law school curricula, bar admission and continuing education pro-
> grams, codes of conduct, etc. Mentoring will be important to sustained
> success. Serving the public – in the form of concrete and measurable out-
> comes – should be an increasingly central feature of professionalism.[54]

The exact processes by which these suggestions will be realized are still to be determined. However, there is no doubt that the Action Committee thinks that essential legal services should be available for everyone if we are meaningfully going to address the gap in access to justice in this country.[55] There is an institutional aspect as well as an individual aspect to this dis-cussion. In terms of institutions and systems, several issues have been raised by the Action Committee. Innovation is needed in terms of making current services more efficient and available and making new services possible. Ideas discussed include unbundling, alternative business structures, legal expense insurance, increases in legal aid services and funding, collaborative and interdisciplinary service providers, innovation in family law, educa-tional and technological innovations, and so on.[56] Some of these ideas have already been realized, while others are still to be experimented with and developed. All of these systemic considerations fit with current institutional mandates to improve access to justice in the context of self-regulated legal services.[57] Furthermore, again from an institutional perspective, creative thinking is needed in terms of legal education, dispute resolution systems, research, and funding strategies.[58] For example, in terms of dispute resolution, the Action Committee contemplates the idea of transforming traditional courthouses into multi-service centres for public dispute resolution – perhaps with both real and virtual components.[59]

Equally important is the individual element of this discussion. Lawyers themselves, in the everyday spaces of how, where, why, and for whom they practise law, need to see themselves as featuring prominently in this conversation. Otherwise, key change makers – those who seek to achieve justice through the fruits of their labour – will not play a meaningful role in the future of progressive and accessible professionalism. More importantly, and more immediately, lawyers need to see themselves as providers of services designed to address – in meaningful and accessible ways – the everyday needs of the public. As we have seen, the gap between what people need and what they can access and afford is significant and growing – leading to a crisis of access.[60] And, though institutional change is a necessary condition for reform, it is not a sufficient condition, not without the meaningful engagement of individual lawyers in the reform of access to justice.

The Action Committee makes some specific suggestions, including first identifying the need for a significant culture shift in the profession.[61] As one court worker put it, in the context of discussions on court administration reform, we need to "change ... how we do business within the context of courts."[62] The same is true for the profession generally, with which the Law Society of Upper Canada, following the recommendations of the Action Committee, has recently agreed:

> The Law Society has responsibility for a broad range of regulatory activities, including standard setting, rule making, policy development and implementation, licensing, investigation and prosecution of complaints against lawyers and paralegals, adjudication of conduct, competence and capacity matters and imposition and monitoring of penalties. Across this range of activities there is significant scope to influence a cultural shift, foster innovation, and stimulate change that will better "facilitate access to justice for the people of Ontario."[63]

Three aspects of that culture shift, flowing from the work of the Action Committee, are relevant to this discussion.

First, problems that clients have need to be understood and addressed, at least at the outset, not from the perspective of legal doctrine and procedural options but from the perspective of those living with the problems. Seeing problems as human experiences, as opposed to legal issues, will help to shift the way that lawyers approach and address these problems.

Second, lawyers need to see their role as part of a continuum of service collaboration to address all aspects of everyday legal and social challenges. Returning to the example of education discussed earlier in this chapter, lasting and meaningful solutions to that issue can be achieved only if it is addressed as not only (or primarily) a legal issue but also as an educational issue, a violence issue, a youth services issue, an employment training issue, perhaps a human rights issue, and so on. The more collaborative and consultative (and imaginative) the approach, the more lasting and fitting the solution.

Third, the Action Committee contemplates a shift in focus from process to outcome. Lawyers have tended to see themselves as procedural experts. In fact, as I have argued more extensively elsewhere,[64] lawyers tend to focus on, if not fetishize, the process-oriented aspects of their trade. Process matters, of course, but lawyers and legal processes are not what clients are looking for ultimately. What clients, and society, want are fair outcomes – for themselves, their communities, and society as a whole. As one respondent to the justice survey stated, "[l]awyers should be on the hook for actually getting good results."[65] Codes of professional regulation have long contemplated the importance of both zealous advocacy and justice-oriented counselling in the lawyering process.[66] Ideally, elements of both are present in many, if not most, retainers. However, to the extent that theories and approaches to lawyering have become increasingly agnostic to those larger social goals, they militate against, as opposed to advocate for, the meaningful improvement of access to justice in this country.[67]

In addition to these culture-based discussions, the Action Committee makes more concrete and action-oriented suggestions in terms of lawyers. In addition to *pro bono* and low *bono* services, lawyers need to consider and further experiment in their practices with some of the institutional innovations contemplated above, including alternative business models, alternative billing structures, unbundling of legal services, collaborative partnerships with non-lawyer service providers (social and health-care professionals), increased use of alternative, collaborative, and consensual approaches to conflict, and so on.[68] All of these innovations, and others, need to be considered and further developed by lawyers in their daily practices, all with a view to servicing not only the long-term health and relevance of legal professionalism but also, equally if not more importantly, the immediate and growing everyday justice needs of Canadians.

If lawyers fail to take up this challenge, then alternative forms of assistance will likely develop. Rather than scrambling to catch up to it, lawyers need to get out in front of the problem.[69] A further challenge to them will come from those who want to read the Action Committee's work as somehow sanctioning the automation of law and the downloading of law primarily to the user (through self-help centres, online information, and online dispute resolution). Of course, many of these initiatives, also contemplated in the work of the Action Committee, will be important in the context of making law more efficient and accessible. However, though some legal problems can be handled without the assistance of lawyers (particularly if problems are caught early), there is no doubt – and the Action Committee agrees – that many problems still need the assistance of lawyers and other trained professionals. The point, therefore, is not to sidestep lawyers. Rather, the point is to encourage innovation and creativity at the bar (and in all legal sectors) so that clients and their problems are handled by the right people, at the right time, in the best ways possible. Lawyers need to see themselves at the centre of this new wave of justice.

Conclusion

I started this chapter with reference to Shakespeare's Brutus and Cassius in the context of their deliberations over marching to Philippi.[70] Although the context is very different, the sensibility of approach is similar. Clearly, a new wave of reform thinking has taken hold in the Canadian justice system – on "such a full sea are we now afloat."[71] It is time fully to jump in – to "take the current when it serves."[72] No longer can we ignore the growing body of research establishing the gap in access to justice in Canada. Nor can we ignore the growing number of Canadians – the voices of those who participated in the justice survey – who cannot access meaningful services to address their everyday legal needs. The legal profession has an obligation to improve access to justice as part of its bargain with society in return for the privilege of self-regulation. To date, this obligation has remained a fairly elusive and opaque concept. If we are going to make real improvements to the legal health of all individuals in society, that obligation needs to come into much sharper relief – both from the perspective of the profession as a whole and from the perspective of everyday lawyers doing everyday legal work.

The Action Committee has provided an accessible and concrete plan for operationalizing improvements in access to justice. According to the Chief Justice of Canada, the Action Committee has brought "accessible justice for all Canadians a significant step closer to reality."[73] It is now time for all justice stakeholders, including all members of the legal profession, to take active and engaged roles in this access to justice exercise. By doing so, all stakeholders will not only renew their commitment to making justice accessible by making meaningful legal services available to all of those who need them but also ensure the continued relevance and sustainability of the profession itself. Doing otherwise will further alienate those who need legal services by increasing the growing justice gap in this country. Returning to the opening passage from Shakespeare, it is time to take the "tide ... at the flood" so that we don't "lose our ventures."[74]

Notes

I am grateful to Alice Woolley and Adam Dodek for helpful comments on this chapter.

1 Although having reflected on this passage many times myself, I heard it most recently connected to access to justice by Justice Thomas A. Cromwell of the Supreme Court of Canada, Toronto, January 28, 2014.

2 This study was done in the form of a survey conducted through the Canadian Forum on Civil Justice (CFCJ). Between November 2012 and May 2013, approximately 500 people were approached, with approximately 100 people agreeing to participate in the survey, conducted at demographically diverse street corners and locations in the Greater Toronto Area. The study was purposely designed to canvass the views of everyday people as opposed to litigants who are currently in, or just completing, a legal process. For a full discussion of the survey, its methodology, the results, my analysis, and acknowledgments, see Trevor C.W. Farrow, "What Is Access to Justice?" (2014) 51(3) Osgoode Hall Law Journal 957 ["What Is Access to Justice?"]. For selected edited excerpts of the video recordings (from interviews with participants who consented to the recordings and their use), see "What Is Access to Justice?," online: CFCJ, http://www.cfcj-fcjc.org/what-is-access-to-justice.

3 Farrow, "What Is Access to Justice?," *ibid.* at 968.

4 For a collection of materials on the Action Committee, see "Action Committee on Access to Justice in Civil and Family Matters," online: CFCJ, http://www.cfcj-fcjc. org/action-committee (I am a member of the Action Committee).

5 See, for example, Action Committee on Access to Justice in Civil and Family Matters, *Access to Civil and Family Justice: A Roadmap for Change,* final report (Ottawa: Action Committee on Access to Justice in Civil and Family Matters, 2013), online: CFCJ, http://www.cfcj-fcjc.org/action-committee (I was involved in drafting that report) [*A Roadmap for Change*]. See also Canadian Bar Association, *Reaching Equal Justice Report: An Invitation to Envision and Act* (Ottawa: Canadian Bar Association, 2013). See, further, Michael Trebilcock, Anthony Duggan, and Lorne Sossin, eds., *Middle Income Access to Justice* (Toronto: University of Toronto Press, 2012); Roderick A. Macdonald, "Access to Justice and Law Reform" (1990) 10 Windsor Yearbook of Access to Justice 287; Roderick A. Macdonald, "Whose Access? Which Justice?" (1992) 7 Canadian Journal of Law and Society 175; Roderick A. Macdonald,

"Access to Justice in Canada Today: Scope, Scale, and Ambitions" in Julia Bass, W.A. Bogart, and Frederick H. Zemans, eds., *Access to Justice for a New Century: The Way Forward* (Toronto: Law Society of Upper Canada, 2005) at 19–31, 99–101; Marc Galanter, "Access to Justice as a Moving Frontier" in Bass, Bogart, and Zemans, eds., *Access to Justice for a New Century: The Way Forward, ibid.* at 147–152; Ab Currie, "A National Survey of the Civil Justice Problems of Low- and Moderate-Income Canadians: Incidence and Patterns" (2006) 13 International Journal of the Legal Profession 217; Faisal Bhabha, "Institutionalizing Access-to-Justice: Judicial, Legislative, and Grassroots Dimensions" (2007) 33 Queen's Law Journal 139; and Patricia Hughes and Janet E. Mosher, guest eds., Access to Justice, special issue, (2008) 46(4) Osgoode Hall Law Journal.

6 For further commentary, see, for example, Farrow, "What Is Access to Justice?," *supra* note 2; Trevor C.W. Farrow, *Civil Justice, Privatization, and Democracy* (Toronto: University of Toronto Press, 2014) at Chapters 2, 5, and 7; Trevor C.W. Farrow, "Ethical Lawyering in a Global Community" (2013) 36(1) Manitoba Law Journal 141 at 152–59 ["Ethical Lawyering in a Global Community"]; Trevor C.W. Farrow, "The Promise of Professionalism" in Benoît Moore, Catherine Piché, and Marie-Claude Rigaud, eds., *L'avocat dans la cité: Éthique et professionalisme* (Montréal: Les Éditions Thémis, 2012) 197 at 208–19 ["The Promise of Professionalism"]. See, earlier, Trevor C.W. Farrow, "Sustainable Professionalism" (2008) 46(1) Osgoode Hall Law Journal 51 at 96 ["Sustainable Professionalism"]; and Trevor C.W. Farrow, "Dispute Resolution, Access to Civil Justice, and Legal Education" (2005) 42 Alberta Law Review 741.

7 See, for example, Patricia Hughes, "Law Commissions and Access to Justice: What Justice Should We Be Talking About?" (2008) 46 Osgoode Hall Law Journal 773 at 777–79. See, further, Action Committee on Access to Justice in Civil and Family Matters, *A Roadmap for Change, supra* note 5 at n. 5 and accompanying text.

8 Farrow, "What Is Access to Justice?," *supra* note 2 at 971.

9 *Ibid.*

10 Chief Justice Beverley McLachlin in Trebilcock, Duggan, and Sossin, *supra* note 5 at ix.

11 Chief Justice R. Roy McMurtry, "Remarks" in Canadian Forum on Civil Justice, Civil Justice Reform Conference: Phase II (December 7, 2006) at 3–4, online: CFCJ, http://cfcj-fcjc.org/sites/default/files/docs/2006/mcmurtry-en.pdf.

12 *York University v. Markicevic,* 2013 O.N.S.C. 4311 at para. 8.

13 See Trevor C.W. Farrow *et al., Addressing the Needs of Self-Represented Litigants in the Canadian Justice System,* white paper prepared for the Association of Canadian Court Administrators (Toronto: ACCA, 2012) at 46, online: CFCJ, http://www.cfcj-fcjc.org/action-committee [*Addressing the Needs of Self-Represented Litigants*].

14 See Farrow, "What Is Access to Justice?," *supra* note 2 at 972.

15 *Ibid.* at 972-73. For a different study involving members of the public, specifically including self-represented litigants who have been involved in the justice system, see Julie Macfarlane, *Identifying and Meeting the Needs of Self-Represented Litigants,* final report (Windsor: National Self-Represented Litigants Project, 2013), online: NSRLP, https://representingyourselfcanada.files.wordpress.com/2014/02/reportm15-2.pdf.

16 *Report of the Treasurer's Advisory Group on Access to Justice Working Group* (Toronto: Law Society of Upper Canada, February 27, 2014) at para. 11.

17 According to Thomas Cromwell, "[b]y nearly any standard, our current situation falls far short of providing access to the knowledge, resources and services that allow people to deal effectively with civil and family legal matters. There is a mountain of evidence to support this view." Justice Thomas A. Cromwell, "Access to Justice: Towards a Collaborative and Strategic Approach," Viscount Bennett Memorial Lecture, (2012) 63 University of New Brunswick Law Journal 38 at 39.

18 See Farrow, "What Is Access to Justice?," *supra* note 2 at 963, citing Action Committee on Access to Justice in Civil and Family Matters, *A Roadmap for Change, supra* note 5 at 2; Canadian Bar Association, *supra* note 5 at 8; Ab Currie, *The Legal Problems of Everyday Life: The Nature, Extent, and Consequences of Justiciable Problems Experienced by Canadians* (Ottawa: Department of Justice Canada, 2007) at 2, 5–6, and 10–12; and Hazel Genn, *Paths to Justice: What People Do and Think about Going to Law* (Oxford: Hart, 1999) at v–vi, 12, and generally Chapter 2.

19 See Farrow, "What Is Access to Justice?," *supra* note 2 at 963, citing Currie, *ibid.* at 23–26; Pascoe Pleasence *et al., Causes of Action: Civil Law and Social Justice* (Norwich: Legal Services Commission, 2004) at 14–31 [*Causes of Action*]; and Action Committee on Access to Justice in Civil and Family Matters, *A Roadmap for Change, supra* note 5 at 2.

20 See, for example, Justice Frank Iacobucci, *First Nations Representation on Ontario Juries,* report of the Independent Review (2013), in which the relationship between the justice system and Aboriginal individuals and groups is described as "dysfunctional" and "in crisis." See paras. 14–15. See, further, Trevor C.W. Farrow, "Residential Schools Litigation and the Legal Profession" (2014) 64 University of Toronto Law Journal 597 ["Residential Schools Litigation"]; and Farrow, "Ethical Lawyering in a Global Community," *supra* note 6.

21 Farrow, "What Is Access to Justice?," *supra* note 2 at 973.

22 *Ibid.* at 964, citing Currie, *supra* note 18 at 49–51, 73; Pascoe Pleasence *et al.,* "Multiple Justiciable Problems: Common Clusters and Their Social and Demographic Indicators" (2004) 1 Journal of Empirical Legal Studies 301; Pleasence *et al., Causes of Action, supra* note 19 at 37–44; Nigel J. Balmer *et al., Knowledge, Capability and the Experience of Rights Problems* (London: Public Legal Education Network, 2010) at 25–26, 42–43; Mary Stratton and Travis Anderson, *Social, Economic, and Health Problems Associated with a Lack of Access to the Courts* (Edmonton: Canadian Forum on Civil Justice, 2006); Action Committee on Access to Justice in Civil and Family Matters, *A Roadmap for Change, supra* note 5 at 3.

23 See Farrow, "What Is Access to Justice?" *supra* note 2 at 964, citing Currie, *supra* note 18 at 33. See, further, Action Committee on Access to Justice in Civil and Family Matters, *A Roadmap for Change, supra* note 5 at 3.

24 See Farrow, "What Is Access to Justice?," *supra* note 2 at 964, citing Currie, *supra* note 18 at 88–89; and Alexy Buck, Pascoe Pleasence, and Nigel J. Balmer, "Social Exclusion and Civil Law: Experience of Civil Justice Problems among Vulnerable Groups" (2005) 39(3) Social Policy Administration 302. See, further, Action Committee on Access to Justice in Civil and Family Matters, *A Roadmap for Change, supra* note 5 at 3. For a current study focusing on the costs of justice, in particular

the costs of an inaccessible justice system, see Canadian Forum on Civil Justice, "The Cost of Justice: Weighing the Costs of Fair and Effective Resolution to Legal Problems," online: CFCJ, http://www.cfcj-fcjc.org/cost-of-justice.

25 Farrow, "What Is Access to Justice?," *supra* note 2 at 981.

26 *Ibid.*

27 Chief Justice Beverley McLachlin in Action Committee on Access to Justice in Civil and Family Matters, *A Roadmap for Change, supra* note 5 at i.

28 Chief Justice Beverley McLachlin in Action Committee, "Media Release" at 2, online: CFCJ, http://www.cfcj-fcjc.org/sites/default/files/docs/2013/Access_to_Justice_Final_Report_Media_Release_draft_5_October_2.pdf.

29 See, for example, Task Force on Systems of Civil Justice, *Systems of Civil Justice Task Force Report* (Ottawa: Canadian Bar Association, 1996); and, more recently, Canadian Bar Association, *supra* note 5.

30 For a list of specific members, see Action Committee on Access to Justice in Civil and Family Matters, *A Roadmap for Change, supra* note 5 at 25.

31 See *ibid.*

32 Chief Justice Beverley McLachlin in *ibid.* at i.

33 *Ibid.* at 2 (references omitted).

34 For copies of the reports, as well as relevant background information, see Reports of the Action Committee Working Groups, online: CFCJ, http://www.cfcj-fcjc.org/action-committee.

35 Action Committee on Access to Justice in Civil and Family Matters, *A Roadmap for Change, supra* note 5.

36 See *ibid.* at pt. 1.

37 See *ibid.* at pt. 2.

38 See, for example, *Constitution Act, 1867* (U.K.), 30 & 31 Vict., c. 3, reprinted in R.S.C. 1985, App. II, No. 5, s. 92(14).

39 See, for example, Macfarlane, *supra* note 15; Farrow, "What Is Access to Justice?," *supra* note 2; and Farrow *et al., Addressing the Needs of Self-Represented Litigants, supra* note 13.

40 Farrow, "What Is Access to Justice?," *supra* note 2 at 974.

41 See Family Justice Working Group, *Meaningful Change for Family Justice: Beyond Wise Words* (Ottawa: Action Committee on Access to Justice in Civil and Family Matters, 2013), online: CFCJ, http://www.cfcj-fcjc.org/action-committee.

42 See, for example, Farrow, "What Is Access to Justice?," *supra* note 2 at 971.

43 For judicial commentary on the need for a culture shift, see *Hryniak v. Mauldin*, 2014 S.C.C. 7 at paras. 1–2, Karakatsanis J. See, further, *Windsor v. Canadian Pacific Railway Ltd.,* 2014 A.B.C.A. 108 at paras. 11–16.

44 See Action Committee on Access to Justice in Civil and Family Matters, *A Roadmap for Change, supra* note 5 at pt. 3.

45 See *Constitution Act, 1867, supra* note 38 and accompanying text.

46 Farrow, "What Is Access to Justice?," *supra* note 2 at 979.

47 *Ibid.*

48 United Nations, Millennium Development Goals, online: United Nations, http://www.un.org/millenniumgoals/, cited in Action Committee on Access to Justice in Civil and Family Matters, *A Roadmap for Change, supra* note 5 at n. 62 and accompanying

text. These UN goals "range from halving extreme poverty rates to halting the spread of HIV/AIDS and providing universal primary education, all by the target date of 2015," and they are designed to develop "a blueprint agreed to by all the world's countries and all the world's leading development institutions." More recently, see United Nations, *Transforming Our World: The 2030 Agenda for Sustainable Development* (2015), online: https://sustainabledevelopment.un.org/content/documents/7891Transforming%20Our%20World.pdfatGoal 16.3.

49 For press releases and media reports of the various aspects of the Action Committee's work, including the working group reports, the final report, and the final colloquium, see Action Committee, selected media reports, online: CFCJ, http://www.cfcj-fcjc.org/action-committee.

50 The colloquium was held in Toronto at Osgoode Hall Law School on January 27–28, 2014.

51 For a summary of the colloquium proceedings, see Action Committee on Access to Justice in Civil and Family Matters, *Colloquium Report* (Ottawa: Action Committee on Access to Justice in Civil and Family Matters, 2014), online: CFCJ, http://www.cfcj-fcjc.org/action-committee.

52 Bob Ward in Action Committee, "Media Release," *supra* note 49 at 2.

53 Richard Zorza, "Canadian ATJ Report Is a Model for the World" (18 April 2014), online: Richard Zorza's Access to Justice Blog, http://accesstojustice.net/.

54 Action Committee on Access to Justice in Civil and Family Matters, *A Roadmap for Change*, *supra* note 5 at 15 (references omitted).

55 *Ibid.* at pt. 3.A.2.

56 *Ibid.* at pts. 3.A.2.1–2; 3.A.4; 3.B.7; 3.C.9.

57 See, for example, *Law Society Act*, R.S.O. 1990, c. L.8 at s. 4.2. The Law Society, motivated expressly by the work of the Action Committee, has recently reconfirmed the importance of its role in the context of improving access to justice in light of this statutory mandate: "It is apparent from all of the above that access to justice comprises a broad category of issues and responses that cannot all be addressed at once or by one entity. While not alone in shouldering the responsibility for promoting access to justice, it must be recognized that the Law Society does play and must play a central role in shaping and guiding the legal professions and in influencing change and innovation." See *Report of the Treasurer's Advisory Group on Access to Justice Working Group*, *supra* note 16 at para. 33. For further discussions, see, variously, Farrow, "Sustainable Professionalism," *supra* note 6 at 96; Brent Cotter, "Thoughts on a Coordinated and Comprehensive Approach to Access to Justice in Canada" (2012) 63 University of New Brunswick Law Journal 54; Richard Devlin, "Breach of Contract? The New Economy, Access to Justice, and the Ethical Responsibilities of the Legal Profession" (2002) 25 Dalhousie Law Journal 335; and Alice Woolley, "Imperfect Duty: Lawyers' Obligation to Foster Access to Justice" (2008) 45 Alberta Law Review 107. See also Action Committee on Access to Justice in Civil and Family Matters, *A Roadmap for Change*, *supra* note 5 at n. 101 and accompanying text.

58 Action Committee on Access to Justice in Civil and Family Matters, *A Roadmap for Change*, *supra* note 5 at pts. 3.A.3; 3.B.6; 3.C.8–9.

59 *Ibid.* at pt. 3.A.3. For a recent collection of papers looking at various aspects of systemic court reform, see Trevor C.W. Farrow and Patrick Molinari, eds., *The Courts*

and Beyond: The Architecture of Justice in Transition (Montreal: Canadian Institute for the Administration of Justice, 2013).

60 See, for example, *supra* notes 10–12 and accompanying text.

61 Action Committee on Access to Justice in Civil and Family Matters, *A Roadmap for Change, supra* note 5 at pt. 2.

62 See Farrow *et al., Addressing the Needs of Self-Represented Litigants, supra* note 13 at 29.

63 *Report of the Treasurer's Advisory Group on Access to Justice Working Group, supra* note 16 at para. 12.

64 See, for example, Farrow, "The Promise of Professionalism," *supra* note 6. See, more recently, Farrow, "Residential Schools Litigation," *supra* note 20.

65 See Farrow, "What Is Access to Justice?," *supra* note 2 at 971.

66 See, for example, Federation of Law Societies of Canada, *Model Code of Professional Conduct,* as amended December 12, 2012, r. 3.2–8, com. 6; r. 5.1–1, com. 1. For discussions of these various issues, from different perspectives within the Canadian legal academy that deal with different areas of legal practice, see, for example, Adam Dodek, "Lawyering at the Intersection of Public Law and Legal Ethics: Government Lawyers as Custodians of the Rule of Law" (2010) 33 Dalhousie Law Journal 1; Alice Woolley, "In Defence of Zealous Advocacy" in *Understanding Lawyers' Ethics in Canada* (Markham: LexisNexis, 2011), Chapter 2 at 33; Allan C. Hutchinson, *Legal Ethics and Professional Responsibility,* 2d ed. (Toronto: Irwin Law, 2006) at Chapters 1–3; and Farrow, "The Promise of Professionalism," *supra* note 6.

67 See, for example, Farrow, "Sustainable Professionalism," *supra* note 6. Of course, not everyone agrees. For a useful discussion of these issues, see Alice Woolley *et al.,* eds., *Lawyers' Ethics and Professional Regulation,* 2d ed. (Markham: LexisNexis, 2012) at 16–64 and Chapter 12.

68 Action Committee on Access to Justice in Civil and Family Matters, *A Roadmap for Change, supra* note 5 at pt. 3.A.2; 3.A.4.3.

69 For a useful discussion on the need for innovation in the legal profession, see Richard Susskind, *The End of Lawyers? Rethinking the Nature of Legal Services* (Oxford: Oxford University Press, 2008). See, recently, Nicole Aylwin and Trevor C.W. Farrow, "The Winkler Institute for Dispute Resolution: Responding Creatively to Complex Justice Problems" (2014) 23(2) Canadian Arbitration and Mediation Journal 16.

70 See *supra* note 1 and accompanying text.

71 *Ibid.*

72 *Ibid.*

73 Chief Justice Beverley McLachlin in Action Committee on Access to Justice in Civil and Family Matters, *A Roadmap for Change, supra* note 5 at i.

74 See *supra* note 1 and accompanying text.

9

Michelle's Story

Creativity and Meaning in Legal Practice

ALICE WOOLLEY

What would it mean if you couldn't be a lawyer anymore? Take money out of the equation, and assume that you have enough to live comfortably. But a degenerative illness has taken away the physical and mental energy required for legal practice. What would you lose if that happened to you? Who would you be?

Most lawyers never have to answer such questions. They might never ask them. Michelle,[1] whose story this chapter tells, was not that lucky:

> You asked me something about how I feel, about how my life is different without my practice. The more I've thought about that, the more I've kept feeling like I'm hollowed out. I'm still useful. If I were holding up a plate, and you hollowed out the centre, you will still be holding up the plate, but its core is gone. I do feel hollowed out.
>
> A tree trunk, you hollow it out, and it's a canoe. It's just not a tree anymore.
>
> It took me a long time to accept that I was the canoe and not the tree. My shape is different. And my shape might be different tomorrow. That's a reality for me every day.[2]

For Michelle, as for others who leave legal practice, these questions cannot be avoided, nor can the deeper question that they reflect: what role did being a lawyer play in the construction of the ethics of my life, in making my life meaningful, in making it moral, in making it count as well lived?

That question can be considered personally through reflection on one's life and what it means to have lived the life that one has. It can also be considered philosophically. The question of whether a lawyer's life counts as well lived matters not only for the lawyer but also for the broader human question about the roles that our society wants people to occupy and about what it means to be one of the people who does so. The general ethical question "how should I live?"[3] is one that I answer for myself (it is, after all, about how *I* should live) but also subject to impartial analysis (since it is also about how I *should* live).

Because of these subjective and objective aspects, the ethical question of how one should live can include a wide variety of things. But in terms of understanding the social role of the lawyer, of what that role ought to require, and the ethical consequences of occupying it, two concepts are especially important: morality and meaning. Morality refers to the duties and obligations that follow from the universal and impartial principles that govern human interaction.[4] Morality identifies what each of us owes to each other by virtue of our common humanity. It imposes duties and obligations and its concerns are universal and general, not particular and specific.[5]

In terms of the lawyer's role, the question posed by morality is whether that role, normally understood, necessarily results in violations of moral values. If it does, then the next question is whether some morality-based justification constrains or explains what lawyers ought to do on behalf of clients.

Meaning is more subjective and particular than morality, though it still has an objective component. Meaning as a philosophical concept has roots in the work of Bernard Williams. Williams suggests that each of us has "ground projects" – "a project or set of projects which are closely related to his existence and which to a significant degree give meaning to his life."[6] Ground projects are distinct from morality in that they are not impartial or universal in their significance, but they are also not just those things that happen to interest or attract me. They are foundationally important; they make my life worth living, and they might be worth dying for. Pursuit of my ground projects is as much part of my ethical life as is my compliance with moral norms.

Susan Wolf has further defined meaning as a philosophical concept. For an activity to be meaningful, it must be something that grips, excites, or engages us; it must be something that we love.[7] It must also be something worth focusing on, something of value in an objective sense.[8] The objective criterion for establishing meaning is not necessarily onerous or rigid. It is not some "sort of pure, subject-independent metaphysical property."[9] It only connotes the idea that meaning is not wholly self-generated but also involves some external assessment. Meaning occupies a halfway point between the pure subjectivity of self-interest and the pure objectivity of morality. It is found in "loving something (or a number of things) worthy of love, and being able to engage with it (or them) in a positive way."[10]

When considering the ethics of the lawyer's role, the question raised by meaning is whether being a lawyer can be a legitimate subject of engagement, a source of meaning for the person who occupies that role. Or does being a lawyer in some way disrupt the ability to achieve a meaningful life, to find and pursue things of value to her?

Perhaps surprisingly, legal ethics theories, which use philosophical concepts to assess the lawyer's role, have generally focused on the morality of that role.[11] They identify the lawyer's role as creating a moral problem – it involves lawyers in advocating for morally suspect (but lawful) causes through morally doubtful (but lawful) procedures.[12] They then consider whether what lawyers do can be justified through the principles of moral or political philosophy or whether what lawyers do ought to change.

The answers to those questions do not tell us much, though, about the meaningfulness of the life of the person who fills the lawyer's role. The morality (or immorality) of being a lawyer can affect the person's experience of it as meaningful, but it does not necessarily do so given that morality and meaning are distinct ethical qualities.[13] The translation of moral principles into a source (or disruption) of meaning requires some shift between the impartial moral idea and the subjective personal commitment to that idea. The principle can't just matter. It has to matter to *me*.

So how can meaningfulness and the lawyer's role be assessed? One way is by exploring the lives of ordinary lawyers, and the complex interactions between their passions and interests, the things that mattered to them and that ought to have mattered to them, and the work that they did. Through a careful telling and consideration of the stories of those lives, we can develop a more general understanding of the intersection between being a lawyer and having a meaningful life.[14]

Michelle's professional life is one such story. If Michelle could have practised longer, then professional renown likely would have come her way. But she couldn't. Her life in law was consequentially an ordinary one, in biographical details akin to those of her peers. But ordinariness does not preclude interest. Michelle's story is one of an intelligent, warm, serious-minded, engaged, social, loved, driven, and sometimes self-doubting woman whose "ordinary" legal career included challenges, disappointments, and fulfillment. I know her story because Michelle is my friend, but I tell her story because what law was for her, and the loss that she experienced when it was taken away, show us something that legal ethics scholarship has not accounted for – the possibilities and challenges of accomplishing a meaningful life in law.

Michelle did not fall accidentally into legal practice; it was not a post–arts degree move of desperation. Although not having any lawyers in her family, she doesn't remember ever not wanting to be a lawyer. She grew up in British Columbia in the late 1970s, and politics mattered there a great deal. Engaged with the stark political divide between the governing free-enterprise Social Credit Party and the opposition New Democratic Party, and the public protest of the "Solidarity Movement" in the early 1980s, Michelle followed and cared about political questions. She saw politics as a "tool for making the world a better place," and many politicians, including Prime Minister Pierre Trudeau, whom she greatly admired, were lawyers. Law and politics seemed to go together.

Law and lawyers could also ensure fairness, and fairness mattered. Her parents divorced, and her father, a disengaged parent, sought custody. To Michelle, that was unfair – how could someone who spent no time with his children claim the right to take care of them? The litigation was resolved in her mother's favour, and, though the adult Michelle views each of her parents in a different emotional light than the preteen Michelle did, that outcome, and her involvement in it, gave her the perception that being a lawyer meant helping people and making sure that things worked out fairly.

Michelle also saw law as a way of obtaining financial security, of knowing that there would always be enough. Her life had begun in affluent circumstances, with her father a successful businessman, and she began her education at a private girls' school in Vancouver. But her father lost his business, and after that money was always an issue, especially in the immediate aftermath of her parents' divorce. Becoming a lawyer was a way of ensuring that she would not face that insecurity or anxiety again.

As Michelle got older, other experiences cemented her interest in law. During high school, she was fortunate to be taught by a teacher who placed significant emphasis on law and social justice and who himself was involved in politics, which reinforced her beliefs about what law could be and accomplish. Michelle completed her undergraduate degree in central Canada, where she was heavily involved in student journalism and student politics, serving on the student union executive for several years. During her time in student politics, she learned a great deal about advocacy, political strategy, and government relations. It was a taste of what being a lawyer might be like, and by then she was confident that this was what she wanted to do and whom she wanted to be.

The next year found Michelle in law school, though her academic and LSAT performances did not ensure her admission. She was accepted as a special applicant and arrived at law school feeling as if she didn't deserve to be there, that, though it was a step toward accomplishing the goal of her life, her admission was granted only because she had "pulled the wool over somebody's eyes." Those feelings faded with academic success, and her law school experience was happy. Michelle found the law school environment collegial and not competitive, and she quickly developed many close friend-ships, including with her future husband. And law school was intellectually rewarding, building on the political theory that she had studied in her undergraduate degree:

> It was fun. The thinking was fun, the learning was fun, the challenge was fun, the overwhelming amount of work almost was fun. It was an absolute challenge. And then when I did well I thought, "oh, okay, I guess I'm going to be okay here after all."
>
> I liked the intellectual pursuit of it. At the very least, it helped me fill in the understanding from [my] undergraduate degree. Helped me under-stand the structure, how the law influences our structure.

Michelle also appreciated her law school's commitment to public service and the community, which she thought imbued the culture of the school.

It was not a purely satisfactory experience, though. Some professors were ill prepared and taught classes that were poorly organized and did not challenge the students. During her third year, her cousin, with whom Michelle was very close, committed suicide, and she found it hard to deal with her grief. She went back to school, hoping that the gossip networks would have done their job and that people would know why she had been gone. But they didn't, and cheerful inquiries about why she had been on holiday were hard to take. The time that she was away from school also meant that she could not participate in the competitive moot for which she had been preparing, and this was a significant disappointment.

With a degree of hindsight, though Michelle believes strongly that law school gave her the needed intellectual grounding for legal practice, it did not help her to make decisions about how and where she was going to work after graduation, crucial decisions that she was ill prepared to make on her own, especially given that she did not know any lawyers. She thinks that three years of law school cannot teach you everything that you need to know to be a lawyer: "Law school would have to be ten years long to teach you everything that comes with legal practice, the business, file management, and all that stuff." However, it could have helped her to frame and understand her choice about where to work:

> The way the university should have prepared me for practice is [by] examining what kind of articles were available. Helping me make that choice. Help me fully understand the choice I was making. I got bamboozled. [The firm] took us out for these very expensive dinners, the most expensive dinners ... It was like the draft ... I was so naive ... I was naive in how I approached all that and how I perceived that.

If Michelle were advising someone to go to law school today, then she would tell that person to be more careful than she was in deciding where to practise after graduation: "I saw the underbelly of legal practice and the toll it takes on a person, and so my advice is now tempered ... Go to law school because it's interesting and a lot of fun, but think about what you're going to do when you get out."

After graduation, Michelle moved back to Vancouver with her husband to begin articles at the relatively small local office of a Toronto-based national firm. It felt like an arrival. The lawyers were young, bright, and totally engaged with their work. The firm paid articling students better than any other firm in the city, and there was no doubt that this was the place to be, with the best work, the best students, the best lawyers, and the tightest team. The firm paid the tab for a weekly breakfast for articling students, gave them supper and a cab ride home if they worked late, and always paid for drinks at the bar if a partner was there. But the work was overwhelming. The transition from law school was almost brutal in its difficulty, especially since the firm was willing to give the students and junior lawyers as much responsibility as they could take and sometimes more. The learning curve was steep and the hours demanded were long.

During that time, Michelle was articled to a lawyer specializing in employment law and immediately was exposed to that work, which she enjoyed very much. When the lawyer left the firm halfway through her articles, Michelle and a more senior lawyer picked up many of his files. As a consequence, by the end of her articles, she had an area of practice on which to concentrate, along with a great deal of practical knowledge and skill.

Michelle also began to sense some of the personal and power dynamics in the firm. Her articling principal had left along with three other partners, and the circumstances of their departure sensitized her to the fact that some people in the firm had more power than others, and it was not always obvious from the signs on their doors.

Her transition to being an associate at the firm was aided by the senior lawyer working on the employment files with Michelle, and by a partner hired as a lateral, both of whom mentored her through employment and human rights litigation and through managing the employment law aspects of corporate mergers and acquisitions. Gradually, she started to accumulate expertise and gain the sense of knowing what she was doing; although she was not an expert, she had enough competence in the field to advise someone effectively, and that was rewarding. Michelle also thought that employment law had a structure of fairness built into it. A lawyer cannot guarantee anyone a job, or prevent someone from losing a job when a corporation is restructured, but employment law ensures fairness in the process. She thought that her advice ensured that people received the notice or other entitlements that the law provides. There was an element of problem solving, and the problems were not always the same; every client and every file had something different that needed to be addressed.

Those emerging rewards, though, were coupled with some significant challenges. Although being given more responsibility was fulfilling, Michelle felt overwhelmed when the responsibility was beyond her knowledge or ability. In her third year, she assisted in the conduct of a trial, except that the senior lawyer was out of town until a few days before it was scheduled to begin, and she tried to do all of the prep work on her own. Yet Michelle had never done a trial before and did not know basic requirements such as how to deal with the transcripts from the discoveries. She also knew that this was not what the client had expected to happen, that the client had no idea that she was carrying that much of the trial preparation without effective supervision.

When Michelle looked more closely at the tight firm culture, it also seemed to be more complicated than when she had started. When she praised the courtroom skills of a lawyer whom she admired to a senior partner, that partner responded, "well, there's more to practice," with an evident dismissiveness and a lack of respect. Eventually, Michelle learned that his partners despised the lawyer whom she admired, condemning his disorganized practice and failure to bill clients. Whatever the closeness of the culture, it did not preclude judgment or ensure loyalty. And the things valued by the partners were not necessarily a lawyer's quality or skill as an advocate for clients.

The financial and business aspects of the practice began to seem as if they determined relationships and status in the firm. Only a few could stick it out. Of the lawyers there when Michelle began, over 50 percent had left by the end of her five years. Some partners aimed to be available to their clients 24/7, and the expectations for billable hours were high. It seemed that the hours billed were significant in a way that the quality or efficiency of the work was not.

The dynamics at the firm could also complicate practice issues. Michelle was asked by a partner to take on a wrongful dismissal case for a family member of a client of the firm, but the employer of the dismissed family member was connected to another client of the firm, represented by a different partner. Michelle was caught between the two clients and the two lawyers, and her representation had the added difficulty of not being obviously meritorious. It left her feeling "boxed in by things completely outside of my control."

The general culture and attitude of the firm became unmanageable for Michelle after she had her first child. No female lawyer at the firm had taken a full maternity leave; the expectation was that the women would return to work as soon as possible. Michelle took six months; she had planned on only four, but a combination of postpartum depression and problems arranging child care kept her away from the firm for an extra two months. The firm was financially supportive during her leave, but on her return, expectations were not adjusted in any way. She was immediately drawn into a significant litigation file, and in her first month back, a February, she billed 220 hours. Yet at the end of that month, during her annual review, the partners who reviewed her said, "you are an exceptional lawyer, but you didn't bill enough hours last year." When she pointed out that she had been on maternity leave, the response was that she should have billed more before she left or come back early to meet her target.

Michelle decided then that she would leave the firm, and after a few months she was able to arrange an in-house position advising on employment-related matters. Although in many ways she did not find the in-house culture especially amenable – it was nice not to have to bill hours, but the culture seemed to go too far in the other direction from the firm's obsession with work – it provided her with the opportunity to work on a significant international transaction and on human rights litigation. At that point, her five years of practice began to feel like emerging expertise, which translated into a sense of competence in doing the work. "I felt confident, and I felt helpful."

After a year in-house, Michelle joined a small firm in which she did work for a more diverse client base, individuals as well as corporations. She found individual client work stimulating and memorable, the importance of the files was "more easily touchable," and the lawyer whom she worked with the most was smart and affable. He was also experiencing some changes in his life, though, that made viability of the firm doubtful.

Now pregnant with her second child, Michelle made the difficult decision to return to practice at a large firm, joining the local office of another national firm. This firm immediately felt different from the one at which she had articled. When she told them that she was pregnant and would take a maternity leave soon after joining the firm if she was hired, the lawyer who hired her responded, "what's a maternity leave in a career"? This time, feeling no pressure, she took only a four-month maternity leave.

The firm was also strongly non-hierarchical; at a retreat, lawyers would draw numbers from a bowl to determine the seating plan rather than seating being determined by a committee on the basis of power and position. They also seemed to live more modestly, within their incomes rather than at or beyond them. And they were intellectually engaged, writing articles about legal practice or new developments in law. There was significant expertise in the firm in labour and employment law, and Michelle became part of this expertise. She concentrated on employment law, acting in both corporate transactions and litigation. Her practice was busy and supported, and though now mainly corporate it continued to include individual clients.

When acting for individuals, Michelle used her advocacy protectively to ensure that clients avoided legal consequences that they ought not to suffer and received the legal benefits to which they were entitled. A client referred to her by the Law Society of British Columbia referral service had been employed at a corporation, and Michelle helped him to settle his wrongful dismissal claim. The client, who was disabled, sought government benefits but, misunderstanding his obligations regarding confidentiality, did not disclose the settlement amounts to the government. Michelle was able to explain to the benefits administrator what had happened and to ensure that the misunderstanding did not result in the disallowance of his benefits. Another client was fired after twenty-four years of employment on the basis of cause, even though cause had not been proven. That matter was also settled, but as part of the settlement Michelle ensured that her client spoke to the human resources manager of the former employer and explained what it had meant to him to be fired in that unfair way. She achieved for him voice as well as money.

When representing employers, Michelle felt able to ensure that businesses could operate effectively and efficiently but also fairly. Employers can be reluctant to have "full-sentence conversations" with employees and to tell them honestly what is expected of them and when those expectations are not being met. They also have to accommodate employees' disabilities and develop systems to work through conflicts in the workplace. Michelle put it this way:

> I loved doing HR [human resources] reviews, going to [the client], and finding all the ways in which they were breaching the *Human Rights Code* ... Someone with a bad back can't be told "you're going to get fired unless you continue to lift those boxes." The law requires them to accommodate the disability to the extent they're able. Surely you can find a job that works for the person with a bad back. I loved doing the teaching on all that, or the workplace mediations, working through conflict, system conflict. I'd always say to my employers, if you have good communication with your employees, they won't have a need to unionize. I loved all of that. I loved the employers who called and said, "I have a big problem. One of my employees stinks. We've bought her soap and bath balms for Christmas, but it doesn't help." [I would respond] that, if she's good at what she does and you want to keep her, you're going to need to have that conversation with her ... You can't just duck it.
>
> It really suits my personality ... It suits my personality because I'm a bit of a practical head. The idea of researching, or working through the courts, that's just not my personality ... Human beings are interesting to me. And they get themselves into all these kinds of knots because they don't ... want to hurt each other's feelings.
>
> We want to fire someone on maternity leave, what do we do? The law says you're not allowed to terminate someone on maternity leave. And that's to protect women, families, and prevent discrimination, which makes absolute sense. However, it fails to recognize that, as she's coming off maternity leave, that woman is trying to come back to work, so she needs to know. So don't fire her, but let her know what it's going to be like for her when she comes back, what's changed in the company, letting her know they may not need her services. You have to have the up-front conversation

because it's fairer all around. In that way, the law doesn't allow that wiggle room, but as a lawyer you help people find that wiggle room.

Or you're buying a business, and 40 percent of the staff is going to get fired. That's a hard thing to do, but it's fair to have a system so that people know how much they're getting paid, and what's going to happen to their job, to live with all the rumours and stress of that. It's fair to the employees to say, "if you stick around, we'll pay you this extra amount of money as a retention bonus, and this is what's going to happen to you, and this is what's going to happen to your position, and this is what's going to happen in severance if you're not kept on by the employer." It's easier to do that in advance, to have that straight-up communication. It's not fair to just sell the business and give them their severance.

Michelle actively practised at the firm for three years, becoming involved in firm hiring as well as continuing with her practice. In March 2003, she travelled to negotiate a collective agreement, and she found herself exhausted and could not feel her feet. She began to develop other symptoms, losing feeling in her hand, so that, when she picked up a glass to drink water, she had no sensation of holding the glass. The exhaustion also continued. Her mother has had multiple sclerosis since Michelle was a child, and Michelle began to be concerned about what these symptoms might indicate. After losing sensation in both her hand and her foot, she went to her family doctor and was quickly referred to the emergency neurology clinic, seeing a neurologist within a few days. She was put on the emergency list for an MRI, and within a few weeks she had an MRI at the Children's Hospital, which had a unit available.

I remember leaving work that day and [my colleague] handing me a disc for the MRI, and I had this feeling of ... I guess I had a feeling of resolve but also a feeling of dread. And fear. My recollection is that my in-laws were visiting, and they took me to Children's for the MRI. And what's funny about that is, because it was Children's, there's all these posters and colours and cute little things, and you kind of feel like an imposter, like I was there by accident in more ways than one.

And so when they called me ... I was at my desk ... And I remember [the doctor] saying, "so we got the MRI results, this is not going to be a surprise to you, you have eleven (or whatever the number was) holes in your central nervous system. All indications of multiple sclerosis."

Exhaustion kept Michelle at home, but she thought that she would be back at work in a month. Yet a month later, in July, she lost her ability to see properly. She could not read or drive until a heavy dose of steroids corrected the problem.

Throughout this period, the firm was supportive. It had excellent short-term and long-term disability benefits, and it made efforts to incorporate Michelle in practice where possible. "Everyone thought I was coming back. I thought I was coming back. They took me to lunch. They put me in RFPs and brochures. I felt like they believed in me."

But the need to reduce stress and manage her exhaustion to keep further attacks at a minimum prevented those efforts from coming to fruition. Michelle also had to deal with regular attacks and an attendant increase in the severity of her symptoms. Over the years, subtle indicators pushed her to the understanding that she was not going back, that she would never go back. After six months, she told her assistant to find another job. After a time, her phone was disconnected. After a few years, the insurer required that Michelle apply for her permanent disability pension from the Canada Pension Plan. And eventually she moved from active to inactive status with the Law Society of British Columbia. The development of that understanding was a process:

At the beginning, I think I thought "this is just one more thing I have to get through." There's a sense of brutal unfairness. My parents are divorced ... My cousin committed suicide. I have alcoholism in my family. This was one more thing I had to overcome. At the beginning, I felt resigned to just getting through it. Figuring out a way so I could get back to my life.

And losing my whole identity. I didn't feel that at the beginning. I didn't feel like I was going to give up. So it's kind of ... been a slow chipping away, ... slowly coming to understand that I was going to lose all of that. All of my purpose for being, all of my reason to get up, all of my efforts, my everything. Being a lawyer to me was so much part of who I am and how I think. I still think like a lawyer whether, you know, I'm talking about teacher reviews or how to divide the costs for something or assess a risk for something. I think like a lawyer. It's still part of the way I approach the world. It's just that I can't use any of those [skills] to help anybody who is paying me anymore.

Part of my identity, that I was compensated for, exercising all those parts of my brain that I had trained to be a certain way, learn a certain topic ... I lost all my contacts. Nobody called me anymore. It just sort of gradually happened. It's like a slow leak. No one called me for lunch. I didn't get invited to the Christmas parties after a few years. The last time I went to one I felt like the token disabled person in the back. You're not part of it anymore. It took me two years to stop going to firm events.

I wanted to come back, and then I'd just get sick. I don't know how ten years have passed, and other than that one time, when I worked on that deal, I can't believe I haven't found a way to do [it]. And it's funny, because that's what people say to me: "Oh, Michelle, there's got to be a way for you to work."

But I can't give anymore. Even these meetings [with you] leave me just spent. It's been a slow realization. A slow acceptance of where I'm truly at. Lots of counselling. Lots of tears. Lots of grieving for all of that. For the collegiality in a firm. For the intellectual work and rigour. For being useful in a way that I knew, that I just had become. That's the sad thing. I had really felt like I had properly become an expert at what I did. Not that I wasn't still learning, but overall I felt a level of competence.

Michelle's life after practice has not been bleak or unhappy. Her close network of friends is a source of happiness and support. Michelle lives in a tightly knit community. And her husband remains her best friend and unwavering in his love and commitment. Her children are still in school, and she feels grateful to have been present for them over the past ten years. She has been as active in their education and in her community as she is able to be, including getting involved in some local issues of policies and politics. She has also found peace through yoga: "That discipline of yoga has been absolutely essential for my healing and my grieving and ... me taking the shape that I am now."

There is nothing perverse or surprising about Michelle's sense of loss. When you consider what attracted Michelle to being a lawyer, why it engaged her passion and her interest, you would not say that she was wrong or that her sense of loss was misguided. It was meaningful to her, and it makes sense that it was so. Some might argue that employment law could be fairer or more just than it is. But inarguably it creates a fairer and more just world for employees than would exist without it. It also achieves law's function of social settlement, perhaps not satisfying everyone's sense of justice and fairness but settling on a form of justice and fairness between employers and employees that is recognizable and legitimate.[15] For Michelle, the impartial principle derived from political philosophy, that what lawyers do can be justified because it helps to achieve law's social settlement, was something that she experienced in her work as a lawyer. It was part of her motivation to become a lawyer, and it was what she believed she was doing when she ensured that employers talked to employees and that employees who had been wrongfully dismissed received the payment and dignity that they deserved. Her passion and commitment, and the impartial objective justification for her work, were matched in her experience.

For that reason, the classic moral problem for lawyers – that they advocate for morally suspect (but lawful) ends through morally dubious (but lawful) means – was not an observed feature of her practice. Michelle did have some legally weak cases, and at times there was external pressure to pursue cases that created challenging and unsettling situations. But her passion for and engagement in her work were not disrupted by any sense that she was participating in a morally corrupt system or process.

Michelle's engagement with her work also arose from values and experiences not specific to law – participating in the intellectual community of a law firm, educating and assisting those who could benefit from her knowledge, and developing that knowledge into expertise. When you engage in an activity worth doing, and you develop your skills in that activity to a form of excellence, they can be meaningful, as they clearly were for Michelle.

The challenges of legal practice to the meaningfulness of her life were when profit orientation overwhelmed the practice, when the emphasis was on billable hours, and when the focus was on fitting into an intensely profit-driven culture. These aspects created obvious challenges for Michelle as a parent; immediately after her return to work from her first maternity leave, she did not spend any waking hours with her child, let alone have the opportunity to be actively engaged in parenting her. But they also disrupted the pursuit of what was meaningful to her about being a lawyer. In those moments being an excellent lawyer, helping or educating clients or ensuring fairness, was more difficult because they weren't how success was measured or valued. They were still what mattered in one sense – certainly they were what mattered to Michelle – but it is hard to hold on to that when those around you are not interested in looking at it or in valuing your efforts to achieve it.

I have told Michelle's story because it shows us things about being a lawyer that the academy does not always see. It certainly has a claim to our attention as scholars. But that isn't the whole truth. I have also told her story because I want people to know it. I want them to know her gifts and the work that Michelle was capable of doing. I want them to know the challenges that she overcame and her determination to find a place to practise where she could be the lawyer that she wanted to be. And I want them to know that being a lawyer can mean a great deal, that when it is taken away it can break your heart.

Notes

1 Her name and some minor identifying details have been changed to protect her privacy.

2 Interview transcript, May–June 2013. Any quotation without direct citation in the remainder of this chapter is also from the interview transcripts.

3 Bernard Williams, *Ethics and the Limits of Philosophy* (Cambridge, MA: Harvard University Press, 1985) at 6.

4 The idea that morality is a subcategory of ethics is from *ibid.* at 6 and 14. Ethics, including morality, are often also distinguished from legality in understanding the duties of lawyers. See, for example, Thomas Shaffer, "The Legal Ethics of Radical Individualism" (1987) 65 Texas Law Review 963. For Shaffer, ethics and morality are one thing; law is another. I am using Williams to suggest further that ethics and morality are not the same and that morality is only one aspect of ethics.

5 Bernard Williams, "Persons, Morality, and Character" in *Moral Luck: Philosophical Papers 1973–1980* (Cambridge, UK: Cambridge University Press, 1981) at 2, defining morality as "impartial" and requiring "abstraction from particular circumstances and particular characteristics of the parties, including the agent."

6 *Ibid.* at 12. His identification of ground projects is most notable for his claim that an ethical life does not necessarily require that we sacrifice our ground projects to the claims of ordinary morality. This aspect of his philosophy has been criticized. For our purposes, the proper intersection between morality and ethics does not need to be resolved. For criticisms of Williams, see Barbara Herman, "Integrity and Impartiality" (1983) 66(2) The Monist 233; Alasdair MacIntyre, "The Magic in the Pronoun 'My'" (1983) 94(1) Ethics 113 at 119–20; Sarah Buss, "Needs (Someone Else's), Projects (My Own), and Reasons" (2006) 103(8) The Journal of Philosophy 373 at 401; and Lisa Rivera, "Sacrifices, Aspirations, and Morality: Williams Reconsidered" (2007) 10(1) Ethical Theory and Moral Practice 69.

7 Susan Wolf, *Meaning in Life and Why It Matters* (Princeton: Princeton University Press, 2010) at 9.

8 *Ibid.*

9 *Ibid.* at 129.

10 *Ibid.* at 26. Like Williams, Wolf views meaning as having a claim against morality. That claim does not require that morality be revised, only that one accept that morality and meaning might conflict with one another (at 58). Wolf does not, though, think that morality and meaning are as likely to conflict as Williams suggests (at 61).

11 For a general discussion on the methodology and history of legal ethics theory, see Alice Woolley, "If Philosophical Legal Ethics Is the Answer, What Is the Question?" (2010) 60 University of Toronto Law Journal 983. Some of the key works include Richard Wasserstrom, "Lawyers as Professionals: Some Moral Issues" (1975) 5 Human Rights 1; Monroe Freedman, "Personal Responsibility in a Professional System"

(1977–78) 27 Catholic University Law Review 191; David Luban, *Lawyers and Justice: An Ethical Study* (Princeton: Princeton University Press, 1988); David Luban, *Legal Ethics and Human Dignity* (New York: Cambridge University Press, 2009); Reid Mortensen, "The Lawyer as Parent: Sympathy, Care, and Character in Lawyers' Ethics" (2009) 12(1) Legal Ethics 1; Gerald Postema, "Moral Responsibility in Professional Ethics" (1980) 55 New York University Law Review 63; W. Bradley Wendel, *Lawyers and Fidelity to Law* (Princeton: Princeton University Press, 2010); Tim Dare, *The Counsel of Rogues? A Defence of the Standard Conception of the Lawyer's Role* (Burlington: Ashgate Publishing Company, 2009); William H. Simon, *The Practice of Justice: A Theory of Lawyers' Ethics* (Cambridge, MA: Harvard University Press, 1998); Thomas Shaffer, "The Legal Ethics of Radical Individualism" (1987) 65 Texas Law Review 963; Allan Hutchinson, "Calgary and Everything After: A Postmodern Re-Vision of Lawyering" (1995) 33 Alberta Law Review 768; and Trevor Farrow, "Sustainable Professionalism" (2008) 46 Osgoode Hall Law Journal 51. A partial exception to this is the work of Daniel Markovits, who assesses in *A Modern Legal Ethics: Adversary Advocacy in a Democratic Age* (Princeton: Princeton University Press, 2008) whether one can be a lawyer and achieve an ethical (well-lived) life. His inquiry, however, is relatively narrow. Although he is concerned with the ethics of a lawyer's life, he is concerned only with the intersection between the moral challenge of being a lawyer and the ethics of the lawyer's life.

12 This is the "standard conception" of the lawyer's role, normally identified as having three features: the lawyer must be a partisan advocate for her client, neutral toward the morality of her client's aims, and without accountability for the morality (or immorality) of those aims (see Dare, *supra* note 11 at 5–11.

13 As noted by Williams, *supra* note 5.

14 For a discussion of the philosophical principles, see Alice Woolley, "Context, Meaning, and Morality in the Life of the Lawyer" (2014) 17(1) Legal Ethics 1–22.

15 This is the explanation for the "moral problem" of the lawyer's role offered by those emphasizing explanations from political philosophy. See Wendel, *supra* note 11; and Dare, *supra* note 11.

10

Ian Scott

Renaissance Man, Consummate Advocate, Attorney General Extraordinaire

W. BRENT COTTER

Many Canadian lawyers have distinguished themselves in their commitment to public service. A number of Premiers and Prime Ministers come to mind,[1] as do leading judges[2] and distinguished Attorneys General.[3] Not to be overlooked are many men and women who have served with distinction in the offices of the Attorney General or Departments of Justice throughout Canada.[4] Among the many outstanding Canadians who have distinguished themselves in their contributions to public service, I have elected to devote this chapter to Ian Scott, QC, former Attorney General of Ontario. The choice of Scott is arbitrary in one sense – why him rather than another distinguished government lawyer? – but in another, highly appropriate. Although others have served with great distinction in law-related positions in public service, few have done so much to advance the public interest in so short a time as did Scott. Few have articulated the role of leading lawyers in public service with as much eloquence or precision, and none was more committed to living that role in his time in public service.

Who Was Ian Scott?
On the surface, understanding Ian Scott is a relatively easy task. With Neil McCormick, he wrote a thoughtful autobiography.[5] He had a wide circle of friends and was greatly admired in the Ontario and Canadian legal and political communities. His extended family cherishes his memory and continues to celebrate his life and contributions to law.[6] His advocacy and writings on

the role of the Attorney General are often cited in professional circles and legal education. At the same time, Scott lived a very private life and in many respects remains an enigma.

Ian Scott was born in 1934 into a distinguished Canadian family that was part of the Ottawa, Ontario, and Canadian establishment. The Scotts trace their ancestry in Canada to the late 1700s and early 1800s. Family members have served for more than a century in distinguished roles in public service. His maternal great-grandfather, A.J. Blair, served as a provincial Attorney General, a Premier, and eventually a federal Cabinet Minister under Prime Minister Laurier. His paternal great-grandfather, Sir Richard Scott, served as Mayor of Bytown, the predecessor of Ottawa, and as government leader in the Senate. He was also influential in establishing the constitutional principle that Canadian education be divided along religious lines. The Scotts were devout Catholics, and though Ian ultimately drifted away from the faith later in his career, he used his immense gifts in the fight to preserve the terms under which funding for Catholic education was established.[7] A deep interest in law and public life continued in subsequent generations of the Scott family, always from the perspective of the Liberal Party, and it is not surprising that both Ian and his younger brother David followed in their father's and grandfather's footsteps to become lawyers.[8] David Scott himself is one of Canada's most distinguished and widely respected lawyers and one of the most committed to the cause of access to justice.

Despite being steeped in the traditions of a great Canadian family, Ian Scott did not easily fit in. Having heard him speak when he was at the peak of his career, I was amazed to learn that as a young person he suffered from a severe stutter. Yet in his effort to overcome it he chose to place himself in situations where he had to confront challenges – debates, drama, and public speaking – and either survive or fail.[9] This seems to presage much of his professional career – the courage to take on daunting challenges and, for the most part, prevail.

Although Ian benefited from outstanding educational opportunities in his early years, and appears to have been popular and admired at school, he struggled to fit in. This was most evident as he came to terms with a "difference" from other students, which he came to appreciate in his teen years as homosexuality.[10] Ian recognized that pursuing further education and a career in Ottawa would be problematic and that he would be better off studying and working in a larger, more anonymous environment. He moved to Toronto to attend university there, and though he visited Ottawa often, he never lived there again.

Scott studied at St. Michael's College at the University of Toronto and enrolled in law at Osgoode Hall Law School, where he was active in student life though by no means a diligent scholar. Upon graduation in 1959,[11] he articled with the McMillan Binch firm in Toronto, after which, declining an invitation to return to Ottawa to join his father's firm, he found a position as a junior lawyer with Andrew Brewin, who subsequently became an NDP Member of Parliament. The practice was apparently busy and often disorganized, an environment in which Scott thrived. His opportunities to appear in court seemed to be endless, and, benefiting from the somewhat haphazard approach of Brewin himself, Scott built a reputation as a skilled lawyer and an outstanding orator, exposed as he was to interesting legal cases and to the outstanding advocates then practising law in the courts of Toronto. The firm evolved and grew, and Ian actively recruited outstanding young lawyers to what was now the law firm of Cameron Brewin and Scott. Additions to the firm in the late 1960s and early 1970s – notably Stephen Goudge, Ian McGilp, and Chris Paliare – established a remarkable team of lawyers that, later in Scott's career, actively supported his entry into provincial politics. Scott himself took on a wide range of cases, from complex issues of administrative law, to high-profile criminal matters, to land and zoning issues, to the representation of prison guards. It appears that he was attracted to cases that interested him, that were matters of high principle, or in which he thought that someone had been wronged or the law had simply gone astray.

By all accounts, Scott was a brilliant courtroom lawyer, perhaps the most outstanding advocate of his generation. Even as great a counsel as John Sopinka noted this talent in a major case dealing with the processes to be followed by a Commission of Inquiry into land acquisitions by the Government of Ontario. Scott recounts that, at one point during his oral argument before the Ontario Court of Appeal, Sopinka interrupted his submission to warn the judges that they were in danger of losing sight of the law by listening to his "eloquence".[12] His friend and colleague Stephen Goudge, until recently a senior member of the Ontario Court of Appeal and a highly respected litigation lawyer before becoming a judge, has seen hundreds of lawyers in court. He described his friend's abilities in this way: "Ian Scott was uniquely eloquent. *Uniquely eloquent.*"[13] In his keynote address at a symposium honouring Scott at Queen's University in 2003, the Honourable Ian Binnie, himself one of Canada's greatest advocates, said of Scott: "In his heyday, Ian Scott was a charming, bantering, eloquent, successful, abrasive, brass-knuckled partisan advocate. He prevailed not only at the appeal court level, but before every type of court and tribunal where advocacy skills and chutzpah win cases. He is so scary that it is entirely appropriate that he will get his honorary doctorate on Hallowe'en."[14]

This ability was perhaps most evident in the one case that Scott argued in the Supreme Court of Canada in his capacity as Attorney General, an office that he held after his time in private practice. The case was a challenge to the constitutionality of a provincial Bill to fully fund Catholic schools in Ontario. By this time, Scott was no longer a Roman Catholic, but he believed deeply that separate school funding, which his great-grandfather had helped to establish, should be preserved. He argued from only a few lines of notes, and his eloquence persuaded the Supreme Court that the legislation was constitutional. James MacPherson, a highly respected member of the Ontario Court of Appeal and a constitutional law expert, appeared on the same case for another party. MacPherson described Scott's argument before the Supreme Court that day as "the finest courtroom performance he had ever seen."[15]

His career in private practice ultimately led Scott to serve as commission counsel for several public inquiries. The first was an inquiry into the cause of riots at the Kingston Penitentiary, where he saw first-hand the circumstances in which inmates lived. Later, with Goudge, he served as commission counsel for the Berger Pipeline Inquiry in the Northwest Territories. And, shortly before his entry into provincial politics, he was involved in the Susan Nelles Inquiry.

The Berger Inquiry was one of the most significant and unique public inquiries in Canadian history. Commissioner Tom Berger charted a course for the investigations that had never been seen before. The report described the project this way:

> We look upon the North as our last frontier. It is natural for us to think of developing it, of subduing the land and extracting its resources to fuel Canada's industry and heat our homes. Our whole inclination is to think of expanding our industrial machine to the limit of our county's frontiers. In this view, the construction of a gas pipeline is seen as the next advance in a series of frontier advances that have been intimately bound up with Canadian history. But the native people say the North is their homeland. They have lived there for thousands of years. They claim it is their land, and they believe they have a right to say what its future ought to be.
>
> The question whether a pipeline shall be built has become the occasion for the joining of these issues.[16]

The Berger Inquiry, and the ways in which it gave voice to those who hitherto had no voice, had a profound impact on Scott and Goudge. As Scott noted, "[o]ne of Berger's great insights was that the commission could be used as a great exercise in democracy, to explore the needs of indigenous peoples and to explain those needs to the great mass of the Canadian people who had little direct experience of the North."[17] Goudge described the Kingston Penitentiary Inquiry and the Berger Inquiry as two of the most significant pieces of legal work that Scott undertook in a remarkable career. Goudge saw this as the beginning of Scott's direct engagement in the public life of the law.[18] Exposure to Berger's imaginative approaches, combined with first-hand encounters with injustice, may well have inspired in Scott the bold approaches that he took in his subsequent work as Attorney General.

It is not self-evident that a young man growing up in relative opulence in Ottawa, a member of a distinguished and well-established family (even one with some sense of being an outsider), would easily come to see the need for justice for disadvantaged people. Yet, in much of his later work as Attorney General, his greatest achievements occurred when Scott challenged institutions and institutional wisdom in a search for justice. Perhaps his work at the Berger Inquiry gave him the chance to appreciate the lives and challenges of people far from the centres of influence in Canadian life, inspired his interest in pursuing justice in public life, and hardened his resolve to achieve justice in ways that honoured ordinary Canadians.

And perhaps as a gay man he felt a sense of affinity with the excluded people and communities that he encountered in his legal career. Given his position of relative privilege in Canadian society, Scott could initiate changes to make that society more respectful and inclusive of those who were marginalized. On this front, he did not explicitly acknowledge his sexual orientation during his legal career or during his period in public life. Despite his courage in taking on so many challenges in his life and career, this was one that he avoided. Perhaps his voice would have led Canadian society to become more accepting, at an earlier time than it ultimately did, of the legitimate place of gays and lesbians and transgendered people in our society. But balanced against this are three important points. First, it is easy to see these issues through the eyes of the early twenty-first century, and not through the eyes of the 1970s and 1980s, the decades in which Scott lived and worked in the public eye and during which time discrimination against gays and lesbians was socially accepted.[19] Second, seen in this light, coming out in those years might well have prevented his election to public office as well as his achievements as Attorney General, including those related to human rights for gay and lesbian people.[20] Third, who are we to say of someone who did so much for public life in his province and country that he could have sacrificed even more, done even more?

Ian Scott's Life in Public Service

Getting Elected

By his own account, Scott's first attempt to enter provincial politics, at the age of forty-six, was a failure. As someone whose family had been steeped in Canadian and Ontario political life for generations, and as someone who had great interpersonal gifts, Scott likely had the possibility of a political career in the back of his mind. Nevertheless, as he tells it, Scott began to consider politics seriously only when encouraged to do so by a group of young law students at Queen's University while on a sabbatical from his law practice in 1978.[21] A lifelong opponent of the Tories – consistent with his family history – Scott chose to align himself with the Liberal Party and to run in his own riding of St. David, then held by a Conservative Cabinet Minister, Margaret Scriviner. He built an enthusiastic and idealistic but unseasoned campaign team,[22] led by Stephen Goudge. They campaigned hard, but Scott lost, and the Conservatives were re-elected.

Four years later Scott agreed once again to be a candidate in the Ontario election. The Conservatives entered the election with a new leader and Premier, Frank Miller, as well as a significant lead in the polls. Scott had become fond of the new Liberal leader, David Peterson, and was unwilling to disappoint him by declining to be a candidate in the 1985 election. Nevertheless, he held out little prospect of electoral success, either for himself or for the Liberals. Both Peterson and Scott ran professional and effective campaigns. Scott's campaign was once again led by Goudge. Scott won his own riding, and the Liberals had the highest percentage of the popular vote, but the Conservatives won the largest number of seats. An early accord between the Liberal Party and the NDP doomed the Conservatives, and the Liberals came to power supported by the NDP. Scott sought and received an appointment to Cabinet as Attorney General.

Becoming Attorney General

Although Ian Scott was the Attorney General of Ontario for only five years, compared with other Attorneys General that this country and its provinces have produced, his achievements in those five years are breathtaking. His accomplishments began virtually from his first day as Attorney General, with his commitment of $1 million in funding to the Legal Education Action Fund (LEAF) and his concession on behalf of the Government of Ontario of the discrimination inherent in prohibiting a girl from playing on a boys' ice hockey team.[23] Although it might thus have been appreciated from the outset that the lawyers at the Ministry of the Attorney General had an Attorney General at the helm whose like it had never experienced before, it is unlikely that anyone imagined the breathtaking ride that they were about to experience.

Scott's contributions as Attorney General can be divided into two categories. The first is his principled articulation of the responsibilities of the Attorney General and the ways in which a person in that position must carry them out. The second is the set of his specific legal accomplishments. I will examine his career in public service through each lens.

Responsibilities of the Attorney General

Generally speaking, in Canadian public governance, the Ministry of the Attorney General is traditional and conservative in orientation. The Ministry supports and defends the laws of the province and their application, including laws that have been around for a long time. This is made clear in the early sections of the *Ministry of the Attorney General Act.*[24] Sections 2 and 5 of the *Act* provide that

> 2 (2) The Attorney General shall preside over and have charge of the Ministry
>
> …
>
> 5. The Attorney General,
>
> (a) is the Law Officer of the Executive Council;
> (b) *shall see that the administration of public affairs is in accordance with the law;*
> (c) shall superintend all matters connected with the administration of justice in Ontario …(emphasis added)

Embedded within this language are significant duties and responsibilities, many of which are difficult to reconcile within the framework of Canadian parliamentary democracy. In Canadian political culture, the Attorney General is a member of the provincial or federal Cabinet. As a member of Cabinet, he or she shares responsibility for the policy and political direction of the government. Law, and the laws of the jurisdiction, do not always accommodate every political or policy interest of a government in power. Yet the Attorney General remains legally obligated to ensure that the "administration of public affairs is in accordance with the law." No other Cabinet Minister bears that explicit responsibility. And it is fair to say that this tension – the politician's desire and obligation to advance political and policy interests on the one hand, and the duty to the rule of law on the other – can be a challenge for anyone; however, it is a greater tension for the Attorney General.

In Canada, we have been blessed with governments in general, and Attorneys General in particular, who have had great respect for the rule of law. More importantly, Attorneys General have wisely understood that a central part of their role is to preserve and protect the rule of law. Scott is part of this history and legacy. But he did much more. His work to inform himself and then to educate lawyers in public service, other politicians, and the public about the nature and fundamental importance of the role of the Attorney General is nearly unprecedented in modern Canadian legal history. Only the published works of Professor J.L.J. Edwards offer a more complete assessment of the role of the Attorney General.[25]

In two papers, Scott discusses the role of the Attorney General in his typically clear and engaging way. In each paper, he celebrates the value of a society governed by the rule of law and articulates the fundamental contribution that an Attorney General makes to its protection and preservation. At the same time, Scott recognized the boundaries of the role, acknowledging that the Attorney General does not have the ability or right to use the position to simply oppose policy choices with which he or she disagrees. His most insightful comments, in my opinion, appear in "Law, Policy, and the Role of the Attorney General: Constancy and Change in the 1980s."[26] In that article, Scott examines various dimensions of the role of the Attorney General and articulates a comprehensive guide for fulfillment of the role in these various contexts. It ought to be required reading for any Attorney General, Deputy Attorney General, or agent of the Attorney General.

Scott's most insightful comments address the role of the Attorney General in relation to criminal prosecutions, the duty to uphold the law (in particular the Constitution and *Charter of Rights*), and civil litigation.

On the first point, Scott recognized that the Attorney General plays a limited role in decision making in criminal law matters, since the lion's share of this work is done by his or her agents. Nevertheless, he is clear about the working principles that ought to be applied:

The confidence of the public in the administration of justice prohibits the use of the criminal law for partisan purposes. Moreover, as a guardian of the public interest, the attorney general must act in accordance with the interests of those whom the government represents, and not simply in the interest of the government to which he belongs.[27]

And, though Scott recognized the value of receiving input into the assessment of what is in the public interest, including Cabinet input, he endorsed the view that the decision was that of the Attorney General. He quoted with approval the views of Lord Shawcross on this point: "The responsibility for the eventual decision rests with the Attorney General, and he is not to be put, and is not put, under pressure by his colleagues in the matter."[28]

With respect to the duty to uphold the law, Scott recognized the primacy of the legal obligation set out in section 5 of the *Ministry of the Attorney General Act*. In his exploration of this question in "The Role of the Attorney General and the *Charter of Rights*,"[29] Scott commented on the dramatic changes to the responsibilities of the Attorney General wrought by the *Charter*. Nevertheless, on the important point of principle, he was steadfast:

In advising on questions of constitutionality, the Attorney General must give paramount consideration to the obligation to ensure that government action complies with the law, in this case the supreme law of Canada. The giving of constitutional advice must be carried out with the same independence and detached objectivity with which the Attorney General approaches questions of prosecution policy.[30]

More directly, he states that, "[i]f the Attorney General gives a legal opinion that a suggested course of action is unconstitutional, a decision by the government to proceed in the face of the opinion would place the Attorney General in direct conflict with the obligation to ensure that government action meets legal requirements."[31]

Nevertheless, Scott did not succumb to the temptation of omnipotence. He recognized the limits of the authority of the Attorney General. As he writes in "The Role of the Attorney General and the Charter of Rights," "no direct conflict would arise if, in selecting between two possible courses of action, both of which were considered constitutional by the Attorney General, the government chose to reject the Attorney General's policy preference."[32]

Indeed, Scott recognized that the "legal" role of the Attorney General was a limited one,[33] and he was understandably more interested in the office's policy-making role (a topic that I will address in examining some of the changes in policy and law that he introduced). Nevertheless, even here he was guided by principle:

> I believe that it is the function of an independent attorney general to bring the focus of justice to questions of politics ... I believe it is wrong to imply that issues of principle cannot also be a primary concern of persons in the political process. Indeed, my claim is that the attorney general's special responsibility must be to ensure that issues of principle remain a central concern of policy-making. An attorney's role, in other words, is precisely to ensure that democratic decision-making in our community takes into account questions of human rights and constitutionalism.[34]

Where does this take us? Scott set out for the legal profession the framework for understanding the roles and responsibilities of the Attorney General, for future Attorneys General, and for those who aid them. He also inspired and provided guidance to subsequent generations of lawyers working in the public service.[35] His analysis does not answer all of the questions.[36] As Adam Dodek and I have argued in different ways elsewhere,[37] the lawyer in public service has greater ethical responsibilities as a result of the role that he or she plays in the exercise of public authority and on behalf of a larger public interest than those that apply to other lawyering roles. That Scott did not definitively answer this question – of where the lawyer's public duty ends and where appropriation of political discretion begins – is evident in an article on government lawyers in which Patrick Monahan asserts a lesser duty for public sector lawyers than do either Dodek or I.[38] Nonetheless, without Scott's analysis of the Attorney General's roles and duties, none of that later scholarship would have been possible. Scott was the first person to provide serious and thoughtful consideration of what is required for the lawyer discharging a public duty.

Achievements as Attorney General

Thinking about Ian Scott's brief but remarkable career as Attorney General, Stephen Goudge recently constructed a list of his achievements:

> Court Reform
> Pay Equity

Meech Lake
1985 Accord
Separate School Funding
Freedom of Information
The Elimination of QCs
Judicial Appointments
Human Rights
Women's Directorate
Class Actions
Land Claims
No Fault Auto Insurance
LEAF[39]

This list is impressive by any measure, but when one considers that Scott served as Attorney General for fewer than six years it is a set of achievements likely unmatched by any Attorney General anywhere. Although each achievement is worthy of extended discussion and analysis, I have chosen to highlight and examine four of them: separate school funding, court reform, judicial appointments, and the Women's Directorate, and Legal Education and Action Fund (LEAF). His work on the *Meech Lake Accord* and land claims, which is well known, has also received significant analysis. I have chosen these achievements because, though perhaps lesser known, they capture his mix of an unwavering support for conventional values (*e.g.*, separate school funding) and an apparently contradictory determination to challenge conventional values – long entrenched in the status quo – that he thought were unresponsive to modern societal needs (*e.g.*, court reform, judicial appointments, and QCs) or unfair to a poorly represented dimension of Ontario society (*e.g.*, LEAF, Women's Directorate, pay equity).[40]

Separate School Funding
Separate school funding was a Scott family legacy. Several generations of men in the family had advocated for funding, dating back to Ian Scott's paternal grandfather, Sir Richard Scott, who had proposed a system for local taxes to be allocated to the particular taxpayer's school system of choice, including Protestant schools in Quebec and Catholic schools in Ontario.[41] This approach was incorporated into the *British North America Act*.[42] Both his grandfather and his father worked to extend the tax base available to Catholic schools, after the Privy Council held in *Tiny Township*[43] that separate school funding would be available only up to grade ten.[44]

Before retiring in 1984, Bill Davis (the Premier at the time) announced that the provincial government would bring in full funding for Catholic schools. However, his successor as Premier was defeated, and the Liberal government under which Scott served would be tasked with drafting the legislation. The resultant legislation, Bill 30,[45] was designed to implement full funding to Roman Catholic high schools and to provide to Catholic school boards access to government grants and local property taxes.[46] The legislation was challenged as being unconstitutional.[47] Scott chose to defend the legislation himself as Attorney General. Ultimately, Bill 30 was found to be constitutional, and his advocacy was highly influential in the outcome. As former Chief Justice of Ontario Roy McMurtry described it in his eulogy to Scott in 2007, "[h]is arguments before both the Ontario Court of Appeal and Supreme Court of Canada were judged by many who witnessed them as the finest courtroom performances they had ever seen."[48]

In this case, Scott strongly embraced the status quo and advocated for a position that, in an increasingly pluralized Canada, is more difficult to justify. Nevertheless, his remarkable advocacy in support of continued separate school funding shows the degree to which he identified both with the importance of respect for constitutional values and with an honourable past, one with which he was personally connected. Although it appears to have been a curious position for someone who was no longer committed to Roman Catholicism, seen through this historical and constitutional lens it is more understandable. Scott, above all, respected the supreme law of the land. And he was deeply respectful of the contributions that his own family had made to our country.

With respect to other issues, Scott had no hesitation in remaking Ontario law and policy in ways that rejected obsolete traditions or advanced the interests of long-excluded members of Ontario society. Perhaps the best examples of the former are his determination to reform the courts, eliminate the QC designation, and reform the provincial court appointment process.

Court Reform

Court reform is no easy task. Scott was a good friend of "the Courts" as an institution and was a personal friend to many of the people who sat as judges on the Supreme Court of Ontario. He respected many of the judges of the Court and had a successful career appearing before them. The status and hierarchy of the courts are also deeply entrenched in a societal perspective.

Before the proposed court reform undertaken by Scott, there were various levels of courts in Ontario. Under section 96 of the *British North America*

Act,[49] the federal government appoints to the superior courts of Ontario judges who had the same powers as English superior court judges in 1867 did. District and county courts were created later, with judges being appointed under section 96 but with less authority than those in the Supreme Court of Ontario. Finally, there are provincial courts, whose judges are appointed by the province and have their powers fixed by statute. In Scott's opinion, the existing system set up an artificial distinction between which courts had jurisdiction to hear which cases, increasing uncertainty in a process already too expensive and difficult to comprehend for the average layperson.[50]

In addition, Scott strongly believed that local matters should be dealt with locally, and decentralization of the functions of the superior court to regional centres around Ontario could only be achieved if the superior court was merged with the county court.[51] Arguments that supported court merger included streamlined procedures, reduction of jurisdictional conflict between county and superior courts, and cost savings through integrated court administration.[52] As well, six other provinces had already merged their superior and county or district courts.[53]

Scott was determined to succeed in reforming court administration where his Conservative predecessors had failed.[54] Before taking action to reorganize the courts, he asked Justice Thomas Zuber to conduct an inquiry into the court system. It was the first general examination of the organization, management, and operation of the Ontario court system in fourteen years.[55] Zuber faced numerous challenges. The previous inquiry had made no recommendations. There was a backlog of unresolved issues. And there was growing public concern over court effectiveness.[56] Upon receiving the Zuber Report, and in the face of significant judicial opposition, the government proceeded to pass legislation by which the superior court merged with the county and district courts to create the Ontario Court of Justice (General Division), the family and criminal divisions of the provincial court merged with the Ontario Court of Justice (Provincial Division), and the Court of Appeal became a separate court.[57]

Elimination of the QC Designation

In a similar vein, Scott eliminated the honorary distinction of Queen's Counsel or QC. The title of Queen's Counsel or, more accurately, Queen's Counsel Learned in the Law, is the adoption by the Canadian legal profession of a status accorded to senior barristers who appear before the courts of the United Kingdom. In that country, it is a status accorded to the most outstanding barristers, and the distinction confers both honour to and duty upon the barrister so designated. In Canada, at least for the past number of generations, the QC designation has conferred only honour. The title is much sought after by lawyers, who often lobby for the designation, either directly or through intermediaries. In some provincial jurisdictions, the QC has been used to recognize long-standing members of the legal profession, or lawyers who have held certain offices, whether or not the recipient lawyer appeared regularly in court. In some cases, award of the QC designation was also used by governments as a form of low-level patronage, denigrating the distinction. Scott believed that the designation had fallen into the latter of these categories, and he decided to eliminate it by refusing to recommend to Cabinet the appointment of any new QCs. He faced significant negative commentary from the legal profession, but he modified his position only to the extent that he did not try to remove retroactively the QC status from those, including himself, who had already received it.[58] Although little of import turns on the presence or absence of the QC designation in the Canadian legal profession, this policy change highlights what was most admirable about Scott. He saw a small injustice, or perhaps a small misrepresentation of status, and sought to correct it. And in this he gave up an asset of some value to a politician – the ability to confer patronage. A politician who loses something in the process of "doing the right thing" deserves our admiration. This "tradition" of not awarding QCs, if it can be so called, has continued in Ontario since Scott's five-year tenure as Attorney General ended.[59]

Reform of Judicial Appointments

In a more significant vein, Ian Scott gave up one of the most valued forms of political patronage when he reformed the process by which provincial court judges are appointed. It is no secret in the legal profession that many judicial appointments are made on the basis of politics. Much has been written recently on the problems associated with the judicial appointment process in Canada.[60] Public confidence in the independence and competence of our judiciary is essential to citizen confidence in the rule of law.

Nevertheless, most governments in Canada have continued to be guided by processes that jeopardize these principles, and they steadfastly avoid processes that would appoint the most qualified candidates to the bench. Once candidates are assessed to be qualified for appointment, Attorneys General are entitled to make appointments from the pool of qualified candidates, regardless of relative merit. These archaic procedures accommodate and encourage problematic, even inappropriate, factors in the appointment process. People perceive that some judicial appointments are politically motivated or based on "who you know." This inevitably results in well-qualified but politically unconnected lawyers being passed over for appointment in favour of less-qualified appointees. And, generally speaking, the idea that someone other than the most qualified candidate obtains a position is problematic and unjust enough, let alone that the position under consideration dispenses justice to citizens. We rarely tolerate such an approach to hiring or appointments in any other walk of public life.

Although someone has to select judges and be accountable for their appointments, one of the most problematic features of the conventional judicial appointment process is the degree of discretion residing in, and patronage authority of, the Attorney General. The use of political patronage in the appointment of judges influences lawyers to join political parties and make financial contributions to them in the hope that, if it becomes relevant in the future, they can call in the favour of their political support to enhance the prospect of a judicial appointment.

Scott did not need a series of academic or public critiques to appreciate the problems associated with judicial appointments. But his decision to give up this virtually unfettered discretion to make judicial appointments required courage and commitment. He implemented a new judicial appointment process that dramatically diminished the Attorney General's discretion, virtually eliminated political patronage, and made merit the key consideration. The resulting process works like this: whenever a vacancy exists in the provincial court, an independent and widely representative screening committee considers a list of potential candidates for appointment and recommends a short list of at least two persons for the position, from which the Attorney General chooses.[61]

Scott embarked on this significant reform of judicial appointments fully aware of the degree to which a process focused on quality and representativeness would strengthen the Provincial Court of Ontario and the degree to which his own discretion in the appointment process would be severely curtailed. The process that he instituted has continued to be used in Ontario since the 1980s. It remains one of the most principled and least political processes for the appointment of judges in Canada.

Equality-Seeking Initiatives
Equally important, Ian Scott was a charter member of the "equality-seeking community" long before the term was coined. This is best exemplified by his

early commitments to equality for women and his determination to entrench equality on the basis of sexual orientation in Ontario's *Human Rights Code.*

With respect to the former, Scott set an early precedent with the position that he adopted in *Blainey.*[62] Justine Blainey, a talented twelve-year-old hockey player, was denied the opportunity to play on a boys' team in Ontario. This denial, part of the Ontario Hockey Association's policies, was insulated from human rights oversight by section 19(2) of the Ontario *Human Rights Act.*[63] Justine challenged this legislation and ultimately succeeded in establishing that section 19(2) was a violation of the equality provision of the *Charter of Rights and Freedoms.* In argument before the courts, at Attorney General Scott's direction, the Human Rights Commission took the highly unusual position that its own legislation was unconstitutional. This view was rejected by the trial judge but ultimately accepted at the Ontario Court of Appeal. As Justice Dubin stated,

> I think it appropriate to add a short comment on the position taken by the Ontario Human Rights Commission on this appeal. Counsel for the commission supported the appellant's contention that s. 19(2) of the Human Rights Code was unconstitutional. Normally counsel for a tribunal, where its enabling statutory authority is under attack, supports the jurisdiction conferred upon it by its enabling statute or submits its rights to the court. However, it is well known that with the introduction of s. 15(1) of the Charter, all branches of government are giving close scrutiny to legislation previously enacted with a view of satisfying themselves that it is now consistent with the Charter. That study has obviously been undertaken by the Human Rights Commission and, under such circumstances, I think it quite appropriate for counsel to provide the benefit of that review to the Court. That is the position that I understand counsel for the commission took in this appeal.[64]

Similarly, Scott recognized early the need to support the cause of women's equality rights through advocacy in litigation. In its early stages, LEAF faced significant struggles in its efforts to finance a wide range of cases challenging the status quo in which the rights of girls and women were marginalized. In many of these cases, the challenge related directly to laws or regulations or government actions. It is not an obviously attractive choice for a government to make meaningful contributions to "cause lawyering" that will bring its own laws, policies, and practices within the crosshairs of court and public scrutiny. It requires an unwavering commitment to the value of equality and fairness in a society, and it requires the courage of one's convictions to facilitate the means by which such equality and fairness will be achieved, even if it leads to criticism of one's own government. Nevertheless, Scott was, without hesitation, willing to invest public resources – including $1 million within days of becoming Attorney General – to facilitate this commitment to equality. In a similar and visionary vein, he took up the cause of pay equity and shepherded through the Ontario legislature the most advanced framework for pay equity in the country at the time.[65]

By his own account, Scott was fully engaged in every aspect of this initiative. First, he recognized the fundamental inequity that existed for women in the workplace. Second, he set about to persuade his colleagues and members of the public that it was an unfairness that needed to be corrected and that it could be corrected without great societal or economic upheaval. Third, he worked with a knowledgeable team to develop the policy to guide the move to pay equity. Fourth, he oversaw the development of the necessary amendment of fifty-eight or more separate pieces of legislation to make pay equity a reality.[66]

All of these achievements in support of the weaker and more vulnerable among us are a testament to Scott's ability to see clearly the needs of others and the ways in which legal mechanisms can help to address those needs. This, combined with his determination and the courage of his convictions, has made our society a better one.

Conclusion

There is little doubt that Ian Scott was a man ahead of his time. Using his consummate skills as a thinker and orator, combined with a truly remarkable sense of what would make his province a better and fairer place, he achieved much. In some respects, he did truly revolutionary things. Yet, in keeping with his own confidence in the legal system and the rule of law (touchstones for his own life, career, and family history), he anchored these achievements in wise public policies and democratic laws. His life and career are a testament to the adage that, "to whom much is given, much will be asked."[67]

Much of what Scott achieved was the result of his position of influence within the institutions of government. But an equally important dimension of his achievement was found in the personal values that he espoused. This is captured elegantly by Professor Edwards in relation to the role of the Attorney General: "No matter how entrenched constitutional safeguards may be, in the final analysis it is the strength of character and personal integrity of the holder of the [office] of Attorney General ... which is of paramount consideration."[68]

Abraham Lincoln is said to have remarked that "[n]early all men can stand adversity, but if you want to test a man's character give him power." The character of Scott shone through in how he used his power and authority as Attorney General not for his own purposes but to achieve what was in the best interests of the administration of justice in Ontario and the betterment of its people.

In a more personal way, Scott's courage and determination to make Ontario a better and fairer place remind me of the attitude of the great Cree Chief Poundmaker, who is reputed to have said that

> [i]t would be so much easier just to fold our hands and not make this fight. To say that I, one man, can do nothing. I grow afraid only when I see people thinking and acting like that. We all know the story of the man who sat by the trail too long, and then it grew over, and he could never find his way again. We can never forget what has happened, but we cannot go back. Nor can we just sit beside the trail.[69]

Ian Scott never folded his hands or took the view that, as one man, he could do nothing. Nor did he let the trail grow over and cause him to lose his way. And we should all be grateful for that.

Notes

Cindy Chow assisted in the preparation of this chapter.

1 Recent such individuals include nearly every Prime Minister since Pierre Trudeau as well as leading Premiers, including Frank McKenna, Jean Charest, Peter Lougheed, Alison Redford, and my personal favourites, Allan Blakeney and Roy Romanow.

2 Notable are Roy McMurtry (the former Attorney General of Ontario and recently retired Chief Justice of Ontario), Frank Iacobucci (former Deputy Minister of Justice of Canada and retired Justice of the Supreme Court of Canada), Ian Binnie (former Associate Deputy Attorney General of Canada and retired Justice of the Supreme Court of Canada), Andromache Karakatsansis (former Deputy Attorney General of Ontario and Clerk to the Premier of Ontario, currently a Justice of the Supreme Court of Canada), Jacques Chamberland (former Deputy Attorney General of Quebec and currently a Justice of the Quebec Court of Appeal), Robert Richards (former Director of the Constitutional Law branch of the Department of the Attorney General of Saskatchewan and currently Chief Justice of Saskatchewan), and James MacPherson (former Director of Constitutional Law with the Department of the Attorney General of Saskatchewan, former Dean of Law at Osgoode Hall Law

School, and currently a Justice of the Ontario Court of Appeal). The building in which the offices of the Department of the Attorney General are housed in Toronto is the McMurtry-Scott Building, aptly named after Roy McMurtry and Ian Scott.

3 In addition to those already mentioned are names such as Anne McLellan, QC (former Attorney General of Canada), Alan Rock, QC (former Attorney General of Canada and currently President of the University of Ottawa), Wally Oppal, QC (former Justice of the British Columbia Court of Appeal and former Attorney General of British Columbia), and Robert Mitchell (former Deputy Minister with the Government of Saskatchewan and former Attorney General of Saskatchewan).

4 John Tait, QC (former Deputy Attorney General of Canada and in whose honour the Canadian Bar Association's annual award for Integrity in Public Service is named), George Thomson, QC (former Deputy Attorney General of Ontario and Canada and former Executive Director of the National Judicial Institute), John Whyte, QC (former Dean of Law at Queen's University and former Deputy Attorney General of Saskatchewan), and Doug Moen, QC (former Deputy Attorney General of Saskatchewan and currently Deputy Minister to the Premier of Saskatchewan).

5 Ian Scott, *To Make a Difference: A Memoir* (Toronto: Stoddard Publishing, 1999).

6 For example, the Scott family has made generous contributions to construct an innovative working courtroom, the Ian Scott Courtroom, at the University of Ottawa, officially opened on October 23, 2013. This project was supported by a literal "who's who" of the Ontario legal and judicial community. See http://commonlaw.uottawa.ca/en/news/common-law-section-news/grand-opening-of-the-ian-g.-scott-courtroom.html.

7 See a brief discussion of Ian Scott's involvement in this case below.

8 A visit to David Scott's law office in Ottawa brings this family history to life. The walls are packed with photos of the Scott family from the 1800s to the present, elegantly articulating the family's deep commitment to Canadian political life.

9 Scott, *To Make a Difference, supra* note 5 at 12.

10 *Ibid.* at 8–9.

11 York University, Media Release, "Justice deCarteret Cory, Ian Scott, and Mel Lastman to Receive Honorary Degrees from York University" (May 30, 1997), online: York University Release Archives, http://www.yorku.ca/mediar/releases_1996_2000/archive/053097.htm.

12 Scott, *To Make a Difference, supra* note 5 at 69.

13 Interview with Stephen Goudge, August 26, 2013.

14 Justice Ian Binnie, "Mr. Ian Scott and the Ghost of Oliver Mowat" (2004) 22 The Advocates Society Journal 3 at 3.

15 Scott, *To Make a Difference, supra* note 5 at 151.

16 *Northern Frontiers, Northern Homeland: The Report of the MacKenzie Valley Pipeline Inquiry* [the Berger Report], vol. 1, *The North* (Ottawa: Supply and Services Canada, 1977) at 1.

17 Scott, *To Make a Difference, supra* note 5 at 58.

18 Interview with Stephen Goudge, August 26, 2013.

19 The laws criminalizing sodomy in Canada were repealed only in 1969.

20 Scott, *supra* note 5 at 45, expresses this sentiment: "After Pierre Trudeau took the state out of the bedrooms of consenting adults, prejudices still lingered that might have hampered my career had I been open about my sexuality."

21 *Ibid.* at 71. If so, then all of us who care deeply about law and public service are deeply indebted to those young law students who encouraged Scott in this direction.

22 The team included David Rubin, Chuck Birchall, Pete Lukasiewicz, John Ronson, and Bob Hawkins. *Ibid.* at 76.

23 *Re Blainey and Ontario Hockey Association* (1986), 54 O.R. (2d) 513, 26 D.L.R. (4th) 728 (O.N.C.A.). The case is described in more detail below.

24 *Ministry of the Attorney General Act,* R.S.O. 1990, c. M.17.

25 J.L.J. Edwards, *The Attorney General: Politics and the Public Interest* (London: Sweet and Maxwell, 1984); J.L.J. Edwards, *The Law Officers of the Crown: A Study of the Offices of Attorney-General and Solicitor-General of England, with an Account of the Office of the Director of Public Prosecution* (London: Sweet and Maxwell, 1984); J.L.J. Edwards, Commission of Inquiry Concerning Certain Activities of the Royal Canadian Mounted Police, *Ministerial Responsibility for National Security as It Relates to the Offices of the Prime Minister, Attorney General, and Solicitor General of Canada* (Ottawa: Commission of Inquiry Concerning Certain Activities of the Royal Canadian Mounted Police, 1980); J.L.J. Edwards, Royal Commission on the Donald Marshall Jr. Prosecution, *Walking the Tightrope of Justice: An Examination of the Office of the Attorney General in Canada with Particular Regard to Its Relationships with the Police and Prosecutors and the Arguments for Establishing a Statutorily Independent Director of Public Prosecutions* (Halifax: The Commission, 1989).

26 Ian Scott, "Law, Policy, and the Role of the Attorney General: Constancy and Change in the 1980s" (1989) 39 University of Toronto Law Journal 109 ["Law, Policy, and the Role of the Attorney General"].

27 *Ibid.* at 120.

28 United Kingdom, House of Commons, *Parliamentary Debates,* vol. 483, cols. 683–84 (January 29, 1951) (Sir Hartley Shawcross).

29 Ian G. Scott, "The Role of the Attorney General and the Charter of Rights" (1986–87) 29 Criminal Law Quarterly 187 ["The Role of the Attorney General"].

30 *Ibid.* at 193.

31 *Ibid.* at 195.

32 *Ibid.*

33 Scott, "Law, Policy, and the Role of the Attorney General," *supra* note 26 at 112, suggests that no more than 15 percent of his time was spent dealing with cases.

34 *Ibid.* at 112.

35 See, for example, Patrick Monahan's recent article, "'In the Public Interest': Understanding the Special Role of the Government Lawyer" (2013) 63 S. Ct. Law. Rev. 43 at 46. Scott's perspective on the role of the Attorney General was extremely valuable to me as a provincial Deputy Attorney General in the 1990s in Saskatchewan.

36 As the British Columbia Court of Appeal observed in *British Columbia v. Davies,* 2009 B.C.C.A. 337, the interplay of judicial authority and authority of the Attorney

General, in particular the Attorney General's autonomy with respect to the exercise of prosecutorial discretion, is complex.

37 Adam Dodek, "Lawyering at the Intersection of Public Law and Legal Ethics: Lawyers as Custodians of the Rule of Law" (2010) 33 Dalhousie Law Journal 1; Brent Cotter, "The Legal Accountability of Governments and Politicians: A Reflection upon Their Roles and Responsibilities" (2007), 2 Journal of Parliamentary and Political Law 63. Dodek's argument at p. 18 is that, "[a]s a matter of public law, Government lawyers should owe higher ethical duties than private lawyers because they exercise public power." Cotter's argument at pp.70-71 is that, since governments owe to their citizens a higher duty of "fair dealing," so do lawyers representing governments.

38 Monahan, *supra* note 35 at 50–52.

39 Personal notes of Stephen Goudge, in the possession of the author.

40 My impression is that some of these achievements parallel Scott's own eclectic, some might say "catholic," choices of cases to take on. However categorized, they are remarkable.

41 Scott, *To Make a Difference, supra* note 5 at 148.

42 *British North America Act, 1867* (U.K.), 30 and 31 Vict., c. 3, reprinted in R.S.C. 1985, App. II, No. 5, s. 93.

43 *Tiny Roman Catholic School Board v. Ontario,* [1928] 3 D.L.R. 753, [1928] 2 W.W.R. 641 (P.C.).

44 Binnie, *supra* note 14 at para. 75.

45 *An Act to Amend the Education Act,* S.O. 1986, c. 21, amending R.S.O. 1980, c. 129.

46 R.D. Gidney, *From Hope to Harris: The Reshaping of Ontario's Schools* (Toronto: University of Toronto Press, 1999) at 133.

47 *Reference re Bill 30, An Act to Amend the Education Act (Ont.),* [1987] 1 S.C.R. 1148, [1987] S.C.J. No. 44.

48 Chief Justice Roy McMurtry, "The Honourable Ian Scott: A Life Courageously Lived" (2007) 25(4) Advocates' Society Journal 4 at para. 6.

49 *British North America Act, 1867* (U.K.), 30 & 31 Vict., c. 3, reprinted in R.S.C. 1985, App. II, No. 5.

50 Scott, *To Make a Difference, supra* note 5 at 178.

51 Binnie, *supra* note 14 at para. 67.

52 *Ibid.* at para. 67.

53 Carl Baar, "The Zuber Report: The Decline and Fall of Court Reform in Ontario" (1988) 8 Windsor Year Book of Access to Justice 105 at 110. Ontario, British Columbia, and Nova Scotia had not merged their superior and county or district courts, whereas Quebec was the only province that did not have two s. 96 courts, so a merger was unnecessary.

54 Ian Greene, "The Zuber Report and Court Management" (1988) 8 Windsor Year Book of Access to Justice 150 at 157.

55 Baar, *supra* note 53 at 106.

56 *Ibid.*

57 *An Act to Amend the Courts of Justice Act (No.1),* S.O. 1989, c. 55, amending S.O. 1984, c. 11, s. 2. These changes were reflected in the *Courts of Justice Act,* R.S.O. 1990, c. 43. It has been speculated that another dimension of Scott's agenda was to merge all of the trial courts of Ontario. There is much wisdom in such an initiative,

in light of the fact that in modern times the quality of provincial courts is so much better than in 1967, and in most provinces provincial courts sit in a much greater number of locations, enhancing access to justice for citizens. Such a merger would pose little risk to the quality of justice meted out by a trial court. I regret that Scott did not have the opportunity to tackle this grand but politically and constitutionally difficult project.

58 Scott himself recognized the irony of this position and humorously recounts both the criticisms that he faced and his responsiveness to John Robinnette's advocacy on the question in Scott, *To Make a Difference, supra* note 5 at 137–38.

59 Sadly, this "tradition" of not awarding QCs was not adopted by Canada or other provinces.

60 Eugénie Brouillet and Yves Tanguay, "The Legitimacy of the Constitutional Arbitration Process in a Multinational Federative Regime: The Case of the Supreme Court of Canada" (2012) 45 UBC Law Review 47; Jacob Ziegel, "Promotion of Federally Appointed Judges and the Appointment of Chief Justices: The Unfinished Agenda" in Adam Dodek and Lorne Sossin, eds., *Judicial Independence in Context* (Toronto: Irwin Law, 2010); W.T. Stansbury and B. Thomas Hall, "An Independent Judicial Appointments Commission for Canada" *The Hill Times* (February 8, 2010), online: The Hill Times, http://www.hilltimes.com/stanburys-view/2010/02/08/an -independent-judicial-appointments-commission-for-canada/23262; James Morton, "Why Judges' Politics Matter" *Ottawa Citizen* (September 20, 2010); Jacob Ziegel, "Judicial Appointments Should Be about Merit, Not Politics" *National Post* (August 31, 2010); Lorne Sossin, "Judicial Appointments, Democratic Aspirations, and the Culture of Accountability" (2008) 58 University of New Brunswick Law Journal 11; Carissima Mathen, "Choices and Controversy: Judicial Appointments in Canada" (2008) 58 University of New Brunswick Law Journal 52; Tom Kent, "Supreme Court Appointments: By Parliament, Not PM; and Shorter" (2009), online: Queen's University Institute of Intergovernmental Relations, http://www.queensu.ca/iigr/ pub/archive/DemocraticDilemma/ReformingTheSCC/SCCpapers/KentFINAL.pdf; Nadia Verrelli, "Reforming the SCC: Rethinking Legitimacy and the Appointment Process" (2009), online: Queen's University Institute of Intergovernmental Relations, http://www.queensu.ca/iigr/pub/archive/DemocraticDilemma/ReformingTheSCC/ SCCpapers/VerrelliFINAL.pdf; and Peter McCormick, "The Serendipitous Solution to the Problem of Supreme Court Appointments" (2006) 44 Osgoode Hall Law Journal 539.

61 *Courts of Justice Act,* R.S.O. 1990, c. 43, ss. 42, 43.

62 Supra, note 23.

63 *Human Rights Code,* 1981 (Ont.), c. 53.

64 *Re Blainey and Ontario Hockey Association* (1986), 54 O.R. (2d) 513.

65 *Pay Equity Act, 1987,* S.O. 1987, c. 34. The *Act* was the first pay equity legislation in Ontario and applied to all public sector employees and private sector employers who employed ten or more employees.

66 Scott, *To Make a Difference, supra* note 5 at 154–58.

67 This appears to be taken from either the speeches of John F. Kennedy or the New Testament of the Bible, specifically Luke 12:48. Either would likely be an acceptable source of inspiration for Scott.

68 Edwards, *supra* note 25, cited by Marc Rosenberg, "The Attorney General and the Administration of Criminal Justice" (2008–09) 34 Queen's Law Journal 813.
69 Robert W. Mitchell, Attorney General of Saskatchewan, "Blazing the Trail" in Richard Gosse, James Youngblood Henderson, and Roger Carter, eds., *Continuing Poundmaker and Riel's Quest* (Saskatoon: Purich Publishing, 1994), 303 at 314.

11

Gerry Laarakker

From Rustic Rambo to Rebel with a Cause

MICAH RANKIN

Vernon is a small city located in the rolling grasslands of the North Okanagan Valley. Those who have visited it will tell you that it is a friendly place, the kind of place where people raise children or live out their golden years. And, if you are not driven by an insatiable appetite for the next "big deal," Vernon is also a fine place to start a law practice. That is what led Gerry Laarakker to start his practice there. He wanted to be part of a community and to have the opportunity to help regular people with the problems that mattered to them.

It was this affinity for "helping out the little guy" that ultimately led to the disciplining of Laarakker by the Law Society of British Columbia (LSBC). In 2010, the LSBC began a conduct investigation of Laarakker after he sent a letter to an Ontario lawyer whom he accused of "preying on people's embarrassment and naiveté." The Ontario lawyer in question had sent a letter to one of Laarakker's clients demanding that she pay for "losses" arising from a shoplifting incident involving her daughter. From Laarakker's point of view, there was no merit whatsoever in the claim. Indeed, the very idea that a fellow lawyer would threaten an unrepresented person with such a flimsy lawsuit so incensed Laarakker that he was temporarily transformed into a rustic Rambo lawyer determined to annihilate what he called "sleazy operators."[1] When the dust settled nearly a year later, Laarakker was found to have professionally misconducted himself in contravention of British Columbia's *Canons of Legal Ethics*.[2]

But was a disciplinary sanction warranted in his circumstances? This essay explores the possibility that Gerry Laarakker was a casualty of what is now commonly referred to as the "civility movement." Although his conduct was not in keeping with the best traditions of legal etiquette, it is only loosely comparable to the kinds of behaviour that have attracted sanctions in recent "civility" cases.[3] But more to the point, Laarakker was acting out of a heartfelt belief that it was unethical for a lawyer to intimidate an unrepresented person with a meritless threat of legal action. Viewed in this way, his actions can be seen as a well-intentioned (but perhaps misguided) attempt to defend his client, entirely in keeping with the best traditions of the bar.

Portrait of a Mild-Mannered Solicitor

Gerry Laarakker is an unlikely person to find at the centre of an essay on incivility. Born Gerardus Martin Maria Laarakker, he immigrated to Canada from the Netherlands in 1963, spending two decades as a successful professional photographer in Hamilton and counting among his clients former Prime Minister John Diefenbaker. For a variety of reasons, Laarakker was not entirely happy with his career as a photographer. So he began taking courses at McMaster University in philosophy, history, and religion, eventually completing an undergraduate degree that he began in the 1960s. Then, at the age of forty-nine, he wrote the LSAT and enrolled in Osgoode Hall Law School.

Laarakker found the study of law challenging and at times difficult to balance with his family life. Although he knew right away that he had made the right choice in pursuing a law degree, he and his wife were growing tired of life in southern Ontario. Indeed, on a snowy day near the end of his first year at Osgoode Hall, Laarakker and his family decided that they were going to move to British Columbia once he had completed his degree. Over the next two years, they laid their plans for an eventual move. In the summer between his second and third years, Laarakker did temporary articles in Kamloops. He then made arrangements for full articles in the town of Armstrong, just north of Vernon.

Laarakker was called to the BC bar in 1997. He practised law at first as an associate at a small firm in Vernon but decided to open his own law practice there in October 2000. Having spent most of his life as a small business owner, he was ideally suited to life as a solo practitioner. Since opening his firm, he has developed a prototypical small-town solicitor's practice, with particular emphasis on wills, estates, and family law. Occasionally, he takes on small claims matters but only if he thinks that someone is being treated unfairly. He confesses now that he was never very interested in litigation. Although he did some litigation early on in his practice, Laarakker has always preferred working cooperatively with clients to help them structure their estates and to assist them with their personal affairs.

From Small-Town Lawyer to Rustic Rambo

In late November 2009, one of Laarakker's clients came to his office to discuss a demand letter that she had received in the mail from an Ontario lawyer concerning an alleged shoplifting incident involving her teenage daughter. Laarakker knew the client well and could tell that she was upset. The client handed him a full-page letter, and this is how it read:

> I am external legal counsel for ... (the "Retailer") with respect to civil recovery matters. It is alleged that on September 22, 2009, a young person under your care and custody ... took unlawful possession of merchandise from the Retailer's premises [in] Vernon, BC. The Retailer takes the position that it has the right to claim damages from the said young person and/or you as a result of such action based on theft, damages, and conversion. The Retailer's right of civil recovery and payments made to the Retailer are separate and distinct from any criminal proceedings which may be instituted by the police.
>
> The Retailer also takes the position that it has the right to claim damages from you as a parent or guardian of the young person for failing to provide reasonable supervision of the young person. You have a right to be represented by a lawyer with respect to this claim.
>
> The Retailer is prepared to settle its claim for damages in return for payment of $521.97 ("Settlement Amount"), received on or before November 29, 2009. If this amount is not paid, I may receive specific instructions, whether or not to arrange for a law firm in your jurisdiction to commence legal proceedings for a civil court for all damages, plus interest, legal expenses, and other administrative costs incurred by the Retailer in connection with this matter.
>
> ...
>
> Any questions regarding this matter are to be made in writing, and addressed to the undersigned.
>
> Yours truly,
> ["Ontario lawyer"]

Although Laarakker is hardly a meek or hesitating person, he is by no means aggressive. But when he read the Ontario lawyer's demand letter, he was overcome with a feeling that it was nothing short of "extortion by letter-head."[4] Yet something else contributed to his feeling of contempt. Laarakker knew that the accused shoplifter suffered from an eating disorder. His family had also been touched by the difficulty of coping with a loved one who suffers from such a condition. He was furthermore aware that eating disorders are commonly associated with impulsive behaviour such as shoplifting, a phenomenon that has been well documented in the scientific literature.[5] Thus, from his standpoint, the demand letter not only advanced a meritless legal claim but also had the effect of humiliating a hard-working parent already struggling to manage a child suffering from a complex mental disorder.

After reading the demand letter, Laarakker told his client not to worry about it and that he would take care of it. He investigated the legal substance of the claim. In the course of doing so, he came across an Internet blog with anonymous postings from parents who had received similar letters. Laarakker decided to vent his spleen by posting his own comment. He wrote that lawyers who send such demand letters give other "lawyers a bad name," that they were "relying on intimidation and blackmail," and that he "hated these sleazy operators." He added that, "speaking as a lawyer," a retailer "would have little chance of collecting in court."

Laarakker's diatribe did not end with his blog posting. His next step was to fax a letter to the offending Ontario lawyer. This is what Laarakker wrote:

> I have been approached by [my client] with respect to your letter of October 30, 2009. Suffice it to say that I have instructed her not to pay a penny and to put your insulting and frankly stupid letter to the only use for which it might be suitable, however uncomfortably.
>
> It is disappointing when members of our profession lend themselves to this kind of thing. You must know that you are on the thinnest of legal grounds and would be highly unlikely to get a civil judgment against my client. That is aside from the logistics in bringing this matter to court in BC. I am also well aware that by preying on people's embarrassment and naiveté you will unfortunately be able to pry some money out of the pockets of some of the humiliated parents.
>
> I have notified the local paper of this scam. Save the postage in the future and become a real lawyer instead! You must have harboured dreams

of being a good lawyer at one point. Surely bullying people into paying some small amount of money is not what you went into law for.

But then again, someone has to be at the bottom of his class, practising with a restricted license as you appear to be.

Good luck.
Gerry M. Laarakker

Civility on Trial

Laarakker's letter provoked a rapid response from the Ontario lawyer. A few days after receiving the letter, the lawyer wrote to the LSBC complaining about Laarakker's letter and blog posting. In the year that followed, Laarakker, the Ontario lawyer, and the LSBC exchanged correspondence, which culminated in the Law Society issuing a citation alleging that his blog posting and letter contained discourteous and personal remarks that constituted "professional misconduct and/or conduct unbecoming. Less than a year later, Laarakker, who had never been the subject of any disciplinary action before, found himself before an LSBC disciplinary panel representing himself. The only real dispute at the hearing was whether his statements were sufficiently discourteous to amount to professional misconduct or conduct unbecoming of a member of the profession.

The focus of the disciplinary panel's inquiry was on the *Canons of Legal Ethics* and the requirement that a lawyer's conduct toward other lawyers "be characterized by courtesy and good faith" and that "personal remarks or references between lawyers should be scrupulously avoided."[6] For his part, Laarakker accepted that he had been rude but argued that his actions were justified because he was dealing with a "rogue lawyer." He maintained that he was permitted, and perhaps even required, to respond to such a lawyer in the way that he did. He also told the Law Society that he had strong personal feelings about the situation, arising from his client's struggle to manage her child's eating disorder. The Law Society's counsel argued not only that Laarakker was in contravention of his duty of civility but also that his misconduct was exacerbated by his attempts to justify his actions on the basis of the Ontario lawyer's having breached his own ethical duties.

Although the disciplinary panel recognized that Laarakker "may have been upset by the legal position and the allegations set out in the Ontario lawyer's Demand Letter," it "concluded that those feelings do not justify the correspondence and blog posting."[7] It went on to state that, even "if the Ontario Lawyer can be considered to be a 'rogue,' it is not [Laarakker's] place to pursue some form of vigilante justice."[8] In the disciplinary panel's view, "the appropriate avenue for [Laarakker] to take would have been to file a complaint either with the Law Society of Upper Canada or the Law Society of British Columbia."[9] The panel concluded that his conduct amounted to a "marked departure from the conduct the Law Society expects of its members" and that his belief "in the correctness of his position does not relieve him of culpability."[10] In the end, the panel issued a $1,500 fine to Laarakker and ordered him to pay $3,000 in costs.[11]

The Civility Movement and Its Proponents

The LSBC's decision to discipline Laarakker for incivility is one of a spate of recent high-profile cases in which lawyers have been found guilty of professional misconduct for incivility.[12] In the past few years, the legal profession, courts, and scholars have paid increasing attention to the role of civility in the practice of law, with proponents arguing that civility is integral to the public's perception of lawyers and to the maintenance of a well-functioning system of justice. The decision to cite and ultimately discipline Laarakker can only be understood in the context of the recent debate concerning regulated civility.

Although civility has gained more prominence in the past few years,[13] there seems to be no dispute that the legal profession has long valued civility as a virtue. It is visible, for example, in Shakespeare's 1592 play *The Taming of the Shrew*, in which two competing suitors agree to put aside their quarrel and "do as adversaries do in law, / Strive mightily but eat and drink as friends."[14] But much of the recent attention paid to civility results from a fear that civility in the legal profession is in perilous decline.[15] Although certain scholars dispute the notion that there ever was a golden age of civility in legal practice,[16] there is no question that there is at least a perception that incivility is on the rise.

Those who perceive a decline in civility offer a number of explanations for it. Some argue that incivility is on the rise because of the increasing size of the legal profession, making "uniform definitions of professionalism impossible."[17] Some say that, because lawyers do not deal with one another on a regular basis, as they once did, there is no longer an economic incentive to be civil.[18] Other scholars argue that the increase in incivility has resulted from the transformation of the profession from a public service vocation into a competitive business.[19] Still others argue that clients are the culprits:

under the influence of Hollywood movies and popular television, clients now expect lawyers to use aggressive tactics and reward them for their misbehaviour. As one scholar puts it, "[c]lients want Rambo not Bambi."[20]

Concern about declining standards of civility has led certain commentators to advocate for an increase in judicial and professional regulation of civility. Michael Code, now a Justice of the Ontario Superior Court, has been a prominent advocate for civility in Canada. He argues that incivility by lawyers can "impair the fairness of a trial" and "seriously distorts the proper functioning of the adversary system."[21] Although Code recognizes that incivility is broad, encompassing "mere rudeness and discourtesy," he maintains that litigants should have a legal right to be protected against the tactics of belligerent counsel who make "irrelevant or unfounded personal attacks against opposing counsel."[22]

Commentators have endorsed a similarly robust approach to the regulation of civility outside courts. Pointing to the costs associated with obstructive litigation tactics (*i.e.*, Rambo tactics), proponents of regulated civility argue that steps must be taken to instill a courteous ethic at all phases of a lawyer's career, including at law school.[23] Regulators and professional associations have responded in a variety of ways, including by adopting various statements, guidelines, or lists of principles that exhort lawyers to be more civil.[24] Although it is not clear that the recent proliferation of civility guidelines has led to increased regulatory intervention,[25] there is no disputing the fact that civility has attracted more attention than ever before. Indeed, the recent cases of Joe Groia, Gille Doré, and Kevin Murphy garnered national media attention and illustrate this increased prominence.[26]

What is perhaps most remarkable about the recent examples of lawyers being sanctioned for incivility is how much their situations appear to differ from Laarakker's circumstances. Consider Joe Groia, found guilty in 2012 of professional misconduct for his aggressive defence of a former Bre-X geologist, John Felderhoff, from insider trading charges by the Ontario Securities Commission (OSC).[27] Groia personally attacked the OSC prosecutors, claiming that they were trying to "win at all costs," "were lazy," "turned a blind eye," used a "conviction filter," and made "promises [that] aren't worth the transcripts they appear to be written on." The situation became so difficult that OSC prosecutors brought an unsuccessful application to remove the presiding judge based on an apprehension of bias arising from his failure to restrain Groia.[28] The judge who heard the judicial review wrote that Groia's "conduct ... resembles gue[r]rilla theatre"[29] and that "the tone of Mr. Groia's submissions ...descended from legal argument to irony to sarcasm to petulant invective."[30] These sentiments were echoed by the Ontario Court of Appeal[31] and paralleled the findings of the Law Society of Upper Canada (LSUC), which described Groia's defence as a "strategy aimed at baiting the prosecution into making mistakes or aimed at convincing the trial judge through rhetoric rather than evidence."[32]

Similarly extreme behaviour led to disciplining of Kevin Murphy by the LSUC.[33] Murphy was defence counsel in a well-known murder trial held before Justice Paul Cosgrove (as he then was). Murphy's trial strategy involved advancing numerous meritless pretrial applications combined with an endless litany of unsubstantiated allegations of prosecutorial misconduct against the Crown. At one point, Murphy went so far as to state that the appointment of new Crown lawyers to the file was comparable to the "last days of the Third Reich where Generals and members of the SS were scrambling, literally like rats deserting a sinking ship, to make arrangements for themselves."[34] Murphy's defence was so egregious that it has been described "as one of the most disgraceful exhibitions that has ever been seen in a Canadian courtroom."[35] Not only was Murphy suspended from practice for six months, but also the proceedings precipitated an inquiry into the conduct of Justice Cosgrove that eventually drove him to resign from the judiciary.

The only high-profile civility case that so far has made it to the Supreme Court of Canada is *Doré v. Barreau du Québec.*[36] Doré was counsel on a complicated criminal trial involving the Hell's Angels motorcycle club. In response to a pretrial application brought by Doré, Mr. Justice Boilard gave reasons denying the application and rebuking Doré for being impudent, for using "bombastic rhetoric and hyperbole," and for doing "nothing to help his client discharge his burden."[37] In reply, Doré wrote a private letter to Boilard in which he described the Judge as "loathsome," "arrogant," "fundamentally unjust," "lacking in social skills," and having a tendency to use his court to "launch ugly, vulgar and mean personal attacks" on counsel. Justice Boilard filed a complaint about Doré with the Barreau du Québec; meanwhile, Doré filed a complaint about Boilard to the Canadian Judicial Council. Both complaints were sustained, with Doré receiving a twenty-one-day suspension and Boilard being chided for showing "a flagrant lack of respect for an officer of the court, namely Mr. Doré."[38] Although the narrow issue before the Supreme Court in *Doré* was the application of the *Charter of Rights and Freedoms* to the disciplinary orders of the Barreau du Québec, the Court observed in *obiter dicta* that "lawyers are expected by the public, on whose behalf they serve, to endure [criticisms] with civility and dignity." Although lawyers are not required to behave like "verbal eunuchs," the Court held that, even when "unfairly provoked," a lawyer is "called upon to behave with transcendent civility."[39]

This brings me back to Laarakker's situation. Whether or not Groia, Murphy, or Doré should have been disciplined for incivility has itself been the subject of heated debate. However, in comparison with these cases (and most reported civility decisions[40]), Laarakker's conduct appears to be rather trifling or puerile. His offensive blog posting, for instance, did not refer to the name of the Ontario lawyer and focused on the merits of such demand letters generally, and it expressed a more general disappointment with lawyers who send them (*i.e.*, the "sleazy operators"). As for his letter, Laarakker's situation is perhaps most comparable to that of Doré. However, unlike the private communication sent by Doré to Justice Boilard, Laarakker's letter was not purely a personal attack but addressed the substance, albeit crudely, of the legal claim. Although his choice of wording left much to be desired, it was not a purely personal attack divorced from the substance of the Ontario lawyer's threatened action. In any case, in an adversarial system of justice such as ours, there is clearly a difference between an aggressive letter sent to a lawyer connected with a dispute and one sent to a member of the judiciary. Permitting abusive or threatening letters to be sent to judges as a result of their decisions in court might have implications for the independence and impartiality of the judiciary itself.

A more important distinction between Laarakker's case and the situation in the Groia, Doré, or Murphy case (or most civility cases) is that it arose from conduct that took place outside formal litigation. In most civility cases, there is not a single rude letter or email but a pattern of disruptive and abusive conduct that worsens over time.[41] Moreover, many civility cases involve ongoing litigation of some form or another, with the belligerent conduct spilling over into court proceedings. This is an important distinction since one of the objects of regulated civility is preservation of the appearance of the justice system as a whole. Thus, in contrast to most civility cases, Laarakker's actions seem to represent a relatively isolated incident that had no real connection with the courts.

Regulated Civility and Its Opponents

Although there is clearly much to commend a professional ethos that values civility, the civility movement also has its detractors. These naysayers worry that the regulation of lawyer civility will have a chilling effect on zealous advocacy. As the oft-quoted *dicta* in *Rondel v. Worsley* goes, "every counsel has a duty to his client fearlessly to raise every issue, advance every argument, and ask every question, however distasteful, which he thinks will help his client's case."[42] Critics of regulated civility point out that lawyers are under an ethical duty to do whatever it takes, within the confines of law, to advance a client's cause. It is worth pointing out, in this regard, that Joe Groia was successful in defending his client against all odds.

A further criticism is that "civility" is simply too vague (or overbroad) a concept to be a meaningful regulatory standard.[43] Indeed, even the civility movement's proponents admit that civility is an "elusive ideal"[44] capable of meaning anything from impoliteness and discourtesy to a consistent pattern of disruptive, provocative, or rude conduct. Legal regulators have not done much, in this regard, to help define the concept. The existing guidelines and principles of civility are largely a list of best practices, often laden with ambiguous qualifiers or descriptors. Although some scholars suggest that a core set of concerns can be distilled from the various guides to civility, no law society in Canada has yet defined the concept.[45]

Laarakker's situation illustrates the problems that arise from the absence of a common definition of civility. In finding against Laarakker, the LSBC relied on the *Canons of Legal Ethics* and two previous LSBC decisions, holding that it had jurisdiction to enforce "the Canons with respect to correspondence."[46] There was nothing, however, that even approached a discussion of the meaning of civility or whether any particular incivility threshold had to be met before a professional sanction was warranted. In contrast, in the *Groia* proceeding, the LSUC concluded that "a consistent pattern of rude, provocative, or disruptive conduct by the lawyer, as well as ill-considered or uninformed criticism of the competence, conduct, advice, or charges of another lawyer, might merit discipline."[47]

The LSBC's failure to discuss the meaning of civility was compounded by the fact that the disciplinary decisions cited involved much more egregious behaviour than that exhibited by Laarakker. In *Law Society of BC v. Lanning*, for instance, the respondent lawyer exchanged numerous letters and emails with an unrepresented mother in a custody and family maintenance dispute over a period of months. The lawyer wrote that she should "stew in your self-imposed bitterness," that she took "pleasure in self-indulgent complaining," and that "[y]ou read as badly as you write."[48] Although Laarakker's description of the lawyer as being the "bottom of his class" was impolite, it is less clear that it was sufficiently uncivil to warrant regulatory intervention.

Definitional problems aside, a more fundamental critique of the civility movement is that it can conflate the pursuit of a moral good (*i.e.*, a polite legal profession) with the effective ethical regulation of lawyers. As Alice Woolley has pointed out in her penetrating critique of the civility movement, the term "civility" is used by regulators, courts, and scholars in several different ways. On the one hand, it refers to "the manner in which counsel communicate with each other, specifically the politeness and courtesy, or lack thereof, in lawyer communication."[49] On the other, it addresses conduct that is said to be essential "to ensure the proper functioning of the judicial process, with a specific focus on advocacy."[50] In her view, the problem with regulating politeness is that lawyers often have competing ethical obligations, such as the duty of loyalty, which requires them to say and do things that are unpleasant and at times galling. Although this does not mean that incivility should be celebrated as a professional virtue, it might mean that disciplining lawyers for incivility has other negative ethical consequences.

Woolley's further concern is that an increased focus on civility "tends to obscure the true nature of the ethical misconduct of lawyers subject to discipline for incivility."[51] Put simply, when a lawyer uses Rambo-type litigation tactics, that lawyer is often breaching some other ethical rule. A lawyer's duties with respect to knowledge and skill, the quality of service, the requirement of promptness, his or her duties as an advocate, or as an officer of the court, already occupy an ethical terrain onto which civility unnecessarily encroaches. However, Woolley's objection is not merely that civility is redundant but also that an emphasis on it results in elision of the "complex and difficult ethical issues raised by the behaviour of the lawyers in [civility] cases."[52] The result, arguably, is that lawyers are left ethically diminished and lacking in guidance about "how to resolve the difficult dilemmas" posed by the practice of law.[53]

Laarakker might be an example of the kind of overregulation of civility that critics have feared. Few would endorse the tone of his letter as appropriate, but some might doubt that a disciplinary process was warranted. Yet what might surprise many is that Laarakker himself is a proponent of the civility movement. Although he is not a fan of what he calls the "etiquette police," he strongly supports the notion that lawyers should be courteous and maintain good relationships with one another. As he puts it, in Vernon every lawyer knows each other, and being courteous creates a "fellowship" among legal practitioners. Laarakker is not, therefore, a Rambo lawyer but a well-mannered solicitor who sympathized a little too much with the plight of his client.

The Ethics of Civil Recovery Demand Letters

Gerry Laarakker's story is also compelling because it raises another prickly ethical question: namely, whether there are ethical duties that govern a lawyer's decision to threaten legal action on behalf of his or her client. Laarakker's argument before the LSBC disciplinary panel was that the Ontario lawyer was a "rogue" who had engaged in unethical behaviour by threatening to bring a meritless claim against Laarakker's client. However, the LSBC found no merit in this argument, holding that "the appropriate avenue" for Laarakker was to "file a complaint either with the Law Society of Upper Canada or the Law Society of British Columbia."[54]

Was the LSBC right to dismiss Laarakker's argument in this way? To understand his position, it is worth saying something more about the Ontario lawyer's claim that a shoplifter's parents are potentially liable for the "losses" incurred by a retailer as a result of "failing to provide reasonable supervision" of a young person. The common law rule has long been that parents are not generally liable for the torts of their children.[55] Thus, where a person is injured by a child who negligently shoots him with an airgun,[56] or steals and damages a car,[57] or sets fire to a neighbour's home,[58] the parents are not normally held liable. However, a parent can be held liable for injuries caused by his or her child "if, by negligently allowing a dangerous instrument to be taken by a child, he [or she] thereby affords or allows the child an opportunity of doing mischief."[59] Yet even then parents are not "vicariously liable for the torts committed by their children" but have a "duty to prevent their children from committing foreseeable harm to others."[60]

Although there are only a handful of shoplifting cases, the jurisprudence strongly supports Laarakker's contention that the Ontario lawyer was "on the thinnest of legal grounds." *D.C.B. v. Zellers* appears to be the only reported case concerning a retailer's ability to claim damages against a parent.[61] In that case, a parent successfully brought a claim in unjust enrichment seeking to disgorge money that she had paid to a retailer in settlement of a threatened claim. The parent argued that she had paid the retailer in the mistaken belief that its claim was valid. The trial judge held that the retailer's "claim was not merely a doubtful claim – it was an invalid claim"[62] – and that the retailer could not have "seriously thought that this claim could succeed or ...intended to pursue it to court if it was not paid."[63] As for the lawyer for Zellers, the trial judge said that, "as a competent and responsible lawyer, he knew or ought to have known that the claim had no prospect whatsoever of succeeding in court and that it would be futile to pursue it."[64] The Manitoba Court of Appeal declined to grant the retailer's application for leave to appeal, noting that, if the trial judge had erred at all, "it was on a question of fact, not law."[65]

The jurisprudence on claims against shoplifters personally also supports Laarakker's opinion. *Hudson's Bay Company v. David James White*[66] was cited by the Ontario lawyer in his letter to Laarakker's client. Unlike *D.C.B. v. Zellers*, the case involved an action in trespass brought against a shoplifter personally, not his parents, in which Hudson's Bay sought damages including the prorated costs of surveillance, investigation, and apprehension of shoplifters. Although the trial judge awarded Hudson's Bay nominal damages of $100 and costs, he specifically declined to make an award of damages for the prorated costs of preventing shoplifting. The judge observed that Hudson's Bay should try to convince Parliament and "the police to adopt a sterner stance rather than seek to invoke the aid of the already overburdened civil justice system."[67] The Ontario Divisional Court allowed an appeal in part, holding that "the case cries out for an award of punitive damages."[68]

The only other decision on shoplifting of any note is *Southland Canada Inc. v. Zylik.*[69] In that case, the Alberta Provincial Court rejected two civil claims of debt advanced against two individuals for shoplifting from 7 Eleven convenience stores. The plaintiff claimed damages for the costs of security on a prorated basis. The trial judge was not convinced of the merits of the action, stating that the "damages claimed are not as a result of any wrong committed by the defendants, but rather in anticipation that they would be members of a group of then undetermined individuals who might do something wrong."[70] Although the judge would not foreclose on future claims, he adopted the words of the trial judge in *D.C.B. v. Zellers* to the effect that the action was "not merely ... doubtful" but also "invalid."[71]

As the above suggests, there does not appear to be much question that Laarakker was correct that there was no merit in the claim against his client. What is troubling, however, is that the Ontario lawyer's demand letter suggests that the retailer had a *bona fide* claim against Laarakker's client. Although the lawyer used qualifiers such as "takes the position," they do not change the overall tone or effect of the letter, especially for a humiliated and unrepresented parent. There are passages in the letter, however, that are legally incorrect. Although the Ontario lawyer referred to *Hudson's Bay Company v. David James White* in the demand letter, that case involved rejection of the claim for the prorated costs of deterring shoplifters. In spite of this, the Ontario lawyer requested a settlement amount "based on the costs associated with the detection, apprehension, recovery of goods and damages associated with shoplifting." In other words, the lawyer relied on *Hudson's*

Bay Company v. David James White, yet that case is entirely at odds with the losses being claimed.

The question, then, is whether there was anything unethical about the Ontario lawyer's actions. Although there are no specific rules in Canada's various Professional Codes of Conduct that expressly prohibit lawyers from sending demand letters, there are rules that could conceivably be relevant to this ethical question. For instance, in British Columbia and Ontario, a lawyer has a duty "to carry on the practice of law and discharge all responsibilities to clients, tribunals, the public and other members of the profession honourably and with integrity."[72] Surely the integrity of the profession is not well served by demanding payments based on non-existent causes of action or that request damages unavailable as a matter of law. Lawyers also have duties relevant to their interactions with unrepresented litigants, including the duty to urge such persons to obtain independent legal representation.[73] In this regard, it is worth noting that the Ontario lawyer's letter did not contain any statement that Laarakker's client should seek or obtain independent legal advice. And, of course, lawyers have duties as officers of the court prohibiting them from pursuing frivolous claims,[74] though it is not clear that these duties would be triggered based on the mere contemplation of litigation.

In reality, however, there appear to be few clearly drawn ethical lines that limit a lawyer's ability to threaten unmeritorious claims. It also appears that the LSBC and LSUC are unconcerned about lawyers sending out the sort of demand letter sent to Laarakker's client. After the LSBC made its finding of misconduct, Laarakker took up its suggestion that "the appropriate avenue ...would have been to file a complaint either with the Law Society of Upper Canada or the Law Society of British Columbia."[75] He has since made complaints to both the LSBC and the LSUC – all to no avail. Indeed, the LSUC has taken the position that there is nothing wrong with the practice of sending demand letters to shoplifters' parents. There also appears to be no disciplinary reports involving lawyers being either cited or disciplined for threatening unmeritorious legal claims against unrepresented persons.[76] The irony, then, is that a lawyer can be fined for cussing but is free to threaten unrepresented members of the public with invalid legal claims.

Rebel with a Cause

Laarakker's experience with the civility movement might have led some lawyers to drop the issue of demand letters altogether. But that has not been the case with Laarakker. Although he concedes that his letter was rude, his resolve to fight back against what he calls "civil recovery demand letters" has only been solidified. In the three years since the LSBC fined him for incivility, he has made it his personal mission to make life difficult for the small group of lawyers responsible for sending out demand letters to shoplifters and their families throughout Canada. For a very modest fee, he will take on any case, anywhere, anytime. Since 2009, Laarakker has taken on hundreds of clients. Yet, after sending hundreds of response letters, no legal action has ever been started against one of his clients.

His response to his predicament is the most intriguing chapter, in certain respects, of his story. Laarakker has become a kind of vigilante lawyer, fighting against what he views as the unethical practices of a small cadre of lawyers who represent Canada's megaretailers. The only difference between his current approach and his former approach to demand letters is that he no longer refers to the megaretailers' lawyers as sleazy bottom-of-the-classers. Instead, he calls their threatened claims meritless or baseless, and he asks that all future correspondence be directed to his attention.

For the proponents of regulated civility, Laarakker's continued commitment to helping the public might be viewed as vindication of the idea that civility and forceful advocacy can live together in harmony. But for members of the public who receive meritless demand letters, it might be surprising that Canada's law societies would sanction Laarakker yet remain silent on legal threats made against the parents of troubled children. For some, this might lead to skepticism about the legal profession's capacity to self-regulate.

Conclusion

Gerry Laarakker's story reveals the profound difficulties that arise from the regulation of civility. One thing that his story suggests is that regulators need to attempt to define the kinds of incivility that will attract professional sanction.[77] Although regulated civility appears to be here to stay, Laarakker's actions must surely be at the margin of conduct that warrants intervention by law societies, assuming that his actions warranted regulatory intervention at all. Lawyers are human beings, and, despite our desire to behave at all times with "transcendent civility," even the most measured advocate experiences the occasional Rambo-like moment.

But Laarakker's situation raises other difficult ethical questions. Underlying his actions was a strongly held belief that there was something fundamentally wrong with a lawyer who threatens an unrepresented member of the public with a spurious lawsuit. If a lawyer cannot use more diffuse social sanctions, such as shaming, then how should he or she navigate this situation? Should he or she stand idly by and wait for law societies to develop ethical standards? If not, then how exactly should a lawyer respond? We probably cannot expect all lawyers to become like Laarakker: a onetime rustic Rambo turned into a rebel with a cause.

Notes

1 A "Rambo lawyer" is one who "uses aggressive, unethical, or illegal tactics in representing a client and who lacks courtesy and professionalism in dealing with other lawyers." *Black's Law Dictionary,* 9th ed. (2009). The Rambo lawyer has become a favourite character in legal ethics scholarship; see, for example, Kathleen P. Browe, "A Critique of the Civility Movement: Why Rambo Will Not Go Away" (1994) 77 Marquette Law Review 751. Indeed, the Rambo caricature appears so often in legal ethics scholarship that some argue that it has led to an underinclusive understanding of lawyer professionalism. See, for example, Amy Salyzn, "John Rambo v. Atticus Finch: Gender, Diversity, and the Civility Movement" (2013) 16(2) Legal Ethics 97.

2 *Laarakker (Re),* 2011 L.S.B.C. 29 (CanLII) [*Laarakker*].

3 Many of the post-2007 disciplinary reports are reviewed in Alice Woolley, "Uncivil by Too Much Civility? Critiquing Five More Years of Civility Regulation in Canada" (2013) Dalhousie Law Journal 240 ["Uncivil by Too Much Civility?"].

4 Laarakker attributes this particular turn of phrase to Alice Woolley, "Lawyers Regulating Lawyers?" (November 3, 2011), online: ABlawg, http://ablawg.ca/2011/11/03/lawyers-regulating-lawyers/ [ABlawg].

5 Antonia Baum and Elliot M. Goldner, "The Relationship between Stealing and Eating Disorders: A Review" (1995) 3 Harvard Review of Psychiatry 210 (noting that stealing might serve as a marker of eating disorder severity).

6 Law Society of British Columbia, *Professional Conduct Handbook* (May 1, 1993– December 31, 2012), Chapter 1 [BC Code of Conduct]. The canons are now found in Chapter 2.1 of the *Code of Professional Conduct for British Columbia* (January 1, 2013, updated April 2013).

7 *Laarakker, supra* note 2 at para. 44.

8 *Ibid.* at para. 45.

9 *Ibid.* at para. 46.

10 *Ibid.* at para. 47.

11 *Laarakker (Re),* 2012 L.S.B.C. 2 (CanLII).

12 Although there have been a number of cases on incivility in recent years, the most well known include *Law Society of Upper Canada v. Kevin Mark Murphy,* 2010 O.N.L.S.H.P. 0023 [*Murphy*]; *Law Society of Upper Canada v. Joseph Peter Paul Groia,* 2012 O.N.L.S.H.P. 0094 [*Groia*]; and *Doré v. Barreau du Québec,* 2012 S.C.C. 12, [2012] 1 S.C.R. 395 [*Doré*].

13 The contemporary civility movement in the United States has older roots and is frequently traced to an address to the American Law Institute by the former Chief

Justice in 1971. See Warren E. Burger, "The Necessity for Civility" (1971) 52 F.R.D. 211.

14 William Shakespeare, *The Taming of the Shrew*, ed. Barbara A. Mowat and Paul . Werstine (New York: Washington Square Press, 1992) at Act 1, scene 2, lines 269–77.

15 Donald E. Campbell, "Raise Your Right Hand and Swear to Be Civil: Defining Civility as an Obligation of Professional Responsibility" (2011–12) 47 Gonzaga Law Review 99 at 103 (Campbell provides a complete discussion of the literature in this area).

16 *Ibid.* See also Marc Galanter, "Lawyers in the Mist: The Golden Age of Legal Nostalgia" (1995–96) 100 Dickinson Law Review 549.

17 Jack T. Camp, "Thoughts on Professionalism in the Twenty-First Century" (2007) 81 Tulane Law Review 1377 at 1380–81.

18 Jonathan Macey, "Occupation Code 541110: Lawyers, Self-Regulation, and the Idea of a Profession" (2005) 74 Fordham Law Review 1079 at 1079.

19 Michael Code, "Counsel's Duty of Civility: An Essential Component of Fair Trials and an Effective Justice System" (2007) 11 Canadian Criminal Law Review 97 at 98.

20 Dane S. Ciolino, "Redefining Professionalism as Seeking" (2003) 49 Loyola Law Review 229 at 237.

21 Code, *supra* note 19 at 104.

22 *Ibid.* at 105.

23 Indeed, in his famous remarks on civility, Chief Justice Burger stated that "law teachers" had the "first and best chance to inculcate" aspiring lawyers with "good manners, disciplined behavior and civility." Burger, *supra* note 13.

24 There are too many examples to list here. However, the most well-known initiatives are the Canadian Bar Association's *Principles of Civility for Advocates*, reprinted as an appendix to the *Code of Professional Conduct* (Ottawa: Canadian Bar Association, 2006); and The Advocates' Society, *Principles of Civility for Advocates* (Ontario: The Advocate's Society, 2001). The sets of principles are nearly identical.

25 Alice Woolley has done an empirical study in "Uncivil by Too Much Civility?," *supra* note 3. Despite much greater public attention to civility, there were only ten decisions involving civility from 2007 to 2012.

26 "Law Society Panel Hits 'Uncivil' Lawyer Joe Groia with $247,000 in Costs" *Toronto Star* (April 19, 2013); "Bre-X Lawyer Groia Suspended for Being Rude in Court" *Globe and Mail* (April 19, 2013); "Supreme Court Ruling Lets Lawyers Talk Tough with Judge" *Globe and Mail* (March 22, 2012); "Misconduct Inquiry Continues Despite Judge's Apology" *Globe and Mail* (September 10, 2008).

27 *Groia, supra* note 12.

28 *R. v. Felderhof,* 2002 CanLII 41888 (O.N. S.C.).

29 *Ibid.* at para. 91.

30 *Ibid.* at para. 101.

31 *R. v. Felderhof* (2003), 180 C.C.C. (3d) 498 (Ont. C.A.) at para. 80.

32 *Groia, supra* note 12 at para. 189.

33 *Murphy, supra* note 12.

34 "Report to the Canadian Judicial Council of the Inquiry Committee Appointed under Subsection 63(3) of the *Judges Act* to Conduct an Investigation into the Conduct of Mr. Justice Paul Cosgrove" (June 27, 2008) at para. 88.

35 These remarks are attributed to Earl Cherniak, the independent counsel who investigated the conduct of Justice Cosgrove.

36 *Doré*, *supra* note 12.

37 *R. v. Lanthier*, 2001 CanLII 9351 (Q.C. C.S.).

38 Cited in translation in *Doré*, *supra* note 12 at para. 14.

39 *Ibid.* at para. 78.

40 See, for example, *Law Society of Upper Canada v. Ernest Guiste*, 2011 O.N.L.S.H.P. 24 (CanLII); *Law Society of Upper Canada v. Colin Cameron Leon Lyle*, 2011 O.N.L.S.H.P 34 (CanLII); *Law Society of Upper Canada v. Mary Martha Coady*, 2009 O.N.L.S.H.P. 51 (CanLII); and *Law Society of Upper Canada v. Kimberly Lynne Townley-Smith*, 2012 O.N.L.S.H.P. 52 (CanLII).

41 Even Doré's letter followed from court proceedings and was based on an ongoing pattern of disrespect shown to Doré by Justice Boilard.

42 *Rondel v. Worsley*, [1969] 1 A.C. 191 at 227 (per Lord Reid).

43 Alice Woolley, "Does Civility Matter?" (2008) Osgoode Hall Law Journal 175 at 182 ["Does Civility Matter?"].

44 C.J. Piazzola, "Ethical versus Procedural Approaches to Civility: Why Ethics 2000 Should Have Adopted a Civility Rule" (2003) 74 University of Colorado Law Review 1197 at 1202–3.

45 Discussed in Campbell, *supra* note 15.

46 *Laarakker*, *supra* note 2 at para. 34, citing *Law Society of BC v. Greene*, [2003] L.S.B.C. 30; *Law Society of BC v. Lanning*, 2008 L.S.B.C. 31 [*Lanning*].

47 *Groia*, *supra* note 12 at para. 62.

48 *Lanning*, *supra* note 46 at para. 28.

49 Woolley, "Does Civility Matter?," *supra* note 43 at 178.

50 *Ibid.*

51 *Ibid.* at 185.

52 Woolley, "Uncivil by Too Much Civility?," *supra* note 3 at 242.

53 Woolley, "Does Civility Matter?," *supra* note 43 at 187.

54 *Laarakker*, *supra* note 2 at para. 46.

55 *Moon v. Towers* (1860), 141 E.R. 1306; see also *Black v. Hunter*, [1925] S.J. No. 37, [1925] 4 D.L.R. 285 (C.A.) [*Hunter*].

56 *Montesanto v. Di Ubaldo*, [1927] O.J. No. 69, [1927] 3 D.L.R. 1045 (C.A.); see also *Moran v. Burroughs*, [1912] O.J. No. 66.

57 *Streifel v. Strotz et al.* (1958), 11 D.L.R. (2d) 667 (B.C.S.C.).

58 *495862 B.C. Ltd. (c.o.b. Desert Gardens) v. CDY*, [2003] B.C.J. No. 2401 at para. 30 [*495862 B.C. Ltd.*].

59 *Hunter*, *supra* note 55 at para. 1.

60 *495862 B.C. Ltd.*, *supra* note 58 at para. 30.

61 *D.C.B. v. Zellers Inc.*, [1996] M.J. No. 362, 138 D.L.R. (4th) 309 (Man. Q.B.) [*D.C.B.*].

62 *Ibid.* at para. 12.

63 *Ibid.* at para. 18.

64 *Ibid.*

65 *Bond v. Zellers Inc.*, [1996] M.J. No. 499, 113 Man.R. (2d) 198 (per Twaddle in Chambers).

66 *Hudson's Bay Company v. David James White*, [1997] O.J. No. 307 (Ont. S.C.).

67 *Ibid.* at para. 27.

68 *Hudson's Bay Co. v. White,* [1998] O.J. No. 2383, 1 C.P.C. (5th) 333 (Div. Ct.).

69 *Southland Canada Inc. v. Bradley Zylik,* 1999 A.B.P.C. 107.

70 *Ibid.* at para. 14.

71 *D.C.B., supra* note 61 at para. 12.

72 LSBC, BC Code of Conduct, *supra* note 6, Rule 2.2-1; Law Society of Upper Canada, *Rules of Professional Conduct* (amendments current to January 24, 2013), Rule 6.01(1).

73 Law Society of Upper Canada, *ibid.,* Rule 2.04. This rule parallels the Canadian Bar Association rule on dealing with unrepresented litigants.

74 Indeed, courts can award costs against lawyers personally when they pursue frivolous, improper, or vexatious litigation. See *Young v. Young,* 1993 CanLII 34 (S.C.C.), [1993] 4 S.C.R. 3.

75 *Laarakker, supra* note 2 at para. 46.

76 I have discovered none, and neither has Professor Woolley, who engaged in a similar search. See Woolley, ABlawg, *supra* note 4.

77 In its most recent decision on civility, the Law Society of British Columbia has continued in the pattern of not defining a threshold for when incivility becomes professional misconduct. See *Re Harding,* 2013 L.S.B.C. 25 (CanLII).

Contributors

David Asper is a lawyer, businessman, and philanthropist in Winnipeg.

Constance Backhouse is Distinguished University Professor and University Research Chair at the Faculty of Law, University of Ottawa.

Janine Benedet is Associate Professor and Director, Centre for Feminist Legal Studies, Allard School of Law, University of British Columbia.

Brent Cotter is Professor and former Dean at the Faculty of Law, University of Saskatchewan.

Richard Devlin is Professor at the Schulich School of Law, Dalhousie University.

Adam Dodek is Associate Professor at the Faculty of Law, University of Ottawa.

Trevor Farrow is Professor and Associate Dean at Osgoode Hall Law School and Director of the Winkler Institute for Dispute Resolution.

Allan Hutchinson is Distinguished Research Professor, Osgoode Hall Law School.

Micah Rankin is Assistant Professor at the Faculty of Law, Thompson Rivers University.

Lorne Sossin is Dean of Law, Osgoode Hall Law School.

Alice Woolley is Professor and Associate Dean (Academic) at the Faculty of Law, University of Calgary.

Index

Printed and bound in Canada by Friesens

Set in Segoe and Warnock by Artegraphica Design Co. Ltd.

Copy editor: Dallas Harrison

Proofreader and indexer: Dianne Tiefensee